IN PRAISE OF *GO FORTH*

"The Church Jesus Christ established is a missionary church with a rich heritage of great Apostles and saintly missionaries. We must continually return to a reading of these great examples. But we also need contemporary examples for inspiration and helpful models. That's what you'll find in Go Forth. *Fr. Luke Veronis, in this gripping story, hardly alludes to what I witnessed in* ~~ ~ *'endship with him over many years: careful and* ~~persis~~ *issions, practical short-term mission exper* ~ *h his beloved wife, sensitive exploration wit* ~ *'ea' of taking a young family to a country like* ~ *nd be accountable to his Church. I think that i* ~~... blessing and~~ *success to this young missionary of the 21ˢᵗ* ~~century.~~

> **FR. DEAN BORGMAN,**
> Charles E. Culpeper Professor of Youth Ministry, Gordon Conwell Theological Seminary

∞

"What a story! Fr. Luke Veronis is a warrior for Christ who will help shape the Orthodox Church for the next generation. Concerning Christ's command to preach the Gospel to all nations, he totally 'gets it.' In this page-turner account, Fr. Luke beautifully reveals both the sorrows and the victories of his ten-year missionary adventure in Albania. Read it and prepare to rededicate your life to zealously serve our Lord Jesus Christ."

> **FR. PETER GILLQUIST,**
> Director of Department of Evangelism, Antiochian Orthodox Church

∞

"'Like cold water to a weary soul is good news from a distant land!' As with its first-century Philadelphian counterpart, outside observers of the Albanian Church were able to detect only the faintest flicker of life after decades of relentless state effort to eradicate its members, destroy its institutions, and erase its very memory. It seemed as though the gates of hell—through the ruthless agency of Enver Hoxha—must surely have prevailed. This eye-witness account of the Albanian Church's resurrection is an inspiring reminder that God's promises are true: the gates of hell cannot prevail over His Church; His strength is made perfect in our weakness; and when the One who holds the key of David opens a door, no power on earth can shut it. This book is a 21ˢᵗ-century Acts of the Apostles."

> **JONATHAN BONK,**
> Executive Director, Overseas Ministries Study Center, New Haven, CT

"This captivating personal journal—insightful, honest, and inspiring—recounts Fr. Luke Veronis' mission-field experiences. The author tells an amazing story of Christians on the one hand facing extreme deprivation, persecution, beatings, imprisonments, and death, and on the other hand testifying to dramatic personal conversions, miracles, mass baptisms, unwavering faith, and the astonishing renewal of the Church of Albania. Along the way the reader will be enriched by Fr. Luke's reflections on the Gospel, the Church, the ways and principles of Orthodox mission, as well as the life and work of Archbishop Anastasios, a truly apostolic figure in our times."

REV. DR. THEODORE STYLIANOPOULOS,
Archbishop Iakovos Professor of Orthodox Theology and Professor of New Testament (Retired); Holy Cross Greek Orthodox School of Theology

"No country in modern times has suffered more thorough religious repression than Albania. In the Communist era, every place of worship was either destroyed or turned to some other use. Many churches became armories, reversing the biblical prophecy of turning swords into plowshares. With the collapse of the Communist regime, the Orthodox Church returned to life with astonishing rapidity. Among the participants in that recovery was an American Orthodox priest, Luke Veronis. In Go Forth, *Fr. Luke provides a vivid first-person account of a resurrection he and his family took part in."*

JIM FOREST,
Author, *Praying with Icons*

"Go Forth *is a gem of a book. It tells the miraculous story of the resurrection of a church the communists thought they had destroyed. I pray that it will be used by the Holy Spirit to bring about an awakening of missions."*

FR. ANTHONY M. CONIARIS,
Founder of Light and Life Publishing Co.

GO FORTH

STORIES OF MISSION AND RESURRECTION
IN ALBANIA

LUKE A. VERONIS

WITH A FOREWORD BY ARCHBISHOP ANASTASIOS
OF TIRANA AND ALL ALBANIA

ANCIENT FAITH
PUBLISHING

CHESTERTON, INDIANA

Dedicated to

Faith, my beloved wife and partner in life and ministry,
and my precious children and co-missionaries
Paul, Theodora, Panayiota and Nicholas

"Let all that you do be done in love."
(1 Corinthians 16:14)

CONTENTS

ACKNOWLEDGMENTS

I want to thank His Beatitude Archbishop Anastasios for the charismatic witness of his apostolic life, for his inspiring and challenging writings over the past fifty years, and most of all for his love as a spiritual father to me and my family. I hope this book offers a glimpse of your life and mission!

Our experience in the mission field has led us to encounter many extraordinary people—some whom we considered living saints, others who inspired us with their search for truth, and still more who labored alongside us as co-missionaries and indigenous co-workers and friends. I thank each of you for blessing us in countless ways.

Another important group of family and friends who made our mission possible were those who spiritually and financially supported us during all our years as missionaries. We couldn't have stayed out in the field for more than a decade without the strong and ongoing support of these partners. Thank you to my parents, Fr. Alexander and Pearl Veronis, to the staff of the Orthodox Christian Mission Center, and to all who participated in this adventure.

In the publication of this book, I want to express my appreciation to the editorial staff of Conciliar Press for their willingness to publish this mission journal and the Endowment Fund for Orthodox Missions for covering part of its publication cost.

Finally, I offer my deepest gratitude to my beloved wife Faith, who sacrificed much, labored with me side by side, and experienced the greatest joy of serving our Lord among the nations. We are partners in life and co-sojourners on a path leading into the kingdom of heaven. Thank you for who you are, for all that you did during our years in Albania, and for all that you continue to do in our ministry and life! I love you dearly!

FOREWORD

There is no treasure more precious than the truth that was revealed by the Word of God. Therefore, the people who suffer most in our time are those who have been deprived of the Word, not because they themselves refuse to listen, but for the simple reason that those who have known it for centuries are not interested in passing it on. This certainty guides and inspires those who participate in the mission of the Church. They feel that their faith and love cannot be genuine if they do not try to do something practical to face this problem.

As a young theologian back in 1959, I had started to speak about "the forgotten commandment" (Matthew 28:19). Some people argued that this new missionary flame was due to an influence from Western Christianity. So we started to study carefully the history of the Orthodox Church, not only in order to answer our critics, but also to discover the principles, the methods, and the spirituality of the Orthodox apostolic tradition.

This effort proved to be a blessing for us as we have learned more about the witness of great Orthodox missionaries. The famous Byzantine brothers from Thessalonika, Saints Cyril and Methodios, evangelized the peoples of Moravia and started a movement that Christianized the Slavic peoples. St. Kosma Aitolos traveled throughout the Balkans during a dark period of history for Christianity, planting seeds of faith and reviving the Church. St. Herman and nine other monks left Valaam Monastery, traveled across the vast Russian Empire to reach Alaska, and introduced Christianity to the indigenous people of North America. St. Innocent spent five decades living and traveling throughout Alaska, Siberia, and Eastern Asia. He concluded his ministry as the metropolitan of Moscow, where he created the first Orthodox missionary society. And St. Nicholas Kasatkin entered Japan when Christianity still did not exist there, and died fifty years later, leaving behind more than 30,000 Orthodox Christians.

This inspiring tradition of missions within our Orthodox Church has been rediscovered over the last five decades—in theoretical sectors as well as in the realization of concrete work. The continuous development in missionary areas of Africa, Asia, and even Europe is a blessed contemporary reality. Our Lord's commandment, "Go therefore and make disciples of all nations" (Matthew 28:19), touches more and more members of the Orthodox Church. And they accepted that we can no longer remain passive in the face of this command of our Lord—that, as it was proclaimed in the 1970s, "Indifference to mission is a negation of Orthodoxy," and "A Church without mission is a contradiction in terms." If the Church shows no interest in the apostolic work with which she has been entrusted by the Triune God, she contradicts herself and her essence, and is a traitor in the warfare in which she is engaged. A static Church that lacks a vision and a constant endeavor to proclaim the Gospel to the *oikoumene* cannot be recognized as the "one, holy, catholic and apostolic Church" to which the Lord entrusted the continuation of His work.

The culminating point of this new missionary self-awareness of the Orthodox is found in the third paragraph of the recent "Message of the Primates of the Orthodox Churches" issued on October 12, 2008, in Constantinople. It states: "Inspired by the teaching and the work of the Apostle Paul, we underscore first and foremost the importance of the duty of mission for the life of the Church and in particular for the ministry of us all in accordance with the final commandment of the Lord: 'You will be my witnesses not only in Jerusalem, but throughout Judea and Samaria and to the uttermost parts of the earth' (Acts 1:8). The evangelization of God's people, but also of those who don't believe in Christ, constitutes the supreme duty of the Church. This duty must not be fulfilled in an aggressive manner, or by various forms of proselytism, but with love, humility and respect for the identity of each individual and the cultural particularity of each people. All Orthodox Churches must contribute to this missionary effort respecting the canonical order."

This personal journal that my spiritual child, Fr. Luke Veronis, has put together offers a small taste of the struggles and difficulties, as well as the joys and excitement of one such contemporary missionary effort. (For a much fuller account of the Albanian mission as a whole, read Lynette Hoppe's *Resurrection: The Orthodox Autocephalous Church of Albania 1991–2003*.) Fr. Luke participated, in 1987 and 1988, in the work we tried to accomplish in East Africa from 1981 to 1991, and he and Presbytera Faith were beloved collaborators in our efforts in Albania from 1994 until 2004. Although this is not a detailed account of the resurrection of the Orthodox Autocephalous Church of Albania, Fr. Luke has firsthand knowledge and shares our experiences, mainly from an American perspective and for an American audience, with his stories and anecdotes. These are his personal reflections, insights, and opinions, and of course not all are generally shared.

I thank God for this offering, and pray that those who read it may be inspired to discover their role in the ongoing divine plan of our Lord to "go into all the world and preach the gospel to every creature" (Mark 16:15).

Archbishop Anastasios of Tirana and All Albania
Feast of the Apostles Peter and Paul
June 29, 2009

INTRODUCTION ✠

The heroism of missionaries and their spirit of sacrifice and love always tend to give back to the old churches a new vigor of life.
—Archbishop Anastasios of Albania

These words summarize why I want to share stories from a decade-long journal of cross-cultural missionary work. The amazing miracle that has occurred in Albania since 1991, inspired by the Holy Spirit and under the vision and direction of Archbishop Anastasios, offers a glimpse of vitality, renewal, and vigor that will motivate and encourage our contemporary Church.

How does one proclaim the Good News of our Lord in the only country in recent history that absolutely forbade and persecuted any and every expression of religion for 24 years? The lands of Albania claim Christian heritage from the first century, yet endured the advance of Islam from the fourteenth century onward, followed by the most extreme totalitarian form of communism. Militant atheists crucified the Church and thought they had abolished it.

With the fall of communism in 1991, Archbishop Anastasios Yannoulatos arrived in Albania to see what, if anything, remained of this ancient Christian community. He faced the daunting task of proclaiming the Gospel and reviving a historic Church while confronting the many challenges of a post-communist setting: an enduring atheistic mentality, a broken societal infrastructure, rampant poverty, prevalent corruption, and ongoing religious prejudice.

This journal offers glimpses of how God has resurrected this Church, granting new hope to so many living in despair. In the early 1990s, Albanians struggled to rise above their status as the poorest nation in Europe. As they made great efforts to develop economically, anarchy and war posed unexpected threats. The atheistic spirit left over from communism seemed imbedded in many, while a new form of atheistic capitalism and materialism threatened to entice the people. How should the Church respond?

In my years in Albania, I learned that love and freedom exemplify the path of Orthodox Christian missions. We incarnate the Gospel of love, while respecting the freedom and dignity of every listener to respond as he or she feels touched by God. Authentic mission has nothing to do with coercion, trickery, or superficiality. Proclaiming the Good News implies revealing the love of God's Kingdom in word and deed, and inviting others to join the community of faith on a journey of salvation.

As you peruse these stories, I pray you will discover your own responsibility and privilege to participate in the Great Commission of our Lord Jesus Christ to "go therefore and make disciples of all the nations" (Matt. 28:19–20). For those actively working in the mission field, this diary may inspire you with examples of how God works among us. For those not called to this work, we all need to understand that God expects every Christian to support and participate in His call to all nations. The Church at home and the cross-cultural missionary play on the same team, working as partners for the glory of God's Kingdom to the ends of the earth.

It is imperative for all Christians to understand that whatever happens in the mission field halfway around the world directly affects them. Jesus Christ calls the Church His Body, and reminds each member how every part of His Body is connected to every other. American Christians cannot look at the Church of Albania, or the Church of Kenya, or the Church of Mexico, or the Church of Indonesia, as a community separate from themselves. St. Paul clearly teaches that "there should be no schism in the body, but *that* the members should have the same care for one another. And if one member suffers, all the members suffer with *it*; or if one member is honored, all the members rejoice with *it*" (1 Cor. 12:25–26).

I pray that this missionary journal will help all Christians understand their role in the overall drama of sacred history, and draw each person into a deeper relationship with God along the way. I believe the stories and anecdotes found here will inspire you. You may find gems of wisdom offered by "living saints" whose faith survived the horrors of communism. New believers who discovered the pearl of great price will share their spiritual journeys. You will see the struggles and successes of the servants who have tried to offer a witness of God's love under difficult conditions.

The most luminous example, of course, represents a unique voice in the contemporary missionary movement of the Orthodox Church, as well as in worldwide Christianity. Archbishop Anastasios of Albania describes himself as a candle before the icon of Christ, but he represents one of the brightest lights leading people to our Lord. His example incarnates divine wisdom and grace, inspiring, enlightening, and transforming those he meets. The archbishop offers the greatest example of how, in his own words, "the heroism of missionaries and their spirit of sacrifice and love give back to the old churches a new vigor of life."

Any who have entered the mission field, or who are preparing for cross-cultural service, will find here a source that can help them better prepare for the challenge that awaits them in the field. I have made and seen plenty of mistakes while serving as a short-term missionary in East Africa, and while playing a part in the rebirth and resurrection of the ancient Church in Albania. Missionaries need to learn from one another, and not reinvent the wheel each time they enter the field. This journal can offer some food for thought.

Finally, I want to challenge all of you to rethink your understanding and commitment to God's call to the nations. St. John Chrysostom taught, "There are two kinds of bishops. One is a pastor who says, 'My parish is my universe.' While the other believes, 'The universe is my parish.'" We could easily translate his words into a modern analogy of two types of Christians—the truly catholic and apostolic Christian whose worldview encompasses the universe, and the egocentric and parochial Christian who limits his vision to whatever centers around "me, my, and mine," whether at a personal, familial, ethnic, or national level.

Orthodox Christianity implies looking outward and remembering the other. *The Philokalia,* a collection of writings from the Church Fathers, teaches, "Blessed is the one who rejoices in his salvation, but even more blessed is the one who rejoices in the salvation of the other." St. John Chrysostom affirms this spirit when he says, "I do not believe in the salvation of anyone who does not try to save others."

In every generation, God calls His followers to reach out towards the "other," wherever the other may be—locally, nationally, and globally. God calls us to go to the ends of the world and share His unconditional love through the witness of our lives and words. More than 1.5 billion people, or approximately one quarter of the world's population today, have never even heard the Good

News of salvation that Jesus Christ brings. They have not rejected the Gospel, but have never met any faithful Christians! Can we hear God's voice calling us to respond to this situation?

My challenge to you as you read this book is this: Open your heart and mind, and find out what God is saying to you!

CHAPTER 1

THE ADVENTURE BEGINS

(1994)

EXPANDING MY WORLDVIEW   JANUARY 20

Today I arrive in Albania. As I sit in the Vienna airport, many emotions flood my mind. I'm excited to finally begin this ministry for which I've prepared for so long. I remember my first mission trip, before my final semester at Penn State University in 1987. I was studying to become a high school math teacher and basketball coach. As I thought about my future, I dreamed about doing something more than teaching in a suburban American high school. I inquired into the Peace Corps, but honestly couldn't imagine living outside of the United States for two years.

At this time, I heard that the Archdiocesan Mission Center (later to become the Orthodox Christian Mission Center, or OCMC) was sending its first short-term mission team to Kenya. One month in the bush of Africa sounded exotic and exciting. Although a two-year Peace Corps commitment frightened me, I figured I could do anything for one month, especially on a team with 25 other Americans.

The 1987 mission team to Kenya changed my life. I tasted the third-world reality for the first time, experiencing how a majority of the world lives. I met inspiring missionaries, starting with Archbishop Anastasios, along with Fr. Dan and Nancy Christopoulos. The joyous faith of the pious Kenyans touched me beyond words. In the midst of an exciting month-long project, I began hearing the first murmurs of God's call. I realized, though, that in order for me to hear Him clearly, He needed time to expand my worldview.

During a 1989 short-term mission trip to Ghana, Luke and Jimmy Hatsis dress up in traditional Ghanian robes as they visit the elders of a village.

I graduated Penn State in December, and my desire to return to Kenya only grew with each passing day. As a preparation for my planned six-month mission to Africa, I went to the U.S. Center for World Missions in Pasadena, California, to take an intensive one-month course entitled, "Perspectives on the World Christian Movement." Each day at this center, a different missionary taught the class. For the first time in my life, I met missionaries who had served in different countries for five, ten, twenty, even thirty years.

I entered this course very anxious about my six-month missionary stint. How could I live in Africa for such a long period, away from my family and without the support of a 25-member mission team? At the U.S. Center, however, I met people who had given lifelong service to missions. In addition, most of my two dozen classmates were preparing to enter the field for at least an initial two-to-three-year commitment. My own six-month trip began to look awfully small. Meanwhile, God continued to expand my worldview.

My second trip to Kenya opened my eyes even more to a new world. Horrific material poverty jeopardized countless people, especially the children, while a spiritual poverty hid the eternal hope offered by God. Imagine, more than 1.5 billion people in the world today have never had the opportunity to hear the Good News of Jesus Christ! Our Lord's prophetic voice came to mind: "The harvest truly is plentiful, but the laborers are few"

(Matt. 9:37). This entire experience unsettled me. If I accepted what I had learned in the Perspectives class, then I could no longer stay indifferent. This course helped me hear God's call more clearly. Yet the very thought frightened me. Would I have to reject living a "normal American life"? This thought haunted me for a long time.

I lived in Kenya for what turned into a year of service. Throughout, many doubts tempted me. Could I become a missionary? Did this mean I wouldn't be a high school math teacher and basketball coach? How could my future family grow up in another culture and country, always being a little different from the typical American? Would this mean that I would "deprive" my children of the comforts and advantages of American life? Did this mean that my children wouldn't grow up playing sports like other American children? Did this mean . . .? So many unsettling uncertainties!

I look back on that year of service and see how God gently took me by the hand, step by step, gradually leading me down a path I never dreamed of years before. In His wisdom, God didn't reveal to me how radically my life would change. He simply whispered, "Trust Me. Take this first step in faith, and don't worry about your future."

Taking a step in faith meant returning to the United States and entering Holy Cross Greek Orthodox School of Theology. I realized that I needed a stronger foundation in my own faith and relationship with God. Initially, I didn't go to the seminary with plans of becoming a priest. I desired only to grow in my love and understanding of my Lord, and to learn to commit myself more fully to Him and His Church.

This chapter of life reflects one of my most joyous times, as I began discovering the depths of our Orthodox faith, enjoying the fellowship of dear friends and co-sojourners in Christ, dreaming about how to serve God, and listening to His voice for direction. Over the next five summers, I led three OCMC mission teams to Africa—a construction team to Ghana in 1989, a youth ministry team to Kenya, Tanzania, and Uganda in 1990, and a catechism team to Kenya in 1993—while also traveling to St. Petersburg, Russia, for an exploratory mission team. Each experience enriched my life and understanding of mission in a different way. I learned to adapt to and appreciate different cultures, traditions, and peoples more easily. Each encounter helped me hear the voice of God in a clearer manner.

As a self-assured young American, I made plenty of mistakes. Thinking back, I often cringe at my immaturity and arrogance. Yet I grew from each experience. I learned to listen to people. I discovered one must remain humble and learn from others. I realized that the greatest way to imitate Christ was through loving service. I noted that too many missionaries "served" others in a dominating and sometimes demeaning manner. These missionaries didn't imitate Christ as much as stroke their own egos. Sometimes missionaries forget that we aren't the only ones who have something to offer and teach. We also have much to learn.

Another hard lesson was the way my American mentality focused on completing projects or accomplishing tasks, as opposed to cultivating and developing meaningful, authentic relationships. Other cultures and peoples value things differently than we do. We Westerners make this critical mistake too often. We allow a task or project to take priority over a personal relationship with the people.

As I think about my own past, I reflect on the tradition into which I enter, a tradition of great missionaries from the past—St. Paul and the early apostles, St. Gregory of Armenia, St. Patrick of Ireland, St. Frumentios of Ethiopia, Ss. Cyril and Methodios, apostles to the Slavs, St. Stephen of Perm, St. Makarios Glukarov of the Altai Mountains, St. Kosma Aitolos, Ss. Herman and Innocent of Alaska, and St. Nicholas of Japan. Jesus Christ commanded us to "go therefore and make disciples of all the nations, baptizing them in the name of the Father and of the Son and of the Holy Spirit, teaching them to observe all things that I have commanded you; and lo, I am with you always, *even* to the end of the age" (Matt. 28:19–20). The apostles and missionaries of the past tried to faithfully fulfill this command of our Lord. Of course, I am not placing myself in the same category with these great saints, but they are models I want to imitate in Albania.

WHY AM I HERE? A POST-COMMUNIST REALITY

What am I doing here? Why am I here? Three days have passed, and I am wondering if I was crazy to come. It would have been so much easier to have gotten a job in the States and settled down there. What did I get myself into?

I experienced similar feelings and fears when I first arrived in Kenya in 1988. The devil sure has a masterful way of cultivating fear and uncertainty. I wrestle with my anxiety while trying to understand how best to adjust. I keep thinking about how much easier it would be if my beloved fiancée Faith were here with me. Arduous mountains seem more surmountable when climbed in pairs. Yet I have to wait ten more months for her arrival. Of course, Christ is with me. He always comforts me during times of doubt. This morning, I meditated on the final promise of the Great Commission, "And lo, I am with you always, *even* to the end of the age" (Matt. 28:20). What words of reassurance and strength! I need that as I face the reality around me.

And what is the post-communist reality here? In so many ways, Albania is the forgotten country of Europe. It is isolated in the mountains northwest of Greece and south of Yugoslavia, yet its physical location did not cut Albania off from the rest of the world as much as did its separatist political policies. Albania lived in its own world for half a century. How many people in America even know that Albania exists, much less that it is a country in Europe?

Prior to World War II, Albania was a poor, underdeveloped country. It declared independence from the Ottoman Empire on November 12, 1912, yet found the Italians invading a few decades later. The brutal communist takeover following the Second World War offers a glimpse into one of the most oppressive regimes of the twentieth century. A startling fact for many is the way Albania detached itself from each of its communist benefactors— Yugoslavia (1944–48), Russia (1948–61), and China (1961–78). The Albanian dictator, Enver Hoxha, justified each separation by accusing these communist bulwarks of abandoning the true Marxist-Leninist path. In true Stalinist fashion, Hoxha believed that only Albania represented authentic communism, and thus his country lived in isolation from the rest of the world.

Hoxha did claim certain successes during his rule, such as bringing electricity to every village, raising the literacy rate of the population to 95 percent, and making progress in industry and agriculture. The people of Albania lived in such a time warp, though, that many believed the state propaganda and thought they had the highest living standard in all of Europe.

Hoxha's harsh regime claimed innumerable victims. Political opponents, religious figures, and dissidents suffered in the most unimaginable ways. The sadistic labor camps, prisons, and torture chambers matched the worst in the Soviet Union or any other communist country. In one area, Hoxha outdid the other communist leaders—in religious persecution. Following the communist takeover in the 1940s, the government tried to control all religious groups. The religious makeup of Albania prior to communism was a tolerant mixture of Islam, Orthodox Christianity, and Roman Catholicism. One census in the 1940s showed 69 percent of the country Islamic (50 percent Sunni and 19 percent Bektashi), 21 percent Orthodox, and 10 percent Roman Catholic. In a conversation that Hoxha held with Stalin in 1947, however, he told the Russian leader that approximately 35 percent of the Albanian population was Orthodox.

Hoxha's religious persecution showed no preferences. The state killed, arrested, or exiled many of the clergy, especially the most charismatic and well-educated. The government closed all seminaries and medresahs, forbidding ordination of new clergy without their approval. The state confiscated all religious properties, limited religious activity to within the church or mosque, replaced religious education in schools with atheistic and anti-religious propaganda, and used whatever means possible to weed out this "opium of the people."

The culmination of Hoxha's militant atheism occurred in conjunction with China's Cultural Revolution in 1967, when Hoxha declared Albania to be the first and only totally atheistic state in the world. He closed every place of worship, whether church or mosque, and forbade any public or private expression of religion under the threat of arrest and death. Under its constitution, Albania triumphantly declared itself totally void of the scourge of religion.

The full fruit of this stance became evident only with the coming of democracy. For example, the Orthodox Church's clergy diminished from 440 serving in the 1940s to only 22 old men by 1991. Some estimate that the state destroyed 1600 churches, monasteries, and church buildings. No church infrastructure remained. The religious persecution showed mercy on no one. The Islamic community (Sunni and Bektashi), the Orthodox Church, and the Roman Catholic Church all suffered. The best-educated clergy posed the greatest threat to the state, and thus suffered in the harshest manner. Yet even pious, simple villagers who tried to maintain their faith in any visible way risked their lives and the well-being of their entire families.

Along with the distortion of Albania's soul, communism left a horrible economic and social legacy. Many Albanians believed the lie that they lived under Europe's highest standard of living, but the post-communist situation betrays another reality. Three years after the fall of communism, the city of Tirana is still the poorest capital in Europe. Hundreds of stolen Mercedes Benzes compete on the streets with villagers who enter the capital city riding donkeys or driving horses and carts. Alongside the wide boulevards the Italians built in the 1930s and 1940s run many unpaved side streets that become quite muddy during the winter months. Trees that once lined the streets and boulevards of the city disappeared during the first years of democracy, as people desperate for fuel used the wood to heat their homes.

There is little construction, despite the fact that the communist-era buildings are dilapidated and falling apart. People wait in bread lines in front of stores with broken windows. They say the unemployment rate exceeds 70 percent. When I go to the outskirts of the city, I see only closed or rundown factories that the Chinese built 25 years ago. People looted many of these factories during the first years of democracy. The dilapidated social and economic condition of the country hides her natural virgin beauty—majestic mountains, gorgeous lakes, green hills, and sparkling seacoasts. I think of neighboring Greece with her famous islands and magnificent coastline, and wonder if Albania could rival her natural beauty. For some, the attractiveness of Albania could supersede that of Greece because she remains unspoiled and undiscovered.

On a personal level, certain aspects won't be as bad as I originally thought. The weather is much better than I thought it would be. Very rarely will it snow in the capital. The only problem is that it seems colder inside the homes than out. Concrete homes with no insulation or central heating are the norm. Typically, Albanians will heat up one room with a wood or oil stove. Whenever you leave the warmth of the main room, it is like walking outside. In addition, we don't have electricity for five or more hours a day, so electrical heaters do little good. This means the cold damp air stays inside the homes, and literally, it often feels colder inside the homes than out!

Then we face the problem of water, which runs only three times a day—at 4–6 AM, 1–3 PM, and 7–9 PM—and only if you live in a house or on the first or second floor of an apartment building. For Albanians who live on the third floor or higher, the water pressure rarely is strong enough to push the water up. Therefore, they have to carry containers down to the first floors, fill them up, and carry them back up to their home. Since the water pressure is strongest in the morning, most wake up at four in the morning to fill their containers.

Fr. Martin Ritsi had warned me that water heaters did not exist in Albania, so I thought I'd be taking cold showers. Thank God, though, in the last month water heaters have entered into the Albanian market for those who can afford them. After Day One, I can already say that I am learning to appreciate the simple blessings in life—water and heat!

I conclude today with these words from the missionary John Mott: "Difficulties are not without their advantages. They are not to unnerve us. They are not to be regarded simply as subjects for discussion or as grounds for skepticism and pessimism. They are not to cause inaction, but rather to intensify activity. They were made to be overcome. Above all, they are to create profound distrust in human plans and energy, and to drive us to God."

WE WANT OUR CHURCH BACK!

I walked the streets of Tirana with Fr. Martin to help me get a better flavor of the city. Many old buildings built by the Italians 60 years ago sit next to structures reflecting the drab communist architecture. Masses of people flood the streets following their afternoon siesta, which is a two-hour rest after a typical 3 PM lunch. This beautiful Albanian tradition fills the boulevards and streets of the city, as people dress up in their finest for a late afternoon stroll.

As we walked, Fr. Martin shared his vision about the mission here. He has great ideas, but the Church lacks trained people to fulfill these dreams. When I first visited Albania in May 1993, Fr. Martin was deeply involved with the youth. His involvement has decreased, though, because of administrative responsibilities. The archbishop has prioritized a stable infrastructure for the Church. I can see that Fr. Martin doesn't have the ministerial interaction he would like with the Albanians.

We talked about turning the St. Prokopi Church into a "youth parish." Up until last year, this church functioned as a restaurant. The state used many of the undestroyed churches for other purposes, such as gymnasiums, storage houses, army depots, and clubs. Even with the arrival of democracy, the government refuses to return many of these properties to the Church. Tirana once had three Orthodox churches. In the center of the city, a mosque stood on one corner and the Annunciation Orthodox Cathedral on the opposite side. In 1967, the state destroyed the century-old church and built Hotel Tirana on its property. The second Orthodox church became a gymnasium. St. Prokopi, located on a scenic hill in the middle of the main park, became a restaurant.

Last year on Palm Sunday, the youth of the cathedral marched with a couple of hundred believers through the streets of Tirana following the Divine

Liturgy, surrounding the Church of St. Prokopi. While people ate inside the restaurant, our youth began chanting, "We want our church back!" As the police arrived, the believers began chanting even louder, "We want our church back." After an hour or so, some authorities arrived and promised that they would return the property to the Church. Although skeptical, our believers slowly dispersed.

When nothing happened over the next few months, the youth organized another protest. Once again they marched through the streets of Tirana, surrounded the church-turned-restaurant, and repeatedly yelled, "We want our church back!" Again, the police came. This time, however, the youth refused to disperse. They threatened to stay and begin a hunger strike until the state authorities listened to their plea.

After many discussions, pleas, and bargaining, combined with unceasing prayer, the authorities agreed to give back the church. Fr. Martin shared with me how the archbishop wanted to make this church a youth center, since the youth had played a central role in getting the property back. The university stands close by, so it would be perfect for an outreach to college students.

As I talked with Fr. Martin, I could see myself falling into the danger of taking on too many responsibilities. I will be teaching at least two classes at the seminary. Earlier today, Sister Galini, a nun from the St. John the Forerunner Monastery in Greece, suggested that I begin a youth program in Elbasan, a city an hour and a half away. Sister Filothei, another nun, asked that I go weekly to Korça and Gjirokaster, two cities four and five hours south. On top of all this, I keep thinking about my priority of language learning.

Part of me wants to jump into these ministerial activities because of the need. I realize, though, that one can get involved in many needs and never learn the language well. To be honest, I am surprised and disappointed to see how little Albanian many of our missionaries know. Everyone seems too busy, and language learning isn't a priority. I can see how missionaries could live here for years using a translator and never really learn the language well. I don't want that to happen to me.

We show our love for the Albanian people and respect for their language and culture by learning their language. May I never forget this! Learning a language, though, overwhelms me more than anything else. Adjusting to a new life, a new environment, and new people is easy compared to mastering a language. I've been trying to learn modern Greek for the past eight years and haven't succeeded well. I don't feel linguistically gifted. It will take much effort and time, plus a good dose of God's grace! I pray that I will have the discipline to put in at least three hours a day for language learning.

Tom Brewster's book, *Learning Acquisition Made Practical—LAMP*, emphasizes that one learns a language because he wants to communicate with someone. If I truly want to be a missionary and show my love to the Albanian people, then I have to communicate the Gospel in their heart language. The best way for me to show the love of God to them is to first take the time to learn their language. I can then use this tool as a means of sharing the good news of Christ. Much hard work lies ahead of me. The key will be discipline.

As I reflect on today, I think of what Isobel Kuhn, a missionary to China, once said. "I believe that in each generation God has 'called' enough men and women to evangelize all the yet unreached tribes of the earth . . . everywhere I go, I constantly meet with men and women who say to me, 'When I was young I wanted to be a missionary, but I got married instead.' Or, 'My parents dissuaded me,' or some such thing. No, it is not God who does not call. It is man who will not respond."

LAY ASIDE ALL CARES OF THIS LIFE

What a moving and beautiful Divine Liturgy today. The enthusiasm I witnessed last May is still alive! Several hundred people packed the church. The choir sang magnificently. Although almost all churches throughout Albania follow the Byzantine tradition of music, the cathedral in Tirana uses the Russian-style music of Bishop Theofan Noli. Noli was the first Albanian bishop of the twentieth century, and even the first prime minister of the country in 1924. Albania remembers him as one of the country's modern "founding fathers" and has even placed his picture on the most common currency bill, the 100-lek bill. Noli was an outstanding intellectual who translated many classical works, as well as numerous church hymns and services.

Throughout the Divine Liturgy, constant movement occurred in the church. Hundreds of believers stayed throughout the service, while several hundred others came in and out, lighting their candles, listening to parts of the service, kissing the icons, talking with one another, and then leaving. This makes the church quite noisy, yet it seems to give it life. People are still in the process of understanding what it means to worship in church. Many come in the middle of their morning routine. They go to the open market, buy the few fruits and vegetables they can find, then stop in church for a few minutes before continuing on their way.

Fr. Martin gave an insightful sermon emphasizing how the Church welcomes not only saints, but sinners. Some believers don't like to see former communists enter the Church. Some who suffered persecution now see their former persecutors or informants entering the Church. Fr. Martin asked, "Would Christ not accept the communists and former spies? What about the apostle Paul, that fierce persecutor of the early Church? Paul admitted that he was the 'first among sinners' because he persecuted the Church, yet he became its greatest apostle! We have to accept communists and former persecutors of Christ just as Jesus accepted them. Remember, he does not desire the death of a sinner, but his repentance and salvation."

As I reflected on this liturgical experience, I thanked God for a packed church. Yet this is only one of two Orthodox churches in Tirana. For a city of 350,000 people, filling a church with 500 people isn't something so great. We need to establish other churches on the northwest side of town and in the outlying neighborhoods. Still, I thank God that churches are open and people are interested!

Following the Liturgy, I walked around town and looked at the faces of so many people. I kept thinking about what knowledge they have of God. I saw numerous signs for horoscopes, palm readers, and other superstitious places. How many senseless ways people try to figure out their future, or communicate with the Divine! We have to help these people place all their concerns in the hands of a loving God who truly cares about us.

Today at the Great Entrance of the Divine Liturgy, we prayed, "Let us lay aside all our earthly cares that we may receive the King of all." At that moment, I lifted up my prayer requests—for a translator, a language tutor, a house, my future ministry, the people of Albania, and my dear Faith. I found comfort in the fact that I don't have to deal with these concerns alone. God will look after them and care for them.

I also found strength knowing that in the Divine Liturgy I united myself to my Lord Jesus, as well as to Faith and all my beloved family and friends back home. At each Divine Liturgy, we enter into the Kingdom of heaven. All worshippers, past and present, become one with Christ, and through Christ, with one another. In Christ, we are bonded to one another. Even though I won't see my dear fiancée for several months, I know that every Sunday and each Liturgy we will be united to one another in a mystical way. What a wonderful way to keep intimate contact with Faith!

STEAL THE BRIDE

I went looking for apartments today, most of which are quite Spartan. Most don't have telephone hook-ups, water heaters, or water deposits. The thought of going off on my own still frightens me a bit. I'd love to find an apartment close to the home of Fr. Martin and Renee.

I received a fax from Faith today. She continues to struggle at home with her family. They can't understand or accept our future life as missionaries. Of course, how many families would understand their daughter leaving the comforts of America to live in a post-communist, third-world mission field? Even many pious families would rebel against this.

I try to think how her mother processes this idea, a woman who left her Greek village to find a better life in America. She dreamed that her daughters would reap the "benefits" of life in the States. Isn't this the American dream for all immigrants? Greek-Americans came to the States like so many other immigrants—with nothing but hope for a better future. Three of our four grandparents could recall the struggles and sacrifices they made for their children.

Greeks were a despised minority in America a hundred years ago. I remember reading a newspaper article from the early 1900s that used the acronym PIGS to describe the scum of the immigrants—Poles, Italians, Greeks, and Slavs. My mother used to tell us a story about how my Uncle Harry got fed up with the ridicule he was enduring from his schoolmates and tried to take a butcher knife to school. When my grandmother asked him what he was doing, he responded, "The first kid who calls me a dirty Greek will pay for it with this knife!" Thank God my grandmother stopped him.

The first generation of Greek-Americans worked hard to educate their children and give them unlimited opportunities. The second generation (my parents' and Faith's father's generation) integrated fully into American life, becoming one of the best-educated and wealthiest minority groups in the States. The third-generation Greek-Americans were supposed to reap the benefits of all the previous struggle.

Faith and her family are a classic example. Faith worked hard for her undergraduate degrees in Psychology and Communications, as well as her two Master's degrees in Elementary Education and Special Education. The Greek-American mentality emphasized the importance of family, and close-knit family ties represented the norm in her parents' circles. Allowing the idea of missions to interfere with the "Greek-American dream" was incomprehensible. How could a daughter leave her family and their dreams behind? And to go to Albania of all places! For many Greeks, the thought of Albania conjures up images of a rugged and wild people. Greeks recall when Italy invaded Greece via Albania in World War II. The Greeks held them back, but the memory of war left an indelible mark.

In my morning prayers, I read several inspiring passages which answered the very questions Faith and I are wrestling with. Commenting on the way Peter tempted Jesus to avoid His upcoming crucifixion and death (Matt. 16:20–26), William Barclay writes,

> *The hardest temptation of all is the one which comes from protecting love. There are times when fond love seeks to deflect us from the perils of the path of God; but the real love is not the love which holds the knight at home, but the love which sends him out to obey the commandments of the chivalry which is given, not to make life easy, but to make life great. . . . If we meet life in the constant search for safety, security, ease and comfort, if every decision is taken from worldly-wise and prudential motives, we are losing all that makes life worth while. Life becomes a soft and flabby thing, when it might have been an adventure. Life becomes a selfish thing, when it might have been radiant with service. . . . The person who plays for safety ceases to be a human, for humans were made in the image of God.*

How true this is for our future and all the concerns Faith's parents have. If we place Christ first in our lives, then we should offer everything we have to Him. It may appear crazy to some, yet this "foolishness" St. Paul talks about is the way of ultimate faithfulness and peace.

When I shared with my seminarians that Faith's parents didn't want her to come to Albania, they just laughed and told me to follow an old Albanian tradition. When the parents of the bride don't accept the groom, the groom and his friends literally "steal the bride" in the middle of the night. Once the bride is at the groom's house, the deal is done! Wait until I tell Faith this one. She'd better get ready!

THE DEMONS OF DESPAIR

I am alone in Albania.

I have been staying at the home of Fr. Martin and Renee since my arrival one week ago, but they left today for Greece on a personal retreat. I thought some of the Albanian youth I met last May might come by the house, but they haven't. I miss Faith. It's cold. The electricity keeps going out. I can't understand anyone here. I haven't started my language lessons yet. I feel quite useless and unproductive. It's official: I've been here for one week, and the demons of despair are on the attack!

The last few days I've walked all around Tirana, trying to get used to the city. It's really a small city. I already feel comfortable going anywhere. Each day, I observe the people and see a spiritual battle. The Albanians long to become "European" quickly. Many of the worst elements of Western society have invaded Albania en masse. I walk along the streets and see the newspaper stands selling *Sex Today* newspapers and other pornographic literature. Albanian society is a strange mixture of traditional village life and values, combined with a dominant communist ideology and mentality, intermixed with recent Western ideas and freedom.

How can the Church influence this society? How can Christians be "salt" that flavors such a country, and "yeast" that touches its very fabric? Can the Gospel help these people free themselves from atheistic communism without blindly embracing atheistic capitalism? The future of Albania remains so uncertain. As I walk around observing people, I keep praying that the light of Christ can open their eyes to see the way of lasting peace and serenity of soul.

Despite these challenging thoughts, I'm home in an empty house and the demons of despair keep attacking. I feel lazy and lethargic. I listened to some Albanian language tapes for an hour. I tried to prepare for my two classes at the seminary tomorrow. Yet I feel unmotivated.

I need to lift myself up from this depressed mood, so I decided to read a book on Mother Teresa which I received as a gift before leaving the States. Mother Teresa always uplifts my spirits and is a good antidote for the demons of despair. What an amazing saint of our times. If the Lord wills, I pray that

I may meet her here in Albania one day. Her message is so simple, yet quite profound. "God created everyone in His own image. He loves us. God created us for great things—to receive His love and to share it with others." Her message of love is powerful because her life exemplifies this love like those of few people living. She tells her Missionaries of Charity to proclaim the good news more through their actions than through their words. Of course, whenever someone asks them why they do what they do, they respond clearly, "We do it all because of Jesus."

This message and example offer a powerful model for me as a missionary. Before ever preaching, we have to be in union with Christ. We have to strive to radiate Christ, and Christ alone. We must crucify our ego, which always tries to pop up its ugly head. Everything must begin and end with and in Christ.

FAMILY BLESSINGS   FEBRUARY 1

Mom and Dad celebrate their thirty-fifth wedding anniversary today. My brother Niko celebrated his thirty-fourth birthday three days ago. What a blessing and support my family has been! When I think about my "calling" in missions, I could mention many factors: my experiences in Africa, meeting inspirational missionaries and people of faith, learning about the imperative of missions from our faith and tradition, as well as my excitement at the adventure of a challenge. Ultimately, though, my calling comes from a deep and intimate relationship with God, which began from my earliest years of life.

I credit the initial stages of my love and understanding of God, and a cultivation of my desire to follow Him, to my parents. The faith and life they modeled exposed all five of us children to God in a most beautiful manner. Not only did they offer a powerful example, but they tried to find every opportunity for us to discover this faith for ourselves—whether through our family prayers and Bible time, through the ministries of the Annunciation Church and our diocesan activities (with all the Bible studies, retreats, summer camps, and youth activities), or through finding unique experiences of faith for us to encounter.

My parents instilled a strong foundation of faith within me and cultivated a universal vision of life. For as long as I can remember, my parents have been involved in ecumenical outreach. We children saw them participate in various activities related to the Civil Rights Movement of the 1960s and

'70s. From six years old onward, I walked the Church World Services' CROP Hunger Walks, which my father has been overseeing for the past 35 years. We watched our parents work with Church Women United, the Lancaster Council of Churches, ecumenical activities, in the local soup kitchens and homeless shelters, as well as reaching out constantly to the poor and needy in more ways than I can mention.

My universal worldview expanded as a child when I saw our house full of African students and various missionaries from around the world. Their stories enticed me and filled me with the desire to visit Africa. Then when I went to Africa myself, I was amazed to meet countless people who knew my father's name and praised him for all he had done for them. Some were students who had studied in America. Others were family members of students in America. Still others were people my parents had helped financially or in some other way. The Orthodox Church recognized my parents' pioneer vision of mission when the Orthodox Christian Mission Center named its administrative center in honor of my father.

One of the greatest lessons in life I learned from my parents was to give generously and to love the poor, needy, and defenseless. My parents taught me that if I err, I should err on the side of generosity. Err on the side of helping others. Err on the side of love! Even if a beggar may be deceiving me, God knows. He will take care of that. My job is to help others as much as possible, in as generous a way as possible.

I thank God for my parents and their legacy. I pray that I may be faithful in planting that universal vision and missionary legacy here in Albania!

YOU HAVE CONQUERED ME
BY EXAMPLE   FEBRUARY 2

Happy Birthday to myself! I thank God for 29 blessed and joyful years of life. On this feastday of our Lord, when Mary and Joseph presented their son in the Temple at 40 days old, I was born in 1965. As I look back on my first 29 years of life, I think about how everything has just been a preparation. Now I am ready to begin my life's ministry and calling. God has blessed me richly throughout my upbringing. I have finished school and received two Master's degrees. I have participated in seven short-term mission trips. I have left my childish ways and become a man. Now I can begin. Christ began His ministry at 30. I'm starting one year early. What do I have to offer? How much do I still have to learn? My greatest prayer is that I can serve others in humility, freely sharing all the blessings I have received with others while constantly learning and growing.

I didn't celebrate my first birthday in Albania in any special manner. The Ritsis are still in Greece. The only other person in Albania who knows my birthday is Elton, my translator. Faith sent me a five-page fax, with messages from all the people from my Bible study group in Lancaster.

I began the day in church, celebrating the Presentation of Christ in the Temple. Church was full for a weekday liturgy. I felt God's presence throughout the service. One thought that kept swimming in my head, however, was how to imitate the unconditional love of Christ for all people. No matter what their belief system—whether faithful Christian or nominal believer, whether Muslim, atheist, or agnostic—I must love them unreservedly. All people are children of God, and He loves them unconditionally. Didn't Jesus shock the religious authorities by accepting those outside the accepted boundaries of faith? Look at the "questionable people" Jesus ministered to—the Samaritan woman, the Roman ce turion, the adulterous woman, the tax-collectors, the Syrophoenician woman, the harlots, zealots, lepers, and all kinds of sinners.

Maybe my train of thought came from thinking of Tonia, a Greek-Australian girl I met yesterday. This woman described herself as a feminist and agnostic. She told me how few young people in Australia have anything to do with the Church, other than attending an occasional wedding or baptism. She expressed an absolute faith in herself and in humanity. No need for God! Her worldview challenged my thinking and made me wonder how to reach such people with the Gospel. She is quite a nice person and believes in doing good for humanity. She works in a school for the blind. She expresses a love for others, but finds no need for God. When I tried to share our treasure of faith, she seemed totally uninterested.

Following that conversation, I spent half the day reading *The Keys of the Kingdom* by A. J. Cronin. This provocative novel proved to be a great follow-up to my visit with Tonia. The book helped me reflect on how I view people who don't hold the same belief system as myself. The main character in the novel, a Scottish Catholic missionary priest named Fr. Francis, based his entire life on the idea of tolerance and humility. He didn't judge a person of another belief system. Of course, Fr. Francis believed in Christ as his God, but never tried to coerce anyone to follow Christ. As a missionary, he carefully avoided making "rice" Christians—people who accepted the faith because they received something material from the missionary.

I did not fully accept the philosophy of Fr. Francis, but I wrestled with these ideas. After reading this book, I thought about Tonia and her stubbornness towards God. She saw no reason to believe in God. She claimed to be at peace with her belief system. When I tried to talk about my faith and its impact on my life, she blithely replied, "That's good for you, but if I don't feel any need for such a Savior and if I'm at peace already, then why can't you accept that?" This book reminded me that the best way to minister to such people is to love them unconditionally and show them the value of Christ through the Christianity I live. I may not be able to convince certain people with any words of great truth, but I may touch them with the witness of my life.

An episode in the book exemplified this truth. Mr. Chia was a powerful political figure in the novel who displayed xenophobia, despising all foreigners and their religion. When Fr. Francis healed his only son, after all the local Chinese doctors failed, Mr. Chia grudgingly agreed to become a Christian. He thought the missionary would expect this as repayment for the good he had done for his family. Fr. Francis knew the man did not believe and had no interest in being instructed, so he rejected his offer, saying, "You do not believe, and do not have time to be instructed. My acceptance of you would be a forgery for God. You owe me nothing, so please go."

Thirty years later, after a saintly life of constant sacrifice and humble service to all the people of the area, regardless of their faith, Fr. Francis prepared to return to his homeland. On the night before his departure, Mr. Chia approached the priest and asked to be baptized. The priest was shocked at the request and expressed disbelief in the man's sincerity.

"Once, many years ago, when you cured my son, I was not serious," Mr. Chia responded. "But then I was unaware of the nature of your life. The goodness of a religion is best judged by the goodness of its adherents. My friend, you have conquered me by example. We are brothers, you and I. Your Lord must also be mine. Then, even though you must depart tomorrow, I shall be content, knowing that in our Master's garden our spirits will one day meet."

"I WANT TO SLEEP WITH YOU"

I finally found a simple apartment with four rooms and a kitchen. God answered another prayer through my language classes at the European Baptist Federation. I began ten days ago with a great teacher, Rosa. She told us that if we stick to the program, we will be speaking fluent Albanian within six months. I have classes every day for an hour and a half. In addition to this, I'm studying at home for an hour, as well as trying to practice whatever I learn with my neighbors and all the merchants I pass on the street.

Every day it takes me an hour to walk to class. I stop on the way, practicing my Albanian with the shopowners I meet. I realize that to learn a language, I have to overcome any inhibitions about making mistakes. Today, when I greeted Rosa, I wanted to impress her with my new Albanian vocabulary. I attempted to say, "I want to speak with you," but mixed up the words "flas" and "fle." Instead I told her, "I want to sleep with you." She just laughed and said, "Keep trying. That's the only way you're going to learn!" I'm sure this will only be the first of many mistakes.

COMMUNIST CAMP TURNED SEMINARY

What can I say about my first impressions of our seminary? It is located in a former "workers' camp" on the beach in Durres, a 45-minute drive from Tirana. The Church pays $7000 per month to rent this decrepit building, which has no heat, sporadic electricity, and only cold water that comes three times a day.

Someone told me an interesting history of the building. It was named after a famous Greek communist who fought in the Civil War between the communists and democrats in Greece back in 1945–49. One policy the Greek communists practiced during the war was to kidnap children in Greece and bring them to Albania for communist indoctrination. What poetic justice that a half-century later, a building named after a famous Greek communist is being used to train Orthodox priests!

The school has three classes with around 35 students in each class. Students range from 20 to 50 years old. Presently, I'm teaching two New Testament classes to the first- and second-year students. As in any school, we see motivated students and others who are uninspired. Many of the older students find it difficult to concentrate for five hours of classes per day. Twenty years have passed since many of them have been in school.

Most students see their families once or twice a month. We have tried to offset their financial sacrifice by giving a symbolic monthly stipend to support their families. We are working patiently and diligently with the students in hopes of establishing a strong foundation for the future leaders of this Church.

Fr. Luke teaching at the Resurrection of Christ Theological Academy.

During my first week at school, I didn't make a good impression with some of my students. When I teach, I'm pretty laid back. At one point, I half sat, half leaned, on my desk as I taught the students. Only later did a student tell me how rude and unbecoming this was for a "professor." In Albanian schools, a teacher can never be so casual in front of the students. I have to be careful to respect the norms of this society.

MASS BAPTISMS

Miron and his zealous gang of converts came to Christ two years ago. Most are from Muslim families, although they considered themselves more atheist than Muslim. During their studies at the Academy of Art, several faced illnesses or crises in their lives. They visited a popular Christian "healer," who they claim not only healed them, but guided them into faith and a relationship with Jesus Christ. This group became so zealous for the faith that they started to travel throughout the villages of Albania preaching the Gospel.

Fr. Martin has worked with this group and has tried to direct them in a more structured way to offer catechism to the people, preparing them for baptism. Thus, this group travels the country, staying in a village for several months and gathering a group of interested believers, whom they catechize. After several months of training, Fr. Martin and an Albanian priest will perform a mass baptism. Today such a baptism was scheduled, and I traveled with them to Rrushkull, a village between Tirana and Durres. Earlier in the summer, Fr. Martin baptized 80 people here. Today, 45 others waited for holy baptism.

Before beginning the Divine Liturgy inside the home of one of the believers, we faced our first dilemma. The big baptismal font we'd brought didn't fit through the door of the house. No problem. The owner of the house simply got a saw and cut out part of the frame of his door!

We proceeded to celebrate the Divine Liturgy with about 30 people inside the house and the remaining 30 outside. Fr. Martin stopped every ten minutes to explain the Liturgy. The baptisms occurred in the middle of the Divine Liturgy. "As many as have been baptized into Christ have put on Christ." Here is the beginning of the Christian walk—accepting Christ and putting Him in the center of our lives. From this time forward, the believer will face many temptations and struggles, but he now does not face anything alone. Christ is with him and in him!

Following the baptism, we went to the house of Vasili, whose Muslim son-in-law had been baptized. He exuded joy that his son-in-law was now a Christian. We made merry in typical Albanian fashion—with a literal feast of four different courses of meat.

Let me say something about Albanian hospitality. No matter how poor a family may be, Albanians consider it a sacred duty to offer hospitality to all who enter their home. In this case, the host expected us to stay for hours. Each course would be served with me thinking this was the final course. A half hour later, they would bring out another plate full of meat. And each plate of meat is offered with a generous refill of *raki*, the homemade Albanian moonshine.

We left the village with our spirits high and our bellies full. I discussed the issue of follow-up to these baptisms with Fr. Martin. Miron and his group feel their call is for evangelism to the villages around Albania. The unfortunate reality for the newborn believers, however, is that following such a baptism, a priest might visit them only once every several months. For many of these areas, a priest will only come for Pascha and Christmas. The need to develop some type of follow-up catechism is urgent.

Simon, one of Miron's co-workers, told me about some of the problems they faced with the many new Protestant missionaries coming from America and Western Europe. In one traditionally Orthodox village, Miron and his group of evangelists taught the villagers about their faith. Many of the older villagers had been baptized before the closure of churches in 1967. Our evangelists helped to catechize and prepare their children and grandchildren for baptism. After the baptisms, however, some Western evangelical missionaries came and confused the villagers. They scolded the villagers for wearing crosses, having icons in their homes, and accepting infant baptism. Many of these missionaries come from a fundamentalist background and don't even consider Orthodox or Roman Catholics Christian.

I'm shocked when I see the arrogance and ignorance with which too many of these missionaries come to Albania. They come thinking they will "save" the people by preaching the Gospel for the first time ever in these lands. Unfortunately, they don't realize that the Gospel has been preached here since the coming of St. Paul in the first century. Christian communities have existed here for twenty centuries. This is a land of martyrs' blood and sacrifice. Sure, the vast number of Albanians know little about faith. Yet missionaries need to come with humility and respect, understanding the people, their history, their faith, their belief. Don't confuse them by saying a Western-style Christianity is the only type of Christianity!

Simon summarized a very valid point. "Since many of the Protestant groups come with material gifts from the West, the people embrace them and become very confused with us. I don't understand. The vast majority of villages around Albania are Muslim. Why can't they focus on these areas first, before confusing the people in traditionally Orthodox villages?"

A JOURNEY OF FAITH   FEBRUARY 27

In today's Divine Liturgy, the archbishop ordained John Fatmir Pelushi to the diaconate. He is a very sincere and humble man, quite smart and well read. He knows the Church Fathers extensively and is constantly sharing stories from the lives of the saints and desert Fathers. He comes across as a well-rounded churchman. He doesn't hold fanatical views about Orthodoxy. He sees the essence of the Gospel as love. He believes we must show this unconditional love and respect for people of all religions. Maybe his sensitivity towards other faiths comes partly from the dynamics of his own family, which includes Orthodox, Catholic, Muslim, and Bektashi members.

John's immediate family comes from a Bektashi background. Bektashi are a mystical Islamic sect that began in the thirteenth century in Asia Minor. The sect spread to the lands of Albania after the sixteenth century. Bektashism combines numerous practices and beliefs of Islam and Christianity. They have a type of baptism, honor some Orthodox saints, and reverence icons. They have three ranks of clergy, and their clergy are celibate. They drink wine. In other words, Bektashism is not an orthodox Islamic group. John told me his region became Bektashi two centuries ago in order to avoid paying the tax the Ottoman Empire imposed on all Christians. Before that, his people and their region had been Christians for centuries. Maybe in order to alleviate their guilt at having left Christianity, they kept numerous Christian features within their faith, and adopted a sort of pseudo-Islamic faith.

John's own journey of faith is fascinating. His formative years coincided with the anti-religious propaganda following the closure of churches in 1967. In 1975, as a high school senior, he had a passion to learn French. One night, he had a dream that St. John the Theologian told him about Christ. Of course, he did not know who St. John the Theologian was. The next day, which happened to be the feastday of St. John, a dear friend who was an underground Orthodox Christian offered the young student Fatmir a French New Testament, telling him this would help him learn French. Of course, this man had other intentions.

Fatmir's reading ignited a spark of faith within his soul. The Gospel of John especially had an impact on him. Only much later did he realize that the man who came to him in the dream was the author of this Gospel. This thirst for God grew as he asked a librarian friend of his to secretly lend him any religious books from the main library in Tirana. He devoured each one. Although the state heightened its anti-religious repression during the following years, Fatmir came into contact with other believers, meeting them at great risk. A special home was that of the Çiço sisters of Korça, where he would celebrate Pascha or Christmas, or participate in secret liturgies.

Four years later, in 1979, Fr. Kosma Qirjo secretly baptized Fatmir in the basement of his home. Fatmir took the name of John, after the author of the fourth Gospel. Of course, Fr. Kosma endangered his life to baptize John at this time. The past decades had seen plenty of priests suffer terribly for trying to practice their faith. Fr. Kosma was one of the bravest of the Orthodox priests, secretly performing liturgies, baptisms, and confessions during all the years of communism.

Years later, John fled Albania to Italy as one of the first refugees in 1990. He and three friends arrived in Rome not knowing anyone, and having only a hundred dollars among them. The first ten days they slept outside, even though it was quite cold. Finally, they found a guard of an apartment building who allowed them to sleep in a room next to the heating room in the basement for a small fee. They stayed there for three months, just happy to be in a room that was heated. They ate in the soup kitchens of the Missionaries of Charity. They eventually found work in the fields, and then in a factory.

John told me, "These experiences were good to have, even though at the time they were difficult. I can say that I was never angry, but my friends looked at the situation differently. 'Why these injustices?' they complained. I was just grateful that we had food to eat and a place to sleep." Eventually, John found a way to go to America, where the Albanian Archdiocese in America helped him study at Holy Cross Greek Orthodox School of Theology in Brookline, Massachusetts. He has now been back in his homeland for less than a year.

Deacon John is already a blessing for this church. He really wants to see the seminary become a school that prepares quality priests and gives the students dignity and self-respect.

As we all cried out, "*Axios! I denjë!* He is worthy!" during his ordination, I thought about his choice of the path of celibacy. This choice may open the way for him to become a bishop in the future. If the Lord wills this, then I think the Church will be in good hands. Of course, I pray that he will stay humble and open-minded, as he is today. May he stay close to and learn from the archbishop as a mentor and spiritual father, and if the mantle of leadership is passed on to him one day, may he continue forward in a similar fashion.

Following Dn. John's ordination, I discussed with Archbishop Anastasios the impact of people converting from so-called Muslim families. The archbishop noted that three men who have integral roles in the Church today were from such backgrounds—Dn. John, who is one of the main teachers at our theological academy; the archbishop's deacon, Sotir, who is one of the solid young clergy we've trained at our academy; and an outstanding iconographer, Gjergj. As I reflected on this, I added Miron the evangelist and a number of his friends. How many other places in the world do you have people from Muslim backgrounds freely entering the Church and taking roles of leadership? I'll definitely have to tell that to my professors at Fuller Theological Seminary's School of World Mission.

Of course, I'm realizing that it is a misstatement to say that Albania's population is 69 percent Muslim. The vast majority of Albanians are nonreligious, atheist, or at best agnostic. They may say, "I am Muslim or Bektashi," referring more to their cultural heritage than to some faith or religion. You can even hear people say that they are "half Muslim and half Orthodox." This means that one parent is from a Muslim background and the other from an Orthodox one. I recently heard a funny comment reflecting this reality. When one Albanian said he was an atheist, the other responded, "Yes, but are you a Muslim atheist or an Orthodox atheist?"

The truth is that many who acknowledge faith in God have no real allegiance to that God. Their lives and actions do not reflect any commitment to a set of religious values. Thus, when we talk about how numerous Muslims are converting, it is proper to explain that most are people with little to no knowledge of Islam. Their conversion often represents a journey to sincere faith for the first time in their lives.

Another example of this is Gjergj, the iconographer mentioned by the archbishop. Like so many other Albanians, he hiked the mountains and escaped to Greece in the early 1990s. He longed to escape the poverty of Albania and heard about the better life in the outside world. Although an artist, he worked as a common laborer in Greece. His interest in art eventually brought him into contact with a pious iconographer. The simple, yet fulfilled life of this iconographer and his family touched Gjergj in an unexpected manner. He admired his friend's icons, and through him, came to see God in these holy images. A combination of the mystery of icons with the example of the simple and holy life of his friend led Gjergj to the baptismal font. Now, he is back in Albania painting beautiful icons for the Church.

The more people I'm meeting, the more I'm fascinated with their stories! We missionaries have to be so careful not to go to other places with arrogant, preconceived ideas about others. We must listen to their stories, learn from their life journeys, and be inspired by their example.

CHAPTER 2

STRUGGLES AND CHALLENGES

We visited St. Vlash Monastery today. Many consider this one of the holiest places in Albania. Thousands of people flock to this centuries-old monastery every year, asking the saint to intercede for various ills and needs. Students at the seminary told me their parents remember as children sleeping overnight at the monastery on the eve of the Dormition of the Virgin Mary, August 15.

On February 11, 1967, when the anti-religious propaganda in the country began its climactic ascent, teachers indoctrinated their students with their militant atheistic party line and encouraged them to do their damage. Interestingly, the students did not attack the Church of St. George, which sat within the city boundaries of Durres. Instead, they marched across the fields to destroy the monastery church, brick by brick. This church, which stood as a symbol of faith, became the first church destroyed.

During my visit last May, the archbishop shared his vision for rebuilding this monastery and turning it into a spiritual center for all of Albania. In addition to the monastery itself, he envisioned a seminary, a training ground, and a spiritual refuge for all people. When I asked him if he had the resources to go ahead with such a dream, he responded, "No. But I have faith. Let us make the sign of the cross, and watch the miracle that God will do."

WATER

Tirana is starting to feel like home. The food situation has improved dramatically since my visit last May. Some "supermarkets" have sprung up. A supermarket here is a small shop that sells more than ten different products. The outdoor markets don't sell only leeks anymore, but have a growing variety of seasonal vegetables and fruits.

I thank God for my fifth-floor apartment. For the first three weeks, I had running water only once a day, from 5:00 AM until 6:30 AM. I've solved this problem by installing a water tank on our roof, something that too few Albanians can afford. People warn me that the water pressure will not push the water above the third floor during the summer months. I'll deal with that problem when it comes.

IN LOVE, FOR LOVE, AND BY LOVE

I had a nice discussion with Fr. Anthony Romeos, a visiting monk from Greece. Fr. Anthony taught at our seminary for the past ten days, and before he left, I asked him for any advice he could give a young missionary. He thoughtfully responded, "Do all things in love, for love, and by love. And not with simple human love, but with divine love. If you remember this, you will do well!"

AFRICA IN EUROPE

I traveled one and a half hours to Elbasan with the archbishop to take part in the Divine Liturgy at St. Mary's Church. Following the Liturgy, the archbishop told the youth that I would begin weekly meetings there. Twenty youth gathered after the service, and we decided to meet every Wednesday. Thus, my youth ministry begins!

After the service, I traveled two hours into the mountains of Elbasan. The dirt roads full of potholes reminded me of my travels in the villages of Africa. The scenery was breathtaking. We heard about the poverty in these regions. When we arrived in the village of Zavollin, Sister Galini had some work to do with a women's group there, so Fr. Justinos, a monk from Mount Athos, offered a sermon to all the others gathered.

As I walked around this village, I thought how interesting it would be to live in such a village for a period of time. Lord willing, if I'll be in Albania for the next five years, I want to stay here for several months. It would be great to live among such people and get to personally hear their stories. Maybe 1000 people live here. I would love to share in their struggles and life, and connect our faith with their lives! I hope I remember this enthusiasm and make it a goal during my third or fourth year to do something like this. When I shared this idea with Fr. Martin, he told me that Miron and his group may live here this summer, trying to evangelize these villages. I'll have to come with them when they do that.

AN UNBAPTIZED TRANSLATOR?

At seminary, an interesting dilemma arose. One of the seminarians confronted my translator, Elton, about not being baptized. Their long discussion raised a question in my mind. Should I, as a missionary, have a non-baptized Christian as my translator? Should I try to encourage Elton to be baptized? My concern is that if I ask him, he may do it solely to please me. I don't want him to do it for my sake, though. I want him to discover who Jesus Christ is and make a sincere commitment. Elton tells me he believes, and he calls himself an Orthodox Christian. Yet he still has a way to go. As he hangs out with me and translates for my classes and catechism lessons, maybe the Holy Spirit will touch him.

I think of the archbishop's translator, Vangjeli. He is a bright young man and an outstanding translator. Although he is from a Christian family, he wasn't baptized. The archbishop kept him close to his side, never insisting that he be baptized. He knew that Vangjeli would hear his words and see his example. In his own time, Vangjeli would decide to be baptized, without any pressure from the archbishop. And this is what happened.

SERVICE OF LOVE

I traveled with Artan to a village near Lushnja and helped deliver boxes of food to 300 families. We distribute food to all the families of the village, regardless of their religion. Even though the boxes of food will not last a long time, this ministry shows the people that the Church loves and cares for them.

During the last three years, many Albanians have suffered in the transition to democracy. Communism left the country bankrupt and poverty-stricken. People misused their newfound freedom to do whatever they wanted. Anarchy reigned. Crime rose. People felt unsafe walking out at night. If someone wore new shoes or clothing, they risked others attacking them and stealing the new items.

The Church has tried to respond to this period of transition by bringing in hundreds of tons of aid—food, clothing, and medicines. Fr. Martin, together with a staff of four Albanian youth, have recently begun a Diaconia Agape (Service of Love) office, which helps distribute aid, as well as trying to establish long-term self-help projects in farming and small businesses. Much of the aid comes from Greece, through friends and supporters of Archbishop Anastasios. Fr. Spyridon, a 65-year-old retired judge from Athens, who became a priest later in life, spearheads this effort that brings tons of aid into the country.

WHEN REVILED, WE BLESS   MARCH 24

Several days ago I saw in the *Liria* newspaper three articles written about the Church and the archbishop. I was dismayed to discover that each article slandered the archbishop in a different way. The first two tried to connect Archbishop Anastasios's ministry with Metropolitan Sevastianos of Konitsa in Greece, whom the Albanians view with grave suspicion. The third article wrote nonsense about how the new three-story archdiocesan center in Tirana will become the personal home of the archbishop. It described how the archbishop will use it to house other Greek nationals and for his own personal gain. It even tried to accuse the archbishop of stealing money from the Albanian Church, instead of recognizing the fact that he actually must find donors who offer millions of dollars every year to rebuild this Church!

Other recent articles have accused the archbishop of working for the Greek government as a spy. Some say that he is hellenizing the Church by not allowing the use of Albanian in liturgical services. Of course, such accusations are baseless. Every liturgical service in Tirana is done completely in Albanian. Rarely will the archbishop say a *"Kyrie eleison"* or *"Eirini pasi"* (Greek for "Lord have mercy" and "Peace be with you") because he knows it may cause a reaction.

These articles left me wondering how many Albanians actually believe such newspapers. The Albanians who come to church and know the archbishop understand the lies of these articles. The average Albanian who never has any contact with the Orthodox Church, though, may believe them. Such propaganda seriously damages the public image of the Church. I discussed these articles with the archbishop, and he showed little reaction. Such newspaper slander occurs almost daily. "If I would focus on these attacks, they would consume my day. Sometimes I think the best response is silence. Let us do our work, and our work will speak for itself."

There seems to be a concerted effort to expel the archbishop from Albania and turn the Church into a political pawn of the government. Papa Jani, the first Albanian priest the archbishop ordained, told me stories of how the police have harassed him. They know that Papa Jani is a firm supporter and spiritual child of the archbishop and one of our outstanding new priests. The police have accused him of not charging any money to perform the sacraments of the Church (baptisms, weddings, funerals), and say that this is a sign that he must be receiving extra money from the archbishop. He is thus an "agent" of the archbishop. When Papa Jani tried to explain that he had no right to charge money for a sacrament of God, and that he only receives the monthly salary of $63 from the archdiocese, his explanation fell on deaf ears. The police warned Papa Jani to take care, or something unfortunate might happen to him or his family. Obviously, some people in power—whether nationalists, atheists, or fanatical Muslims—don't like to see the Church progress.

The archbishop's secretary, Agiro, told me that the slander comes from both sides of the border. Albanian nationalists write against the archbishop because he is Greek. Greek nationalists write against the archbishop because he is building up a strong Church that uses the Albanian language and prepares Albanian clergy. The mean spirit of nationalism is the same, regardless of which flag it waves.

"Remember, Luke," the archbishop said to me, "we must seek only the approval of God and not be hindered by such work of the devil. The evil one tears down any good work. One way we know that we are doing the work of God is by the persecution we receive."

WHEN PERSECUTED, WE ENDURE

Attacks continue against the Church. This past weekend the archbishop celebrated the Divine Liturgy in Korça and planned to bless the foundation for a new cathedral. After petitioning the government for two years, the Church finally received permission to begin construction. The communists turned the old St. George Cathedral in Korça into a library. The cathedral held a prominent position in the center of town. The Metropolis Church of the Life-giving Waters also stood close to the center of town. They converted that into a museum. Since the Orthodox make up more than half the population, and many consider this city to be the center of Orthodoxy in Albania, the Church petitioned the government to return to us a prime piece of property. The authorities finally agreed.

In the middle of the Divine Liturgy, however, a representative of the federal government walked into the church and gave the archbishop an official letter telling him that the church no longer has permission to go ahead with construction. Of course, no mention was made that the Muslims have already received permission to build a mosque in this city. When the people rose up in fury, the archbishop calmed them by reminding them to pray harder.

This event represents an ongoing discrimination against the Church. The monastery at Ardenica, one of the best preserved monasteries in the country, is still being used as a taverna and hotel, even though the government promised to return it to the Church over a year ago. For three years the Church has been trying to get property in the northern city of Shkodra, but the government won't allow the Orthodox to purchase any land. The archbishop has been seeking land near Tirana to build a seminary for the past two years, but with no success. And the same story continues in many other cities. During all this frustration, various newspapers spread lies and poison the mind of the average citizen against the Church and the archbishop.

One Italian source estimated that the communist government destroyed 1608 churches and monasteries in Albania. For a country of only three and a half million people, this is quite an incredible number of churches. In addition to the destruction, the government seized all properties as well. Now, with the coming of democracy, the state is reluctant to give these properties back. Along with property, the government still maintains control over thousands of priceless icons and religious artifacts, as well as church archives. Satan is alive and active in his fight against the Church, despite the coming of democracy.

Of course, persecution doesn't come only from the government. We face a battle with the ultra-nationalist Albanians, who see the archbishop only as a

Greek. Today I saw a newspaper which called itself the "True Autocephalous Orthodox Church." The newspaper served as a vehicle to slander the archbishop, stating that an Albanian autocephalous church must have no foreigners in it. Obviously, such people offer few solutions to the problem of where the Church can find an Albanian bishop to govern it. No such bishop exists in the world at the present time. According to church canons, a bishop must be celibate, and there is not even one canonical celibate Albanian priest in the world.

Many of the Albanian Orthodox leaders in America have supported this opposition voice. They seem to have a greater concern for nationalism than for the Gospel. They seem to care little for the spread of Christ's message to their people, since their suspicion of the Greeks blinds them.

As I traveled with the archbishop today, he didn't want to talk about all our struggles from outside. Instead, he focused on the fact that we need to prepare future leaders with the right spirit. "First, we have to teach them to be thankful for life and all that life brings, whether good or bad. Gratitude is a primary virtue in the Christian life. Second, we have to teach people to sacrifice and be ready to risk their lives for Christ. We don't want people who will simply keep the status quo. An authentic Christian is one who will give his life to Christ with selfless abandonment! Third, we need to help people understand what it means to share in the life of Christ—in His Cross as well as His Resurrection. Walking with Christ means to joyfully accept the sufferings, persecutions, and struggles of life. By doing this, we not only participate in Christ's own passion, but we unite with Him in His glorious resurrection. Finally, find faithful people who can take responsibility and carry on the ministry we do. From the beginning, think of your successors—people who will not only continue our work, but who will supersede it for Christ's glory!"

"YOU DIRTY FOREIGN PRIEST!"

Several days ago, terrorists in southern Albania killed two Albanian soldiers and injured four others. The Albanian government initially blamed the Greek army. The latest rumor, however, was that a terrorist group called "Free Northern Eiperos" did it. The southern third of Albania, or Northern Eiperos as the Greeks call it, is an explosive issue between the two countries.

Historically, Albania has tried to minimize and indigenize the minority Greek villages. Greece, on the other hand, claims that Northern Eiperos belongs to Greece. Since the fall of communism, tension in this area has increased.

This latest terrorist act has given impetus to the government and the newspapers to renew their attack on the Orthodox Church. They reason that since the archbishop of the Orthodox Church is Greek, the Church itself must be sympathetic with these terrorists. Archbishop Anastasios distributed a news release after the incident, condemning all acts of violence and offering his sympathies to the families of the deceased and injured. He called for renewed peace and stability between Greece and Albania. In fact, over these first years of Albanian democracy, the archbishop has tried to play the role of peacemaker between the two countries. In another display of discrimination, however, no Albanian newspaper even published his news release. Only the BBC read it on their radio news.

Shortly after this incident, one of our new Albanian priests, Fr. Kristo, reported that as he walked through the streets of Tirana with his long beard and black robe, some men threatened him, saying, "You dirty Greek priest! We should hang you for killing our men in southern Albania." They thought Fr. Kristo was an accomplice in the entire affair since he worked for the "Greek Church." Even though Fr. Kristo is ethnically Albanian, and ethnic Albanians make up the majority of Orthodox in this country, people still look at the Orthodox Church as Greek. The whole incident will unfortunately become another excuse for the government to continue to hold back our lands, to make life difficult for us, and to discriminate against the Church.

UNDERSTANDING PERSECUTION

Not only do the media accuse the archbishop of being a spy for the Greek government, but now they say his ultimate goal is to use the Orthodox Church as a means of helping Greece annex Northern Eiperos. One recent newspaper article ran a picture of Vangjeli, the archbishop's translator, standing next to Metropolitan Sevastianos of Konitsa. The newspapers were trying to show that Archbishop Anastasios's translator has friendly relations with a Greek nationalist. All the more proof of the archbishop's questionable intentions, they reason. Of course, the newspaper failed to report that the picture shown was from 1991, when Vangjeli, working as a reporter, interviewed the metropolitan. Truth plays little role in contemporary Albanian media.

I asked the archbishop how he handles the constant slander and persecution. Imagine, from the moment he entered the country, suspicion fell upon him because of his Greek identity. In fact, his struggles began before he even entered Albania. He applied for a visa in January 1991 to visit the country, after Ecumenical Patriarch Demetrios asked him to go. The Albanian government refused to give him a visa for six months. He finally arrived on July 16, 1991.

As we discussed this ongoing harassment, the archbishop told me that he comforts himself by meditating on the persecution Christ endured. Christ remained silent during His persecution, and so the archbishop feels that he also should remain silent despite such ridiculous accusations. He quoted Jesus, "If the world has persecuted Me, how much more will they persecute you who are My followers." Then the archbishop said something I will always remember: "How can I expect to be the archbishop of a Church that suffered persecution in the worst ways for fifty years, and not expect to experience persecution myself? I cannot truly serve as their leader if I am not ready to experience suffering. The people can now see that their spiritual leader continues to be persecuted by many of the same forces that persecuted the Church in previous years."

GOING HOME! APRIL 21

I'm writing this from the London airport. I'm on my way home for two weeks. I haven't told Faith yet, but will show up at her school unannounced and surprise her.

We have a two-week vacation from the seminary for Holy Week, Pascha, and Bright Week. I really feel the need to go home and be with Faith. She faces daily pressure to forget Albania. Her family expresses concern only for her safety and what they consider to be her well-being. They can't understand why she would abandon all her dreams of professional success and the comforts of America to live in a third-world country.

Last night, I asked the archbishop for his prayers. He showed his typical fatherly love. "Be careful in trying to convince her parents," he advised.

"Arguments from you will do little good. They will get defensive if you say anything. Allow others to do that. Just make sure you are polite and loving, yet unwavering. Don't try to debate, because when you debate with people who are passionate about something, you will get nowhere. You will achieve little if you lose your temper and get frustrated with them."

In the middle of our conversation, the archbishop shared with me a critical experience from his own life. He admitted that his pious mother had great difficulty in "giving up her son" to monasticism, and her strong overreaction caused him terrible pain. As I understood it, the archbishop came from a well-to-do family. When his mother was pregnant with him, however, the family encountered some financial crisis, and his oldest brother died at a very young age. In addition to this, his mother came down with tuberculosis. The doctors recommended an abortion because she would risk her life if she proceeded with her pregnancy. And if she did give birth, the baby would most likely be born ill or deformed. Distressed and uncertain about what to do, his mother went to the Church of the Annunciation and prayed to the Panayia. She promised the Virgin Mary that if she gave birth to a child, she would dedicate the child to God.

The archbishop reminded his mother about her promise twenty years later, when he chose to enter the brotherhood of *Zoe*. He didn't tell her this in the heat of their crisis, but found the opportunity to remind her after she calmed down a bit. This comment helped his mother eventually accept his path as the will of God. I don't know if his mother could have ever imagined that her "little Tasso" would one day become the archbishop of Albania and one of the outstanding voices in the Orthodox and Christian world. Even mothers of archbishops can react fiercely to the radical call of Christ. In some ways, that's comforting to know.

"If we are going to live a life of missions, then we have to experience the most extreme reactions so that we relate with others," the archbishop concluded. "We have to understand what it means to be misunderstood, persecuted, abused, and slandered. We will see our loved ones suffer through their own hardness of heart. We will see innocent bystanders suffer. People will speak against our Christianity because it challenges their comfortable, lukewarm, and nonconfrontational understanding of faith."

I have to share this story with Faith so that she can see that her own struggles are not unique. Her parents' reaction reflects those of countless "pious" parents, who have faith but don't want that radical faith to upset their lives.

In the end, I appreciated that the archbishop took the time to listen attentively, understand the situation, and then share wisdom from his own experience. When I left, he blessed me and gave me a big hug, assuring me of his prayers. "God will show you the right path to follow in His time."

SURPRISED BY JOY!

Surprised by joy! Faith had no idea I was coming home, so I totally shocked her. My sister arranged to pick me up at the airport, and I took a train home to Lancaster. When I arrived, I immediately went to Faith's school and showed up in her classroom with flowers in my hand.

We spent our time supporting and reassuring one another about our decisions for the future. I wanted to emphasize my love and commitment to Faith, as well as reaffirm our partnership in this mission ministry. Thank God, she is excited about joining me and our mission team in Albania. She has so much to offer, and the Albanians will fall in love with her gentle, caring, loving spirit.

We felt blessed to journey through the Passion of Christ with our Annunciation family. Our church celebrates Holy Week and Pascha in such an inspiring way. We sang "Christ is Risen" in numerous languages, including Albanian. The entire Passion story took on new meaning as my mind raced back to Albania and all that has occurred there over the past decades. Faith and I talked about how this spirit of the Resurrection summarizes what missions means, and represents what we want to transmit to others.

We enjoyed the time spent with our families, despite some tense moments. I understand that full acceptance may come slowly. In the meantime, we will continue to love one another and be patient with those who don't understand. We said goodbye with much difficulty. How wonderful it will be to go back to Albania together. Three and a half months still to go!

KRISHTI U NGJALL! CHRIST IS RISEN!

All week at the seminary, the students shared with me their stories of Pascha. Although I celebrated Holy Week and Pascha in America during my

Approximately 20,000 people gather in one of the main boulevards in Tirana at midnight, Pascha night in 2000, to listen to the Archbishop's Paschal sermon and sing "Krishti u Ngjall" (Christ is Risen).

first year as a missionary, I caught the excitement of our Lord's Resurrection in a land which forbade such festivity for 23 years. I saw a video of the Resurrection service held in Tirana, outside the church on one of the main boulevards, and could not believe my eyes. At midnight Pascha night, an estimated 20,000 people stood in the streets with candles, listening to Archbishop Anastasios's paschal sermon and singing, *"Krishti u Ngjall"* (Christ is Risen)!

The seminarians shared stories of how hundreds, and sometimes thousands, came out at midnight to celebrate Pascha in their villages or cities. Spiro described his village scene. Since his village has no priest, they did not celebrate a liturgical service. Still, hundreds of people gathered at the sight of their destroyed village church with lit candles and red eggs. Spiro admitted that he was unsure what to do. He decided to read the Gospel story of the Resurrection, sing *"Krishti u Ngjall"* countless times, and preach a sermon on the significance of the Resurrection. This simple, spontaneous story seemed like an account of the early Church.

On Holy Saturday, the archbishop baptized 38 adults in Tirana's cathedral. Six university girls I had catechized preferred to wait for me to come back from the States so I could attend their baptism this week. It was a moving experience. Five of the six women came from Muslim families. They exuded excitement at committing their lives to Jesus Christ and being reborn by His grace and mercy. Afterwards, one of the girls proclaimed with a radiant smile, "It's so wonderful to know that all the sins I have committed in the past are forgiven." I knew her past struggle with guilt, and I thanked God for her new beginning.

Isn't this what missions is all about—offering new life, bringing hope to the hopeless, love to the unloved, peace to the troubled, forgiveness to the sinners, joy to those in sadness, and salvation unto eternal life for all people!

MONASTERIES, SNAKES, AND CHRIST'S RESURRECTION

The seminarian John described Holy Week and Pascha at the Nativity of the Virgin Mary Monastery in Ardenica. Although the state still runs this famous monastery as a restaurant and hotel, the Church received permission to use its fifteenth-century church building for liturgical services. John explained that he grew up near the monastery, always frightened by it. For as long as he remembered, his main exposure to the monastery came from state television, which portrayed horror stories about the Church, priests, monasteries, and anything that had to do with religion. In school, he watched films in which bishops ordered priests to kill young children, poisonous snakes filled the "dungeons" of the monasteries, and monks would torture people in these places.

"Growing up with all these images and stories," John confided, "makes it all the more surreal to worship in the very monastery where these films took place. Sometimes as a child, my friends and I would sneak up the hill and enter the monastery grounds. Of course, we were frightened and thought something terrible might happen in this evil place. Yet the 'beautiful house' left an impression on me. That's what we called the church, because of all the pictures we saw on its walls. Who would have imagined that ten years later, we would actually be in the monastery worshipping God at Pascha time. How amazing!"

MISSIONARIES, MONKS, AND MARTYRS   JUNE 2

Today is Faith's birthday. She just faxed me the cover page of my new book, *Missionaries, Monks, and Martyrs: Making Disciples of All Nations*, which Light and Life Publishing Co. just released. The book describes the life and work of ten great Orthodox missionaries ranging from the apostle Paul to our beloved Archbishop Anastasios. When I showed the archbishop the cover page, which lists all the missionaries, he jokingly replied, "You are going to get me into deep trouble. You list my name among nine other saints!"

I thank God for this publication and pray that the book may be a source of enlightenment and inspiration for those who read it. In the Orthodox world in general, and even in America, we don't understand the privilege and responsibility of missions. I pray that this book will open the eyes of at least some people and will challenge them to fulfill God's great command to carry the Gospel to all nations and peoples. I also hope that this book will introduce non-Orthodox believers to our Church's rich missionary tradition.

DOES THE DEVIL TAKE YOU SERIOUSLY?

Faith came to Albania for a two-week visit. She loved Albania, and we had a wonderful time. The trip helped to answer questions she had about life here. She realizes that she will fit in without any problem. The archbishop, along with Fr. Martin and Renee and the other missionaries, all inspired Faith. She loved meeting my Albanian friends and kept talking about how she can't wait to make this her home. We will fulfill this dream after only a few more months.

We had a wonderful two-hour meeting with the archbishop, speaking much about the opposition Faith still faces. He encouraged us with his words of wisdom. "A life without persecution means that the devil does not take you too seriously. We must face difficulties with love and peace, and always try to make peace with others. You have difficult decisions ahead of you. Remember, in all Christ's words, He gave one of His hardest statements to a possible disciple who felt the need to first care for his family. 'Let the dead bury the dead. Come follow Me.'"

As harsh as this may sound, Faith and I have to realize that even those who love us the most may not understand our decision to follow Christ whole-heartedly. Mother Teresa says, "Imagine how God gave His all for us. And can we respond by only giving part of ourselves back to Him?" May we have the courage to give our all to our Lord.

OCMC SHORT-TERM MISSION TEAM   JULY 5

Thank God, the OCMC short-term mission team went extremely well. Six Americans worked hand in hand with five dynamic Albanian youth and put together an outstanding youth program. We decided to conduct four-day "mini-camps" in the places where I have been offering weekly catechism for the past four months—in Elbasan, Durres, and Korça.

Three hundred and twenty children and youth attended our programs. We focused on the theme, "Jesus Christ: Who He Is and How He Transforms Lives." We accomplished our goal of strengthening the already existing youth groups and introducing new youth to the transforming truth of Jesus Christ.

Our program included songs, skits, games, Bible studies, talks, and small group discussions. By the end, both the Albanian and American team members expressed gratitude for their experience. I think the five Albanians who worked with us developed some important leadership skills and came to a better understanding of what it takes to put together an outreach program. As for the Americans, several agreed that the entire experience changed their lives. Jimmy Nakos mentioned the possibility of returning here in October to join our growing team of missionaries.

A highlight for all of us was the baptism of 160 people in a small village in the Shpati mountains near Elbasan. One of my seminarians catechized the people and prepared them for the baptism. Fr. Martin, together with two Albanian priests and two deacons, performed the baptisms.

THANK GOD FOR WATER!

For two weeks now, I have had to wake up at 4:00 AM in order to take a shower and fill my containers with water. The water pressure can push the water to the fifth floor only in the early morning shift, but it can't reach my

Harallambi and other villagers gather water for their homes in the village of Shen Vlash, just outside the Resurrection of Christ Theological Academy.

water tank on the roof of the apartment. Having limited water makes me thank God all the more for the little water I do get. Many homes here in Tirana still get no water at all. These people have to wake up in the middle of the night, walk down four flights of stairs, and wait in line for an hour to fill up their containers of water.

A LONG HONEYMOON   SEPTEMBER 1

Mr. and Mrs. Luke A. Veronis! We're finally married! What a blessed event after ten months of uncertainty and turmoil. On Sunday, August 28, God blessed Faith and me as husband and wife in our Annunciation Church of Lancaster. Thank God, our families and friends all rejoiced with us in a most beautiful sacrament and a delightful reception. Even John, our dear Albanian friend, attended the wedding. We had brought him here to participate and learn from the Boston Diocese Camp. What a special treat to have Albania represented at our wedding.

I feel so blessed to have a partner like Faith. Although we have been friends since high school, our courtship took a long, winding path. I remember admiring this homecoming queen when I was only a sophomore. During our university years, we often got together to play ping-pong and discuss the relationships each of us were in. We kept contact with one another as I traveled around the world and she worked as a schoolteacher. Our friendship turned into something more serious in 1991, yet I foolishly broke it off with my uncertainties. I thank God for her forgiveness, patience, and willingness to try again in 1993. And now in September 1994, we are husband and wife!

How can I properly thank God that I found someone who will walk the long and narrow journey with me, struggling together towards the Kingdom of heaven? What a unique treasure to have such a soul-mate—a partner who has her own sincere love for our Lord and a strong desire to follow Him. She is ready to share life's joys and struggles together, so that we can help one another throughout life's long walk. Faith is such a strong, courageous, and faithful woman. I admire so many of her traits—her kindness, gentleness, patience, compassion, and love for others; her faith, commitment, and desire to continuously grow closer to God; her willingness to sacrifice, struggle, and stretch her limits as she seeks to fulfill the will of God; her talents, skills, and virtues; her tenderness, care, and love for children; her desire to serve and minister to others; as well as her physical beauty, charm, and humor. She is a gem I will always value and cherish!

I remember how Fr. Calivas, the president at Holy Cross Greek Orthodox School of Theology, used to reprimand us seminarians whenever he talked about relationships. "You men are all waiting to find a spouse who is spiritually mature, yet who looks like Miss America. Well, don't count on finding that combination!" In Faith, I can say that I found a woman who combines a beautiful soul with beautiful looks. Proverbs 31 says, "Charm is deceptive and beauty fleeting, but the woman who fears the Lord is to be praised." I found a wife with all three—charm, beauty, and the fear of the Lord!

I told Faith on the day of our marriage, "I cannot promise you a wealthy or comfortable life. Instead, I can promise you an exciting adventure in life—a quest of following God wherever He leads." This adventure began with a brief honeymoon on Martha's Vineyard, but I joked with Faith, "Our real honeymoon begins in a couple of weeks, when we return to Albania." May it be a long, blessed honeymoon!

MY GRACE IS SUFFICIENT
FOR YOU   SEPTEMBER 17

One of the most moving and blessed days of my life occurred today.
I'm not usually an emotional person, but I could barely read my comments
in the middle of my ordination to the diaconate. When Bishop Maximos of
Pittsburgh laid his hands on my head, asking for the Holy Spirit to come and
make me a deacon, I fulfilled part of a dream that started when I first went to
Africa in 1987. Of course, at the time I didn't even realize God was calling me
to the priesthood. Now, though, I see this all as a part of God's plan.

Here is part of my ordination sermon:

*Your Grace, today I come before you with great fear and trepidation—a
sense of awe overwhelms me as I think about the sacrament of ordination. I was filled with fear when I read St. John Chrysostom's treatise
describing his own unworthiness of becoming a priest. I was filled with
fear when I read about St. Gregory the Theologian's flight into the desert because of his own sense of inadequacy at accepting the ministerial duties of the clergy. And I was filled with fear when I read how St.
Augustine was ordained against his own will and wept freely during his
ordination ceremony because of his sense of unworthiness.*

*How should I feel when I read about the pillars of our Church
hesitating to approach this holy mystery because of their own sense of
unworthiness? If they hesitated, then how dare I approach and accept
this calling to the diaconate? My fear of unworthiness and inadequacy
is strong, and yet I take courage and stand before you today because I
feel called by our loving God to serve in this manner. Such a calling is
based upon my awareness and trust in the unfathomable grace of God.
Our Lord said to St. Paul, "My grace is sufficient for you, for my power
is made perfect in your weakness" (2 Cor. 12:9). Well, I respond to that
by saying, "Here I am, Lord, full of many imperfections and weaknesses.
Accept me, cleanse me, transform me, and use me in whatever way You
see fit."*

*I approach today trusting in this amazing grace of God, but also
placing my hope in something else. St. Peter writes that all baptized
believers are a part of the "royal priesthood" of the Church. So I place my*

hope in all my friends, this "royal priesthood" gathered here today, that they may become ministers with me. I don't want them to be curious, idle spectators who simply act as witnesses to my ordination. Instead, I invite them all to be active, faithful partners in my diaconate and eventual priesthood.

I can only take this step toward ordination if I know that there is such a team behind me, supporting me, loving me, encouraging me, and protecting me. First and foremost, I beseech you, Your Grace, and all the faithful to pray that I will be filled with a love which outshines all else. Before being a preacher, a teacher, or a theologian, I want to be a lover— one who sincerely loves God and others.

Please pray that God will grant me the spirit of humble service to others, and wisdom to truly understand the Gospel. Pray that I may avoid the danger to fall in love with books and ideas instead of falling in love with Jesus Christ and His flock. Pray that my zeal may continually be renewed and never wane. God condemns the church of Ephesus for "abandoning the love they first had" (Revelation 2:4). I do not want to be a priest who develops a perfunctory spirit. Pray that my courage and boldness to proclaim the truth may never diminish.

Pray that I may have a tiny portion of the strength of Samson; the prayerfulness of Hannah; the wisdom of Solomon; the courage of David; the patience of Job; the leadership of Moses; the zeal of John the Baptist; the humility of the Virgin Mary; the love of Mary Magdalene; the hope of the myrrh-bearing women; the faith of Peter; the boldness of Paul; the tongue of John Chrysostom; and the missionary zeal of St. Innocent.

Your Grace, if the faithful gathered in this church make a covenant to offer such prayers to our Lord, then I take courage in accepting my ordination.

FREEDOM OF THE CROSS

We returned home to Albania after seven blessed weeks in the States. The expression of love that our family and friends showered upon us throughout our wedding and ordination overwhelmed us. All glory be to God!

We greeted the archbishop last night and returned to the reality of Albania.

Government attacks continue against the archbishop as we hear more rumors of how the authorities want to expel him from the country.

"Despite all these struggles, I can say that I am experiencing the 'freedom of the Cross,'" the archbishop calmly told us. "One can find amazing freedom when we learn to say, 'Your will be done.' I won't allow the nationalists on both sides [Albanian and Greek] to take my peace away. These groups focus more on the politics of their own country than on the Gospel and Church of Jesus Christ."

ORDINATION TO THE PRIESTHOOD   OCTOBER 18

Another highlight of my life! Within the past nine months, I have entered the mission field, married my love and best friend, become a deacon, and now been ordained into the priesthood. My mother and father came to Albania for this special event, and it occurred unexpectedly on Tuesday, October 18, the feast of St. Luke the Evangelist. The archbishop wasn't feeling well on Sunday, so he couldn't perform the ordination as planned, but then thought it appropriate to do it on my feast day. The cathedral was full for this Tuesday service, for which even the church choir came and sang. I felt deeply blessed to have Archbishop Anastasios ordain me, to have Faith beside me, for this is her ordination as well, and to have my parents present.

ARCHBISHOP IN EXILE?

The archbishop discussed at our weekly leaders' meeting the grave situation concerning the upcoming referendum on the proposed constitution. Since the fall of communism, Albania has no constitution. The present government proposed a new constitution that seems to give the president too much power. In regard to the Church, the proposed constitution stipulates total separation of state and Church, while simultaneously including one article that places severe restrictions on the heads of the four major religious groups (i.e. Orthodox, Catholic, Muslim, and Bektashi). In practice, these restrictions would force Archbishop Anastasios from the country.

Everyone thinks the proposed constitution will pass, whether the people vote for it or not. There is too much corruption in the country. The president has publicly stated that if the referendum passes, he will immediately expel the archbishop from the country. Of course, this will cause all kinds of confusion in the Church, and the government will most likely try to create a puppet ecclesiastical structure.

What impressed me about our meeting today was how peaceful the archbishop appeared. He began by asking if anyone remembered what the Gospel reading of the day was. When no one responded positively, he opened his Bible and said, "No matter how hectic and stressed we get during these days, never forget to read the Epistle and Gospel lesson of the day. We will find our strength and nourishment here, as well as the wisdom needed to proceed ahead. What is truly urgent for us is to remain peaceful and prayerful."

Following the meeting, he privately told me, "We must remember that Albania served as an empire of Satan for over 45 years. We came trying to re-establish the Church and begin breaking apart that empire. Satan will not sit back and allow that to happen. We face a serious spiritual battle. As St. Paul says, 'For we do not wrestle against flesh and blood, but against principalities, against powers, against the rulers of the darkness of this age, against spiritual *hosts* of wickedness in the heavenly *places*" (Eph. 6:12).

VICTORY FOR THE PEOPLE!

We have overcome one of the greatest challenges yet to the future of Orthodoxy here. On Sunday, November 6, the people voted down the proposed new constitution. Although the newspapers wrote slander against the archbishop for the past three weeks, he preached a non-political message of peace and love. He emphasized to our own believers the need for unceasing prayer for our Church, the people of Albania, and especially the leaders of government. On the evening of October 25, the night before the feast of St. Dimitrios, we held vigils throughout the country calling people to prayer. In Tirana's cathedral, more than 400 people attended the Vigil from 9:00 PM until 2:00 AM.

When the day of voting arrived, many Albanians themselves feared the outcome was already established, even before people went to the polls. Forty-five years of communism have left many feeling they have no true say in the future of their country. To the surprise of many, the 54 percent to 42 percent outcome reflected a sound rejection of the proposed constitution. Not only could the Church breathe a sigh of relief, but the people won a victory by seeing they have a voice in the future of this country. Democracy may have a chance to work yet. Everyone in the church agreed that we had witnessed a miracle from God. Of course, Archbishop Anastasios always says, "We Christians do believe in miracles!"

THANKSGIVING ALBANIAN STYLE   NOVEMBER 24

What a wonderful Thanksgiving celebration we enjoyed. Our American mission team is now up to thirteen, including four children—the Ritsi family, Hal and Sheila Mischke, Penny Deligiannis, Mike Stavropoulos, and Jimmy Nakos. We all gathered together for a typical Thanksgiving feast in an atypical setting. Fr. Martin began the day by riding his bike into the mountains to find some villager who would sell him a turkey. Once it was secured, he returned home carrying a live turkey tied onto his bicycle. With the axe already sharpened and Renee boiling the water, Faith and Penny each took one end of the turkey and held it down. All seemed well until Fr. Martin lifted the axe. Our Albanian-style Thanksgiving then took a new direction.

Faith didn't realize what it meant to hold a turkey's head and watch an axe come flying down close to her fingers. She flinched, loosening her grip on the turkey's head enough for Fr. Martin's axe to only partially hit its mark. Blood began squirting all over the place as both Faith and Penny released their grips. The turkey began running around the yard with his head half cut off. Fr. Martin had to catch the turkey in the midst of showering blood and finish the job. Following this butchering, Renee, Faith, and the others plucked the feathers and prepared the meat for the oven. This calamity, surprisingly, didn't dampen our appetite, and we proceeded to enjoy a most delicious Thanksgiving meal. Our first Albanian-style Thanksgiving would be one hard to forget.

Not losing the significance of the holiday in the midst of an amusing and traumatic day, Faith and I paused in the evening to reflect on all our blessings. We thanked God profusely for the innumerable gifts He has given us this past year.

Fr. Luke baptizing a camper at the Good Shepherd Summer Camp at St. John Vladimir village, Elbasan.

Facing page, top: Fr. Luke and Faith hold their 15-month-old daughter Theodora and son Paul during the annual Pascha luncheon at the archdiocesan chapel.

Facing page, bottom: Fr. Luke celebrates an all-night vigil in the St. John Vladimir monastery church during the Good Shepherd summer camp in 2001. The church was still not renovated and had no roof.

Above: Beggars line up outside the alleyway in front of the Annunciation Cathedral, Tirana.

Facing page: Paul Veronis, age 3, serves as an acolyte, helping his father at the St. John Vladimir monastery church during summer camp.

Top: Archbishop Anastasios passing out the paschal light, with Hieromonk Ephraim of Simonopetra of the Holy Mountain behind him.

Bottom: In 1988, some Kenyan children gather around Luke in the village of Chevogere.

Top: Faith and Theodora are surrounded by some of the female students at the Resurrection of Christ Theological Academy.

Bottom: Faith and her babysitter Alexandra teach a group of neighborhood children some Bible stories in her home.

Top: Fr. Luke speaking to the seminarians in the St. Vlash Monastery Church.

Bottom: Faith leading a catechism group in the Annunciation Cathedral, Tirana.

Top: The Resurrection of Christ Theological Academy in front of the St. Vlash Monastery.

Bottom: The Annunciation Women's Group gathers outside the home of Fr. Luke and Faith to say farewell in 2004.

CHAPTER 3

PLANTING THE SEEDS OF FAITH

(1995–1996)

LIVING SAINTS

In the city of Korça, I frequently visit the house of three elderly "sisters"— Marika, Demetra, and Elizabeth. Marika and Demetra are blood sisters, while Berta, as they call her, is a sister in Christ. Many Orthodox believers consider these women among the "living saints" of Albania. They range in age from 67 to 88. Each week, I sit enthralled in their home, listening to their stories of faith during the terror of Enver Hoxha.

"Our house was like a little underground church," Demetra shared with me. "Even during the most dangerous years, we would invite Fr. Kosma Qirjo to come from Vlora and celebrate the Divine Liturgy in a back room during the middle of the night. He would come five or six times a year. We would cover the windows with thick blankets, so no one could see light from outside. We spoke in whispered voices, so as not to awaken the children. We never celebrated a liturgy with the children around, because we didn't know if they might slip up and say something at school. One person would keep watch at the front door of the house, to warn us if anyone was coming. We felt like the early Christians worshipping in the catacombs."

On one occasion, Demetra traveled to Vlora and stayed at the home of Fr. Kosma. For 40 days in a row, they celebrated the Divine Liturgy every night in a small room. Fr. Kosma would work during the day, but they worshipped at night. Of course, they understood the consequences if someone discovered their actions. The authorities would send them to prison, or worse. This danger, however, did not hinder their devotion to God.

"Even when Fr. Kosma couldn't come, and we didn't have a priest to cel-ebrate the Divine Liturgy, we would do something else," Demetra contin-ued. "I would bake the prosphoro [the holy bread used in the Eucharist], and

The three holy women of Korça—Marika, Demetra, and Elizabeta.

place the bread and wine on top of our radio. Since we live so close to Greece, we could pick up a Greek station and listen to a live broadcast of the Divine Liturgy. Hoxha strictly forbade anyone to listen to foreign radio, so we realized the great risk we were taking. We would keep the volume very low and pray to God with the radio. At the end, we would eat the bread and wine as our Holy Communion."

"Even when we said our daily prayers, someone would keep watch at the front door and give us warning if anyone was coming," Marika chimed in. "Sure, we were scared, but we had faith that God was watching over us."

Before the closure of the churches in 1967, the women visited Bishop Irineu Banushi. The authorities had taken everything from this bishop and sent him into internal exile in a monastery. In exile, the authorities permitted him to receive visitors, so Demetra and Marika would go from time to time, bringing him food. During one of their visits, this holy bishop taught them about unceasing prayer.

"St. Paul exhorts us to 'pray without ceasing' (1 Thess. 5:17). Bishop Irineu taught us how to do this," Demetra explained. "He suggested that we organize a group of women who could each take a particular shift in the day. Every day, that person would pray during her shift. When her time finished, the next person would pray in her house. For example, if twelve women each take a two-hour shift, then someone would be praying each of the 24 hours in a day. We began to practice this for specific prayer requests before the closure of the churches and witnessed miracles.

"Following 1967, it became more difficult to organize our unceasing prayer chain. We found fewer women who would take shifts, but we continued to pray without ceasing during various forty-day Lenten periods. Our greatest prayer during those times was that we would see the reopening of the Church. Glory to God, we have seen this happen!" The women have continued this practice of unceasing prayer even following the fall of communism. "The Church still faces many difficulties, and we still have a need to pray without ceasing," said Marika.

Demetra, the self-described "evangelist" of the group, described how she "would write the Lord's Prayer, parts of Scripture, the Nicene Creed of Faith, or some other prayers on small pieces of paper. Then I would secretly go to various homes and deliver these spiritual gifts to believers and friends."

Over the years, the sisters even secretly baptized people in their homes. When I asked Demetra if she was afraid, she responded, "Sure. We didn't know what would happen if they caught us. Several times the police took us into their office and questioned us, but thank God, they never imprisoned us or physically hurt us. They weren't sure of what we were doing, so they just tried to scare us."

When communism fell and the government allowed freedom of religion in 1990, the sisters immediately wanted to go to the site of the destroyed Holy Trinity Church at the local cemetery and hold a water blessing. They went to the home of an old priest in Korça, but his children objected to their father going out because of fear. They asked what permission the sisters had received from the authorities, and why they wanted to endanger their father and his entire family.

Demetra proudly told me, "We stood in front of their door very firmly and shouted, 'We have the permission of God!' We then barged into their house and were ready to take the priest by force. The priest consented to come freely, however, and we celebrated the first public worship service in 23 years."

"With the opening of the country and the restoration of religious freedom, we can now die in peace," they all professed. "I always told people that God would hear our prayers and that our churches would reopen one day," Marika told me. "So many people wouldn't believe me. Now we see the fruit of the prayers of so many people. Of course, none of us ever imagined that one day we would actually be sitting in our home with an Orthodox Christian from America sharing stories about our love for Jesus Christ! God truly is great!"

Before I left, they asked me to remember only one prayer request. "Please pray that we may live to see the reopening of the monastery of St. John the Forerunner in the village of Voskopoja. We want to end our lives there as tonsured nuns."*

On my last visit to Korça, I found only the oldest sister, Marika, at home. Demetra and Berta had been staying at the St. Nicholas Monastery in Komanista, which stands in the middle of an all-Muslim village. For the past twenty days, these women had been preaching and teaching lessons to the women and children of the village, preparing them for baptism.

During this visit, I happened to meet Gaqo, another "saint" of Korça. He spent nine years in prison. Although he suffered much, he showed no signs of bitterness or anger, but radiated the joy of the Lord. For over an hour, he held me captive with his story. When the authorities forcibly closed the churches in 1967, Gaqo snuck into his village church and took many of the Church's icons, liturgical books, and the priest's vestments to hide in his house. He wanted to save these items for the time when the churches would undoubtedly reopen. Unfortunately, someone spied on him. The police arrested him, broke all his teeth and ribs, and sentenced him to execution. Later, the authorities reduced his sentence to 28 years of hard labor. After nine years in prison, they allowed him to go home.

Every day during his imprisonment, the three sisters of Korça prayed for him. The police questioned him, asking him if there were any others who were practicing their faith. He would simply answer, "Everyone goes to the churches in secret. They are my group."

He summarized his experience with these words, "God tested me. I have suffered much. They broke all my teeth. I have only one functioning kidney. They took away all my possessions. They made my family suffer. Yet I never denied Christ. I often remembered the words of our Lord when He said, 'Whoever denies Me, I will deny in heaven.' Although I suffered much, I never forgot Him. God says, 'I will test the person I love.' It was easy for me to say 'I

---

* In fact, in 1999 the oldest of the three sisters, Marika, was tonsured a nun in a monastery in Florina, Greece. Demetra and Elizabeta had passed away by that time.

love God' with my words. God wanted to test the sincerity of my love. I thank God He gave me the strength to pass the test!"

LOBSTERS, TERMITES, OR LAMB'S BRAIN?

Adapting to a new culture and all its traditions—this is a fundamental principle of missions. Yet sometimes, accepting this principle challenges our limits. I recently visited Fr. Petro's house to congratulate him on his daughter's recent marriage. Unfortunately, I couldn't attend the wedding itself, but the following day I visited his home, together with the seminarian John, who happened to be from his parish.

Whenever you visit an Albanian home, the hosts will surely bring you food. In this case, Fr. Petro felt especially honored to have a missionary priest from America visiting his home, so in traditional fashion, he brought out lamb. To show special respect to his guest, he placed in front of me a plate with the lamb's head—eyeballs, tongue, brain, and everything else included! I stared at it, unsure how to proceed. John looked at me with puzzlement, his mouth watering, and simply asked if he could eat one of the eyeballs. When I nodded, he proceeded to pluck one out with a fork and chew!

I have to admit that I was still too new in Albania to fully adapt that day, and only ate part of the meat around the cheekbones.*

Someone's treasure is another one's challenge. This story reminded me of an experience with my Kenyan friend Elekiah. When Elekiah and I studied together at Holy Cross, we sometimes traveled to different churches speaking about missions. One day, Fr. Basil Arabatsis invited us to his church in Maine. As we drove up from Boston, I jokingly told Elekiah that maybe the priest would offer us lobster for dinner, since Maine was known for lobster. Elekiah looked at me with disgust and informed me he could never eat lobster. "Lobsters walk on the bottom of the sea eating all the garbage in their path. Eating lobsters sounds disgusting!"

I tried to explain that we understood lobsters as a delicacy. Refusing such an expensive delicacy could be taken in the wrong way. As we debated this point, I reminded him that a fundamental mission principle was that one should adapt to the local culture, including trying all the local foods. We

---

* In fact, it would be many years before I actually tried an entire head—brains, tongue, and everything except the eyeballs.

finally agreed that if he would try lobster that night, then I would eat whatever Kenyan delicacy he chose to introduce me to the following summer. Elekiah just smiled.

Sure enough, that evening we did eat lobster, much to his dismay. Three months after that, as we traveled from village to village in Western Kenya, I remember his delight in finding freshly cooked termites. He put a handful of them in his mouth as I looked at him with uncertainty. He just smiled and said, "If you don't want the wings to get stuck in your teeth, just roll the termite in your hands, and then all the wings will fall out. In this way, you just get to taste the juicy meat!"

A deal was a deal, and I had my first handful of termites.

SUFFERING FOR CHRIST

Fr. Zef Pellumi, a Roman Catholic Franciscan monk, spent 24 years in prison. The Roman Catholic Church sent him to study in Rome and Austria as a young boy, and he returned to Albania in 1945 at the age of 22. Shortly after his return, the state arrested him for being a "spy of Italy and other foreign countries." He spent three years in prison. Following his release, he still wanted to become a priest. The state tried to control the Church, passing a law that anyone who wanted to become a priest had to receive official permission from the government. They denied Fr. Zef permission for ten years, yet the Church secretly ordained him. After a decade, the state gave the Church permission to ordain him.

In 1967, Albania officially became an atheistic country. The government closed every church and mosque and threatened to arrest all who practiced their faith. They arrested Fr. Zef, along with many of the other Franciscan monks, and he spent the next 21 years in prison. He told me unimaginable stories. He remembered how all believers, Orthodox and Catholic, would try to celebrate Pascha in some secret way. Once, when the Catholic priests were trying to figure out the date for Pascha, one priest wrote on a tiny piece of paper "d2p", which meant *"dielli e dyt eshte Pascha"* (the second Sunday is Pascha).

When a fellow prisoner spied on this priest, the authorities placed him in solitary confinement in a room one meter by two meters for thirty days. They stripped him of his clothes, except for his underwear, and then poured cold water under the door on the concrete floor. The cold winter, combined with the constant draft, created a dangerous situation. Although the priest survived his thirty-day punishment, he came out with pneumonia and died shortly after his release.

Fr. Zef shared with me many tortures he endured. For starters, he described how fifteen prisoners lived in a cell three meters by three meters. "We could never all sleep at the same time, because there wasn't enough room to lie down on the ground. The prison system deprived us of sleep. They put us to work doing backbreaking labor and gave us little food. They treated us worse than animals as they tried to break our spirits. Randomly they beat us until we were unconscious. They forced us to take medicines that would make us sick. They gave us the electrical shock treatment, and did so many other unimaginable things.

"In some ways, though," Fr. Zef told me, "it seemed easier back then. All we had to do was suffer for Christ. Each day we would say, 'Lord, give us the strength needed to endure.' Now, we are in charge of leading people to Christ, and it is difficult to care for the souls of others."

One moving story occurred in 1991 after the churches reopened. Fr. Zef became the pastor at St. Anthony's Church in Tirana. One Sunday after Mass, he noticed a big man standing in the back of the church. He immediately recognized the man as one of the worst guards in the prison where he had stayed. The man remained in the back until the service was over and everyone else left. Then he approached Fr. Zef and expressed his desire for confession. This man actually confessed his horrible sins to one of the men he himself had tortured. Fr. Zef witnessed a sincere repentance and conversion of this prison guard. "Today," Fr. Zef explained, "he is one of my most faithful parishioners."

One day I visited Fr. Zef with two Protestant missionary friends, John Johnson and John Quandrud. Johnson is a lawyer working with Advocates International, and Quandrud is a missionary who previously worked in Kosovo before coming to Albania. Surprisingly, Fr. Zef had a very open mind towards these Protestant missionaries. He explained that if we hope to reach many Albanians who come from a Muslim background, it might be difficult for them to become Roman Catholic or Orthodox. Even though the Albanians are not religiously Muslim, they still may feel a cultural loyalty to their tradition. To become Orthodox or Catholic might mean a betrayal to some Muslims. The Protestants offered another option, he thought, and maybe some Muslims could become Christian without a perceived betrayal of their family's religious tradition. It was an interesting, although controversial, attitude for an old Albanian Franciscan monk.

BLACKOUT!

Orthodox churches in Albania open every day from 8:00 AM until 7:00 PM. Clergy celebrate daily matins and vesper services, and one can normally see people walking into the churches throughout the day to light a candle, kiss the icons, and quietly pray.

A beautiful scene I witnessed in Korça related to these open churches. I travel to this southern city every other week and hold a Bible study with about fifty high school and college students. One morning during my last visit, I sat in one of the city's five Orthodox churches and noticed that many children came into the church, lit a candle, kissed all the icons, stood quietly in prayer, then left for school. At least a hundred students entered the church that morning.

As I reflected on that scene, I thought how only four years ago no churches were open for these children to enter and learn about Jesus Christ. The government forbade the children to pray and make the sign of the cross. How things have changed! In addition to this youth group in Korça and my ministry at the seminary, I am holding three different Bible studies in Tirana—one at the church, one at our house, and one in the dormitories for medical students. I also gather between thirty and fifty youth every week in the cities of Durres and Elbasan. The youth are responding to the Gospel!

New magnificent church buildings offer another sign of resurrection around the country, together with the growing ranks of indigenous clergy. In only three years' time, we have built or repaired 63 churches, and are in the process of building another 62. Thirty-two newly trained priests and 28 deacons have joined ranks with the 22 very old priests who survived the horrors of communism.

As for Faith, she becomes busier as time goes on. During her first two months, she concentrated on language learning as well as adapting to married life in Albania. I must say that she has already become a fantastic homemaker. Along with these responsibilities, she holds a weekly catechism class and Bible study for high school girls, while teaching English at the seminary and in Tirana. She also substitute teaches at a school for missionary children that the Ritsi children attend. Presently, she is organizing a Christmas show for all the children involved in our various catechism groups. Thank God she has adjusted so well!

The only thing she has some trouble getting used to is our daily electrical blackouts. For the past two weeks, we lose electricity every evening for three to five hours. The longest blackout has been 48 hours. One of my students told me his entire village will not have electricity until after Christmas. That puts our reality in a different light. After hearing that, we thank God for the electricity we do have!

DON'T DENY GOD IN YOUR HEART

Mihali, one of my seminary students, described himself as a pious young man growing up. He entered the army after eighth grade and stayed in the armed forces until 21 years of age, when his troubles began. In 1969, Mihali wrote a letter to Enver Hoxha, protesting the closure of churches. He understood the danger of writing such a letter, yet felt the need to be honest with himself and defend His Lord.

Needless to say, shortly after he sent the letter, the police arrested him. In prison, the guards beat him mercilessly, kicking his head and all parts of his body. They forcibly gave him large doses of insulin, along with electric shock treatments. During one period, he received no food for six days. Throughout his initial tortures, he prayed for God to have mercy on him. Six months passed in the local prison before they transferred him to Tirana. There, Mihali befriended a political prisoner who had already served twelve years in prison. This man warned Mihali to use diplomacy and change his language. "Don't deny God in your heart," his friend advised, "but don't talk publicly about God. Retract the statements you previously made by saying that you were temporarily insane."

Mihali cried as he told me how he succumbed to this advice and committed his "great sin." When a judge reviewed his case after one year in prison, Mihali rejected all his previous statements and pleaded insanity. Through this confession, and manipulations of family members in the Communist Party, the judge released him from prison.

Mihali himself found no peace within his soul as he relived his denial of God. He tried to suppress these feelings by focusing on school. As a young man in his twenties, he worked all day while completing his secondary education via correspondence. He graduated and, surprisingly, was accepted by the university. In this he saw the hand of God, because the state never allowed former prisoners to study at the university. Four years later, he graduated with a degree and became the head of a farm cooperative.

When democracy arrived in 1991, Mihali dreamed about making amends with God. He heard of the Church's seminary, but feared his age of 46 would hinder the school from accepting him. We saw his good character, however, and accepted him. Now, his sole desire is to dedicate his life to serving God.

He concluded our conversation by sharing a poem he wrote in prison before his denial:

> I am in a prison, in a dark prison
> I can't find rest nor peace.
> My body burns, it burns like an oven
> my soul is in pain, in pain to the depths.
> But the faith I have for my holy Lord
> Gives me the strength to smile, and to die with happiness.
> O very beautiful sun, on whom are you shining?
> Please light my little house, from heaven bring happiness to it.

AN HONEST COMMUNIST

Vlash described to me how he came from a very poor but spiritually rich family. When he was growing up, his parents taught him to have a healthy fear of God. Although his father was a diehard communist, Vlash described him as an "honest communist." He was a communist who never accepted the atheistic propaganda. "There were two kinds of communists in those days—most were thieves who tried to use the system to benefit themselves, and then there were those who truly believed the ideology and were ready to sacrifice everything for the party. My father represented the latter. Although we had little to eat growing up, he would never steal. I remember as a young boy taking some corn from a field. I was very hungry. When I arrived home, my father became angry and insisted that I return the corn to the field. 'We are not thieves!' he reprimanded me."

Vlash repeated that during those years it was unusual to find someone honest like his father. "Through such an example, I learned what was important in life," he proclaimed. "Although I graduated from the University of Tirana in agronomics, I now have the desire to become a priest and serve the people by teaching them about God. It is important to have educated people serving the Church, because our people have seen too many intellectuals reject God and ridicule the faith. It is essential for our priests to be prepared for such people!"

PASCHA 1995

What a joyous and meaningful Pascha we celebrated in 1995! Unlike last year, when the government restricted the Church's activity, this year Christians freely celebrated Pascha throughout Albania. Between 20,000 and 25,000 people showed up at midnight in the streets of Tirana. Most came with candles and red eggs, ready to hear the archbishop's paschal message and sing "Christ is Risen!" The state channel televised the service live for the entire country, and even repeated it the following morning. What a moving sight! It's hard to imagine that five short years ago, the state strictly forbade any religious worship. Yet today, tens of thousands joyously celebrate. Enver Hoxha tried to abolish God for fifty years, and now he is the one in the grave, while his compatriots cry out, "Christ is Risen!" One cannot overstate the symbolism of this feastday—victory over evil, hope for the future, peace in our lives, and salvation for eternity.

PASCHA IN HIMARA

For Faith and me, our Pascha celebration was quite different from the experience in Tirana, but just as powerful. We spent Holy Week and Pascha in a small village five hours south of Tirana, only 50 miles from Greece. The village of Himara is a picturesque coastal town with five thousand inhabitants, divided with the central part of the village along the sea and the "old" village a 45-minute walk up the mountain.

From the moment we arrived on Holy Wednesday, we could sense the excitement of Pascha. The enthusiasm, however, wasn't simply for religious reasons. Since Himara is so close to Greece, almost all the people under 50

Faith gets a taste of village life in Himara during Holy Week, 1995.

have gone there to work. As a result, the village is left with the old grandparents and their grandchildren. Almost every villager told us of their difficult life, and how they now had to live without their children nearby. Yet in
anticipation of Pascha, everyone waited for their children to come home for
the holidays.

Many of the older women expressed delight to know that a priest had come to their village. They could now celebrate the Lord's Resurrection and receive Holy Communion. The last time a priest had been in their village was a year before. They waited during Christmas, but no priest came.

FIRST HOLY COMMUNION IN THIRTY YEARS

On Holy Saturday morning, 150 people celebrated the first Resurrection service in the St. Marina Church by the beach. With what reverence and desire a number of the faithful approached to receive Holy Communion! After the Liturgy, we baptized three people.

The most interesting event, however, occurred in the middle of the Liturgy. Faith was looking out the door of the church when she saw an old lady fall down in the middle of the road. Faith watched her get back up, then fall down again. She rushed outside and met Yiayia Eleni, a 96-year-old woman who seemed ready to pass out. Faith thought she was going to die. After a few minutes of resting under a tree, Yiayia Eleni told Faith, "I heard that there is a priest in the village. I haven't received Holy Communion for almost thirty years, since the church of our village closed. Yet when I heard that a priest has come to our village, I fasted from all food yesterday and today, in order to prepare for Holy Communion! How could I stay away from receiving my Lord?"

The woman was so weak, though, that Faith helped her get back to her house. Following the Liturgy, I went to her home and offered Holy Communion. What a special blessing! Afterwards, I went to the homes of several other older people who couldn't come to church. One woman must have said, *"Doxa to Theo!"* (Glory to God!) a hundred times. After I gave her Holy Communion, she kept kissing my hand and saying, "Thank you! Thank you so much. Glory to God!"

Offering the sacrament of our Lord's life-giving Body and Blood to people thirsting for union with Him was an overwhelming experience. Serving as a priest and offering these grace-filled sacraments has made me appreciate and understand them as never before. I kept thinking, how often do we in America literally cry for joy and thank God from the depths of our hearts for the ineffable blessing of receiving Holy Communion? Both Faith and I came away with a new appreciation of our faith after this experience.

CIGARETTES, CHAOS,
AND CHRIST'S RESURRECTION

The Resurrection service on Pascha night was unbelievable. People packed into the main Church of All Saints. Hundreds of people gathered both inside and out in the courtyard. The day before, several busloads of immigrants working in Greece returned for the holidays. Of course, few of these people know anything about the Church. They simply understand that their grandparents were Orthodox, and one of the traditions of the Orthodox was to go to church on the night of Pascha.

This, my first Holy Week and Pascha as a priest, left unforgettable memories. As I tried to read the Gospel of the Resurrection at midnight outside the church, people were talking, yelling, lighting fireworks, and carrying on as if they were in an outdoor bazaar. Inside the church, things were even worse. At one point, I turned around and noticed people smoking cigarettes. Someone even lit his cigarette from one of the candles in the church. Part of me wanted to yell, "What are you doing? This is a house of God!" Yet another part of me thought, "They are like sheep without a shepherd. This is just another sign of the desperate need to preach the Gospel, so that these people can understand what our faith is all about!"

By the time Matins concluded, the noise had reached such a level that I couldn't even hear my chanter, who stood only ten feet away from the altar. I asked the people (for the tenth time) to please be quiet, but each time I did that, the lull lasted for only a few moments. Finally, I motioned for everyone to stop and announced that whoever wanted to receive Holy Communion should come forward and stand in front of the Royal Doors. About seventy people approached, thinking they would receive Holy Communion at that moment, but we had just begun the Divine Liturgy. John Lena, my chanter, came right next to the Royal Doors so we could hear one another, and we continued the Liturgy in the midst of utter chaos for the next hour and a half. It was like no liturgy I ever celebrated before or after. Yet the power and joy of our Lord's Resurrection radiated in the middle of bedlam. By the end, our voices ached, but our spirits soared!

During Holy Week we stayed with Panos and Yanoula, a 65-year-old Greek couple. Panos spent nine years in prison because he once mentioned to a group of friends that if he had the chance to escape to Greece, he would. Someone reported his comment to the authorities. Panos described the two-meter-by-one-meter cell in which he stayed for the fourteen months prior to his sentencing. His daily rations included a cup of soup, really just hot water, together with 600 grams of bread twice a day. After his sentencing, he stayed in a tiny cell with twenty-five other prisoners and no beds. All the prisoners worked at hard labor from early morning until late at night. Initially, the government sentenced Panos to twenty-eight years, but later they reduced it to fourteen. They released him after nine.

Whenever someone went to prison, the entire family suffered by being labeled as enemies of the state. Panos's wife lost her job and had to find other menial work, toiling twelve hours a day. Their children, ages two to seven, nearly starved. No one, including their relatives, wanted to talk or associate with any member of the family. Even after Panos got out of prison, few people would talk to him.

We met his daughter-in-law, Andonia, who came home for Pascha. She told me that her own father didn't talk to her for a year because she married an "enemy of the state." Only in 1990 did people cease to consider Panos and his family dangerous. Panos mentioned that while in prison, he spent some time with a bishop who was also imprisoned. Today, he faces the new challenge of living on a pension of fifteen dollars a month.

LEARNING TO FORGIVE

Deacon Kristaq spent eight years in prison. One day in class, we discussed the theme of forgiveness, and how unfathomable are God's mercy and love. We forgive, not because others deserve our forgiveness, but because God first forgave us. In a country where so much evil has occurred, and among a people who can be quite stubborn, forgiveness doesn't make much sense. Yet after a long and sometimes heated discussion in class, this deacon came up to me privately and showed me a little list of names he prays for at every Divine Liturgy. Six of those names were people who falsely testified against him, and whose testimony led him to spend eight long years in prison. "It's not easy," he admitted, "but I know that I must forgive them." Such concrete examples of forgiveness and love epitomize the Gospel message.

A FOOL FOR CHRIST?

One day, a friend in Durres introduced me to his mother, a pious and humble woman who abounded with the love of Christ. When I asked Jani to tell me about his mother, he said he remembered when he was a child, she constantly talked about her love for Jesus Christ. She would go around the neighborhood telling people about their need to turn to God. She even wanted to meet the dictator Enver Hoxha and tell him that he needed to repent of his evil ways. Of course, the entire family was scared and told the mother to stop, but to no avail. A number of times the police questioned her, but various doctors concluded that she was "crazy." Thus, her family survived. As I listened to this story, I thought about some of the saints of the Church who were called "fools for Christ." Many people often thought they were crazy as well, yet the Church today lifts them up as saints. Maybe this woman is like them.

CRYPTO-CHRISTIANS   JULY 1995

Crypto-Christians. I had never heard of such a term. Yet this is the term given to people who kept their Christian identity in a secret manner. I spent three days in the area of Spathi and Gjinar, small villages two hours up in the Elbasan mountains. This area, with its fifteen or so villages, claims a unique history.

During the 500 years of Ottoman rule, when most Albanians succumbed to the Islamic pressures toward conversion, these villagers made a pact with one another to hold onto their faith in a secret manner. Although they publicly professed Islam, secretly they kept their true identity as Christians. For example, everyone in the village had two names—a Muslim one used in public, and a Christian one used in their homes. In the secrecy of their homes, they continued to celebrate Christian feastdays and practice Orthodox traditions. Even after centuries of Islamic influence, and surrounded by a sea of Muslim villages, these people fiercely held onto their Christian identity. Over the past decades of militant atheism, however, these villagers began to lose their faith. Today, these people proudly proclaim their Christian identity but understand little of what this means.

In response to this situation, twelve zealous young men under the guidance of Fr. Martin decided to spend the summer in these areas, preaching the Gospel, teaching the faith, and preparing people for baptism. For five or six weeks at a time, these students lived in one village, going out two by two each day into neighboring areas sharing the Good News. Since most of these students attend our seminary, they invited me to come to the villages and participate in their work.

I spent three unforgettable days with them. What zeal and fervor they have to share the faith! Daily, they prayed together, ate together, and encouraged one another in their various ministries. Some walked an hour and a half each way to different villages, offering lessons, visiting with the people, and returning late at night. For two nights, I visited the homes of several villagers with Emmanuel, a third-year student. I was deeply moved as I observed the simple way Emmanuel shared the love of God and the basic teachings of Christ. On the second day of my visit, Fr. Kristo and I baptized 45 villagers. The following day, we baptized 81 others of all ages in another village. The spirit of these students reminded me of what St. Kosmas Aitolos must have done 200 years ago when he traveled the Albanian countryside preaching a similar message.

Along with religious instruction, the Church offers humanitarian aid in these regions. Our Service of Love office oversaw a clean water project and aided the villagers in purchasing their own tractor. Each project has been carefully researched and planned in cooperation with the village leaders, so that the villagers take ownership in the work. Presbytera Renee has begun a new program in which medical students go into these villages and offer practical health care lessons for the women and children. The outreach is symbolic of the holistic mission the Church tries to fulfill.

One evening, I took a walk up the hill to the site where the Church of the Prophet Elijah had been destroyed. The two evangelists who came with me wanted to do a Vespers service. What a moving moment—on top of this hill overlooking the entire village, holding candles in the midst of darkness, singing with all our hearts, "O Joyful Light," "Lord, have mercy," and other evening hymns. Many in the village must have heard our voices ringing from the hill.

The next day we returned home after a very bumpy and cramped ride inside the church's jeep. We were exhausted but spiritually renewed. This is what missions is all about!

A BABY!   APRIL 1996

The Lord has given us innumerable blessings. One of the greatest
recently is the conception of our first child, around March 25. A new life has
begun, and I thank God, our Creator, Giver and Sustainer of life.

> *Lord, thank You for this greatest of gifts. We pray from the moment
> of his or her conception that this child will fulfill his or her potential,
> become a servant of God and a saint of the most Holy. Thank you, Lord,
> for the ability to conceive and for the new life to be created out of the
> deep love we have in our marriage. May this child always live in an envi-
> ronment of love! May we provide a safe and Christ-centered environ-
> ment in which our child may not only hear about You and Your great
> deeds, but more importantly, see You, feel You, and experience You in
> the depths of his or her heart. Finally, Lord, I humbly ask You to comfort
> all those who have difficulty conceiving and all who long to become par-
> ents. Comfort them, and may they, through their difficulty, draw closer
> to You. We give thanks to our Lord and our God.*

AN ARRANGED MARRIAGE

I arrived at the seminarian Sotir's village, four hours south of Tirana,
for the beginning of Holy Week 1996. Our trip here reminded me of my time
in Africa. We traveled for an hour off the main road to reach his village, and
since it had rained the past week, we had to stop several times to push our van
through the muddy roads.

We brought a bell for the new prefabricated church and rang it to welcome
the villagers to celebrate the first service, which was the Vespers for Lazarus
Saturday. Forty people, mostly men, came. Afterwards, we ate a delightful dinner at the home of Sotir. Much of our conversation focused on the engage-
ment of his eldest daughter, which had occurred a month earlier. Sotir had
arranged the marriage of his 15-year-old daughter with a 25-year-old suitor.
He described how many suitors came for his daughter, but after examining
their families' background, economic situation, and the intentions of the
groom to stay in the village or not, Sotir decided on Arben. Needless to say, we
had an interesting conversation on the topic.

The next morning, I woke up to the sound of sheep, a donkey, a boisterous rooster, and plenty of chickens. We celebrated the Divine Liturgy to a full church of 150 people, including many children. They seemed excited to have a priest.

Afterwards, we continued our trip to Himara with two other seminarians, Luka and Deacon Jani. We traveled the road from Vlora to Himara along the magnificent Albanian coastline, with snow-capped mountains on one side and the glistening Ionian Sea down below. We stopped for half an hour in the Greek-speaking village of Palasa to inform them that we would return on Holy Thursday for the Divine Liturgy. Many of the old people expressed such excitement to hear that a priest was coming to their village. They wanted us to come for Pascha as well. They kept repeating, "It's been five years since the fall of communism, and we still don't have a priest. A priest comes here only once or twice a year." After passing through two other villages, we stopped in the Albanian-speaking village of Vuno, and informed them we would be there Holy Tuesday night and Holy Wednesday morning.

HOLY WEEK 1996

We held a Vespers service for Palm Sunday in Himara, but since the people weren't expecting a priest until later in the week, only two people showed up. For Palm Sunday Liturgy, twenty villagers came. After services, we walked down to the lower section of the village, by the sea, and began informing people that a priest had arrived and services would be held in the All Saints Church in the upper village.

After the Presanctified Liturgy on Tuesday, we walked to the village of Vuno an hour away. Alexandra, a medical student from Tirana who is quite active in our university youth group, has a family house there. We visited the Church of St. Spyridon, which is falling apart and quite unkempt. Yet the church has beautiful frescoes covering every inch of its walls and ceiling. Following the Bridegroom service, a villager asked us to come to his café and bless it, in order to protect it from the evil eye. We proceeded to interrupt 25 villagers playing billiards and blessed the café. I also offered an explanation of what this blessing means.

As we did the various services throughout Holy Week, it became so apparent how little these people know of the faith. For example, two of the village chanters who helped us with the Holy Unction Service on Holy Wednesday left the church without even being anointed.

On Holy Thursday morning, we returned to the village of Palasa, where 100 people filled the church. More than 25 women brought prosforo. This was their Pascha Liturgy, since no priest would come Saturday night. Deacon Jani came from Dukat. Afterwards we went to Pirouli, a tiny village 45 minutes up the mountain from Himara. A family wanted a forty-day memorial for their mother. It was a great opportunity to talk about life, death, and resurrection.

We spent Holy Friday in Himara. Many children came with flowers to decorate Christ's tomb. Leonidha and Faith taught the kids how to sing some verses from the Lamentations. The morning and afternoon services were beautiful. The only trouble came when I tried to preach in English and have Nina translate for me in Albanian. After a couple of minutes, several people started to shout out that they didn't want to hear Albanian in the church. When I explained that I had difficulty preaching in Greek, they wouldn't listen. "No Albanian," they said. Afterwards, some people came up to me and apologized. Everyone understands Albanian, but down south among the Greek minority, language is a sensitive issue.

We celebrated the first Resurrection Holy Saturday morning in an Albanian-speaking village. A hundred people filled the church. Everyone seemed pleased to receive Holy Communion. Afterwards we visited a man with leprosy. He spent 14 years in a leprosy colony, where he received treatment. For 20 years, he has stabilized his leprosy with medication. Over the past five years, however, with the collapse of the entire infrastructure of government, he has stopped receiving the medication. He asked if I could help him get the proper medicine.

The midnight Pascha service was a zoo, just like last year—packed with people and extremely noisy. Yet in the midst of chaos, we experienced the joy and wonder of the Resurrection. Very early on Pascha day, we traveled to two villages to take Holy Communion for the people. One village was just below Himara; the other was a 30-minute drive, then a 30-minute walk up a mountain. We arrived in the church with the entire village waiting. We spent two hours there, singing, reading the Gospel, preaching, and visiting the homes of a few shut-ins.

THE "FAIRY TALES" OF FAITH?

After we celebrated the Agape service on Pascha day, someone informed me that an 80-year-old lady had just died in the village. Her family wanted me to come to their house and do a funeral. According to typical practice, the body was laid out in one room of the house, where all the women gathered around it. The men sat in the adjacent room smoking their cigarettes. I first entered the room of the dead woman, and since it was Pascha, began singing the entire Resurrection service. How moving to sing "Christ is Risen" dozens of times as I looked upon the dead body.

After this service, I entered the room with all the men. Their conversations immediately stopped as they saw a priest enter. They just stared at me, so I used the opportunity to preach a few words. Although death is always a tragic end to life, I explained about the hope we Orthodox Christians have in the resurrection. I shared with them the monastic greeting of *"Kalo paradiso"* (A good paradise) when someone dies. Our hope and belief as Christians is that death is not the end, but simply a doorway into fuller union with God, into paradise.

As I continued along this vein of thought, an older man yelled out, "Come on, Papouli [a familiar term for a priest]! We know there is no such thing as paradise. Life is what we see here and now. Nothing exists after death. Quit telling us these fairy tales!"

"You are free to believe what you like," I responded. "Yet for Orthodox Christians, hope in the resurrection is central to our faith. Today is Pascha, and we joyously greet one another by crying out, 'Christ is Risen!' and answering, 'Truly He is Risen!' If there is nothing after death, then Christ did not rise. And as St. Paul says, if there is no resurrection, then our faith is in vain. But for us Christians, the resurrection and paradise make up the cornerstones of our faith."

The man scoffed at my reply, and shouted out, "I am Orthodox! My parents and grandparents are Greek, therefore I'm Orthodox. But I don't believe in such fairy tales!"

I didn't want to make a fuss, especially since this man was in no mood for discussion, so I turned my attention to the others in the room. The whole episode, though, reminded me about the work ahead. This is what missions is all about—patiently yet boldly proclaiming the Good News of our Lord in all situations.

VICTORY OVER DEATH

The day after Pascha, for the feast of St. George, we celebrated the Divine Liturgy in Vuno. The people showed great respect and reverence throughout the entire service. A high point occurred at the end of the service, when I went throughout the graveyard adjacent to the church and sang "Christ is Risen!" in front of every tomb. Each villager had some relative buried there, and some began to cry as we vividly proclaimed Christ's victory over death.

We have nothing to fear when Christ is with us—not even death. As St. John Chrysostom emphasized in his powerful paschal sermon, "Death has been swallowed up in victory! O Death, where is your sting? O hell, where is your victory? Christ is risen and you are overthrown! Christ is risen and the demons have fallen! Christ is risen and the angels rejoice! Christ is risen and life is liberated! Christ is risen and not one dead remains in the grave! For Christ, having risen from the dead, becomes the first-fruits of those who have fallen asleep. To Him be glory and dominion for ever!"

THE DEATH OF OUR CHILD   MAY 29, 1996

"Can a mother forget the baby at her breast and have no compassion on the baby she has borne? Though she may forget, I will not forget you. See, I have carved you in the palm of my hand." (Isaiah 49:16)

Yesterday, we lost our precious child—only two months in the mother's womb. Of course we are sad. Every time we saw a child playing in the streets, or walking hand-in-hand with his mommy, we kept thinking, "That will be us very soon." God must have other plans, though. He created and "carved" this baby in the palm of His hands. What joy the news of a baby brought to us and our family and friends! Now the baby has gone back to his or her Creator.

In the midst of our sorrow, the archbishop showed such love and concern. Presbytera Renee was a godsend to Faith, helping her throughout the miscarriage. Fr. Justinos, a monk from Mt. Athos, shared a nice thought after our tragedy. He told us how his spiritual father reminded people that from the moment of a conception, Christ creates a mansion in heaven specifically and uniquely for that conceived child. God always hopes that each person will fulfill his or her potential and live up to the likeness of God in which he or she was created. In doing so, they will enter into paradise and dwell in that mansion. In the cases when people don't live up to their potential and become saints, the place remains empty for all eternity in memory of that person. So Fr. Justinos comforted us by saying our little baby would now take up his or her abode in his or her mansion in paradise.

O Lord, please accept our precious one into Your loving arms. We said from the moment of his or her conception that we dedicated this new life to You. Please accept this offering with all our love! And in Your time, according to Your will, bless us again and help us to become worthy of another child. Amen.

A GYPSY BAPTISM   JULY 1996

Every Sunday we have a group of a dozen or two beggars that sit in the alley that leads to our church. So often, people walk right past them as they go to church, or at best throw a coin at them to ease their conscience. Last December, our youth group decided to do something special for these beggars. They invited them to come to our youth center after services on Sunday for a delicious lunch.

Something beautiful happened. As these outcasts ate a hearty meal, our young people sat and ate with them. Conversations began, and very quickly one could see how our youth no longer looked upon them as pathetic Gypsy beggars, but as people and children of God. We learned their names and listened to their stories. One of our students began feeding a crippled man. Another cuddled a beggar's newborn baby. Christ's love broke down barriers that day.

During this meal, we came to know Izmir, a paralyzed Gypsy woman, and her husband, Gezim. They told us of their three-year-old daughter, whose birthday was the following week. Several of the students asked the family if we could visit their home and celebrate Viola's birthday together. Izmir and Gezim were shocked and honored. They had often felt the harsh prejudice many Albanians display towards Gypsies, and they couldn't believe we actually wanted to visit their home. The following week, five of us visited their tiny one-room home in a slum of Tirana. Viola looked precious on her birthday and thoroughly enjoyed her cake, presents, and our visit.

Over the following months, many students greeted Izmir and Gezim weekly as they begged in front of the church, and occasionally visited their home. I went to their home to offer a house blessing. By late April, during one of our visits, they expressed a desire to become Christian, asking whether such a thing was acceptable. We enthusiastically encouraged them and explained the need for catechism before baptism. They seemed a little discouraged because of the difficulty Izmir would have in coming to the church twice a week in her wheelchair. It was quite an effort for her to come even once on Sundays. At that moment, though, Spiro, who was a fourth-year medical student, said, "No problem. I can come to your house twice a week and do the catechism." Although the school year was coming to an end and Spiro had finals, he joyously offered to go to their home and share his faith in Jesus Christ with them.

Over the following two months, Spiro discussed with me the lessons he would teach, and then came back afterward with interesting stories. The first week some relatives of Izmir and Gezim came to listen. The second week, ten people squeezed into their tiny one-room shack to hear the lesson. Another week Spiro told me, "They loved the story about the prodigal son and had so many questions!" By the end, Spiro was not only their teacher, but became their godfather. I was thrilled not only with the catechism of Izmir and Gezim, but also with Spiro's enthusiasm. We pray this spirit of love and evangelism will grow among all our youth.

The baptism took place in July. We gathered in the church baptistery with maybe twenty other students. A prayerful presence filled the room. Izmir and Gezim, together with their daughter Viola, prepared for baptism.

Two students tenderly lifted Izmir out of her wheelchair and helped her into the baptismal font, while her husband stayed in the water to offer support. After I immersed her three times, two other students lifted her out. The students expressed such tender love. Izmir took the name Kristina, and her husband, who was such a good caretaker for her, received the name Josif. As Kristina sat back in her wheelchair, she wept and kept repeating, "Thank you so much! Thank you! I love you all!"

Her sister came to watch and literally cried throughout the service. Afterwards, she asked me, "When can I be baptized? I felt deprived by not participating today."

The following day in church, Faith sat in the front row with these new-born Christians. They proudly held their candles throughout the service and received Holy Communion at the proper time. Once again, Kristina cried with joy. At the end of the service, a number of people in church came up to congratulate them and welcome them into Christ's home.

Izmir and Gezim, the newly baptized Gypsy couple, take on the new Christian names Kristina and Josif.

A week later, though, Josif and Kristina faced the reality of the world. The archbishop had warned me, when I shared this story with him, that although he was happy to hear of their baptism, not everyone would be rejoicing at Gypsies becoming a part of our church family. His words proved to be prophetic. Josif and Kristina excitedly came to church on the following Sunday and sat in the front. They piously prayed and participated in the entire Divine Liturgy. At the moment of Holy Communion, they went forward with their baptismal candles and their godfather Spiro behind them.

After we finished the Divine Liturgy, I unvested and came outside the altar only to see Kristina crying. At first I thought she was shedding tears of joy, but quickly realized she was upset. When I asked her what had happened, she told me that a woman had come up to her and told her, "You don't belong here. Why are you here? Go back outside and beg. That's where you belong!"

I was furious. I asked Kristina to show me who had told her this, and to my shock, I recognized the woman as someone who sat in the front row of the church every Sunday. She attended services regularly, yet, like the Pharisees during Christ's time, she never captured the spirit of the Gospel. When I went over to her and asked what she had said to Kristina, she pretended not to understand my question. I repeated myself and pointed to Kristina, but the woman looked past Kristina and said, "What are you talking about?"

Finally, I asked Kristina to come over to where we were, and asked the woman if she had told Kristina that she didn't belong in our church. The woman blushed and stammered, "Oh. She didn't understand me. I just told her that she might feel more comfortable somewhere else, and not here." I proceeded to scold the woman, telling her that Kristina was a baptized Orthodox Christian and fully belonged in this church, just as much as I or she or anyone else.

I left the woman with a stunned look on her face. I apologized once again to Kristina, and reminded her that others might say silly things, but I wanted her to always remember that she was a beloved child of God. This church was her new home now!

CHAPTER 4

ANARCHY
AND CHAOS

THE CRISIS OF 1997

Albania fell into anarchy in 1997. In many ways, one could only describe the events as madness. Senseless destruction. Countless injuries. Meaningless death. Overwhelming despair. Lingering fear and uncertainty.

After some previous crisis, Archbishop Anastasios said to me, "Remember, satanic forces controlled this country for many years. Don't think these forces will sit back and relax now that democracy has come. Satan is always fighting."

The country could note much progress since the fall of communism. Albania had a democratically elected government; the people enjoyed freedom of religion; society had opened up; foreign investment had entered the country; and Albania appeared to be on a path toward a modern European life. Satanic forces, however, returned with a vengeance in 1997. As people around the world watched the violence and destruction on CNN, many wondered what was happening. Many Americans were hearing about Albania for the first time in their lives, and unfortunately they were not getting a good impression.

Seeds of the present crisis were sown with the rise of questionable investment companies. These "Ponzi pyramid" investment schemes promised outrageous returns of up to 300 percent within a three-month period. Although some of the larger companies had operated in Albania for several years, their popularity rose primarily during the second half of 1996. Some experts estimated that as many as 80 percent of Albanian families invested in these schemes. Even the president of the country offered his stamp of approval when he commented that the money from these investment firms was clean and secure.

I talked with my students at the seminary about these investment companies in November 1996. I remembered friends back in the States who had fallen prey to much smaller Ponzi schemes, and thus, I tried to share my concerns and doubts about the validity of these companies. The difficulty, though, was that everyone knew someone who had profited, and the atmosphere of the country made anything believable. Only months later did I discover that after my talk, the students asked one of their old Albanian teachers what he thought about these investments. He simply responded, "We have suffered so much over the past decades, maybe God is blessing us!" So much for my words of warning.

By the end of 1996, the investment firms began to collapse. The government froze the assets of all the companies by January 1997, and tens of thousands of Albanian families faced desperate economic distress. Countless families lost their life savings. Some even lost their homes.

Kristina's family had moved to Tirana five months before from a northern village. They sold their village home but didn't have enough to buy an apartment in Tirana. So they invested all their money, including money saved up by a son who worked as an immigrant in Greece. They figured that if they could earn the promised 300 percent return within four months, they would have enough money to buy a simple two-room apartment. Instead, the company folded, and now Kristina's family has no money and no home.

Jani's three sons worked in Athens for the past five years. They saved $40,000 with sweat and blood that only immigrants can understand. They invested all their savings in the firms and now have nothing to show for their years of labor.

Drita invested her family's money without her husband's knowledge. When the investment firm closed its doors, she didn't dare tell her husband. Instead, she stepped in front of a train. We hear of many such suicides.

Outsiders may criticize these reckless investments, yet they must understand people motivated by desperation and naiveté. Many elderly people try to live on a pension of $40 per month. Villagers long for a new life in the city, which will offer more opportunities for their children. Others witnessed the initial payouts of these investment firms to friends and neighbors, and didn't understand the economics of such pyramid schemes.

Whatever the reason, countless people faced an uncertain future in 1997. Despair and anger boiled up in the streets. Chaos began in the southern city of Vlore, where citizens protested against the government. University students began a hunger strike. When the secret police tried to stop the protesters, angry citizens reacted. Some broke into army warehouses and armed themselves. The police left their posts, and the army disappeared. As anarchy reigned, people looted shops, factories, schools, and other institutions, even opening up the prisons.

In this chapter I offer a perspective on the fear and despair that engulfed this country throughout the early part of 1997.

HOPE FOR THE FUTURE

A Declaration of
Archbishop Anastasios
(FEBRUARY 12, 1997)

Throughout these years of democracy, the Orthodox Church of Albania has tried to stay close to the people, supporting, comforting, and speaking to them through the language of eternal truth. She reminds all people about the duty of solidarity, integrity, responsibility, forgiveness, and proper selection of those who seek the trust of the people. At this critical time, the Church joins in the great trial of thousands of defenseless people. We are obliged to remind every side that to transcend this new trial, all forms of misinformation and violence must be abandoned. Violence gives birth to hatred, and hatred darkens the mind and heart, leading everyone in a vicious circle of exploitation and upheaval. To transcend this crisis, all sides need to reflect more calmness, more truth, a greater disposition for reconciliation, more collaboration, and mostly more justice and love in an effort of compensation. It is not fair to victimize the innocent and uninformed people.

At the same time, we invite all believers to intensify their prayers on Sunday, February 16. We pray that God will enlighten all those who are engaged in these issues to face them with integrity, sincerity, and wisdom. Faith in the God of truth, justice, power, and peace will help us find the right solutions and see the future with more hope.

NO MORE HATRED

A Supplication of Archbishop Anastasios
(MARCH 6, 1997)

During these difficult times, as the Orthodox Archbishop, I have simple words to say in prayer for all people: No more blood! No more fighting! No more arms! No more hatred! "And the God of peace will be with you." (Philippians 4:9)

It is only with self-control, repentance, truth, forgiveness, and reconciliation that substantial peace can be secured and the way for a better future can be opened. The God of love and peace will not leave us.

KALASHNIKOVS FOR EGGS   MARCH 14

Anarchy! The anarchy that has engulfed the southern regions of Albania for the past two weeks, starting on March 1, has come full force into Tirana. For two days, we have heard non-stop machine-gun fire. People have looted the country's military warehouses, and thousands upon thousands have Kalashnikov machine guns in their homes. In fact, yesterday I saw people selling Kalashnikovs for $20 on the street. Some barter guns for eggs.

No one is really fighting anyone else. It's not like two sides battling one another. Part of the shooting seems to be from adolescents finding a thrill in shooting a machine gun into the air. Of course, we also see malicious behavior in the looting.

Chaos reigns. The federal army has disappeared, along with the local police. Thieves freely loot the shops. People are being killed by stray bullets. Those who shoot for fun don't seem to realize that every bullet shot into the air must come down. It's so sad to see people's lives destroyed. We just heard that guards at the main prison outside of Tirana have abandoned their posts and all the prisoners have escaped.

Foreign embassies have begun their military evacuation. Last night, the US Embassy evacuated all women and children. Presbytera Renee Ritsi left with Stephanos and Nicole. Today, Lord willing, the embassy will evacuate others, including Faith and our co-missionaries, Peter Gilbert and Art and Eloise Ware. Fear, uncertainty, and despair fill the hearts of many friends. Unlike expatriates, they don't have the option to evacuate. They're stuck here, facing an uncertain future.

Of course, our archbishop will stay in the country. OCMC missionaries Fr. Martin, Penny Deligiannis, and I, along with our Greek co-missionaries, Fr. Justinos, Fr. Theologos, Fr. Spyridon, and Sister Agiro, will stay as well. We feel a loyalty to our archbishop and a strong solidarity with the Albanians. How could we preach about the love and hope of God, and then abandon the people during a major crisis? Fr. Martin and I received a directive from Archbishop Spyridon of America that we should evacuate immediately. When we responded to his deacon that we didn't think it wise to leave, we received a second fax stating, "The archbishop was not asking you, but telling you that you must leave." In good conscience, though, we pretended not to have received the order and stayed.

We don't know how this will play out. Later today I will move out of our apartment and into the Metropolis building with the archbishop and other expatriates. I'm not sure of what we'll be able to do, but we will stay, praying and doing whatever we can to comfort the people. Archbishop Anastasios has begun organizing massive relief of food and medicines from Greece.

I must say that this whole experience has made me identify much more with the millions of people around the world who suffer from violence and war. It's so easy to see a 30-second clip on CNN and then turn the channel, without thinking about all the fear and suffering people go through. May the Prince of Peace always reign in our hearts, and may we Christians, more than all others, strive to shine forth our Lord's hope and love!

MADNESS   MARCH 15

Via helicopter, the US Marines evacuated Faith and four hundred other Americans. I dropped Faith, Peter Gilbert, and several other American missionaries off at the US Embassy complex. We could hear machine gun fire all around us. Later in the day, the news reported that the US evacuation was halted because of people firing on the helicopters. I wasn't sure if Faith had actually left the country or was stranded at the embassy, until she telephoned me just moments ago from Rome. The helicopter took the evacuees to a US Navy ship in the Adriatic Sea. From there they transported Faith to Brindisi, from where she took a train to Rome. Later this afternoon she'll be on a plane for New York.

Thank God things have quieted down here in Tirana. Last night was the first time we didn't hear continuous gunfire. Today police cruised the streets of Tirana in tanks. They announced by loudspeaker that anyone seen with a gun would be shot on sight. An eerie quiet has taken hold of the capital.

We celebrated Divine Liturgy this morning, and many people were in church. Even though it is the first Saturday of Lent, I thought few people would venture out because of all the chaos. People and cars have begun to fill the streets of Tirana once again. Most shops remain closed. We no longer hear continuous gunfire and are not afraid of bullets landing on our heads. Yesterday, I met a woman who told me that stray bullets had injured both her father and her brother.

Everyone seems in shock. It's quite depressing. People can't understand the madness that has enveloped the country. And it continues in other cities. We hear daily about looting and senseless destruction of factories and buildings. Everyone is trying to understand how all this happened.

The entire situation reminds me of Aleksandr Solzhenitsyn's words, "The line of good and evil does not run between countries or parties or ethnicities; it runs through the heart of every person." How true. Scenes here remind me of the Los Angeles riots in 1992. The answer is not simply the change of a political system, but a radical change of people's hearts, a transformation that occurs in an authentic conversion to Christ. After seeing all this chaos, I keep reminding myself that when things return to normal, we must focus more on getting people to truly encounter Christ in the depths of their hearts.

One frightening thought that persists is the reality that so many people have guns. Yesterday, I saw people buying Kalashnikovs for as little as five dollars. Many have bought guns to protect themselves and their families, but it's crazy to see people walking down the street with machine guns. Yesterday, someone came up to me carrying a machine gun on his shoulder, a pistol at his side, and a bag full of bullets. Fr. John Pelushi keeps saying,

"It's madness. It is as if the entire country has fallen under a spell and become mad!"

RESTORING THE HUMAN ICON   MARCH 16

If we have to find one positive side to all our problems, I can say that many people in America have now learned where Albania is, and have begun praying for the people here. Thank God for this!

We continue to have peace in Tirana. We hear only sporadic gunfire. Movement on the street is returning to normal, although most shops remain closed. Church was packed, as on a typical Sunday. In the center of town, we participated in a peaceful commemoration for all those who have died over the past days.

Of course, fear persists everywhere. Yesterday I walked out of my apartment and saw three kids playing with a bag of unused bullets. Later in the day, Fr. Kristo told me about a funeral of a 17-year-old kid who was fatally shot, along with two of his friends. The plethora of guns will continue to create fear and death for many months ahead. Even if the police try to gather all the stolen arms, it seems futile. Many of our young female students have expressed their fear of walking around town alone, even in daylight.

Chaos continues in many other cities, with riots in Durres. Many Albanians are trying to flee to Italy. So many people feel their only hope is to go abroad as a refugee. The sense of hopelessness is palpable.

Appropriately, today the Orthodox Church is celebrating the Sunday of Orthodoxy. This is the Sunday commemorating the restoration of icons in the churches back in the ninth century. This holy day holds much symbolism for the people here. Icons are not only holy images on wood, but the divine image in each person. As Christians, we believe that God created us in His image. Even though sin has distorted this image in us, and this distortion is so apparent these days, we still remember that we have the potential to recover this image. In fact, the goal of our lives should be to restore the beautiful icon from within. Over the past days, the world has seen the evil side of humanity. Yet good dwells deep within even those who have committed the worst crimes. This Sunday of Orthodoxy offers an opportunity to preach about the good that is within all of us.

On a personal note, I spoke with Faith today. She arrived home safely, thank God! She described her evacuation to me—she traveled by helicopter out to a huge naval ship; sailed to Brindisi, Italy; bused eight hours to Rome (where she met Renee Ritsi and her kids); flew to New York; drove to my sister's house; then took a train to Lancaster. She described her evacuation as efficient and friendly.

AN AGONIZED APPEAL   MARCH 17

Looting and violence continue in various cities, especially in Durres, Shkodra, and Korça. Yesterday, people looted the historic palace of King Zog. In Korça, bandits broke into an orphanage and stole everything, including the beds, and then ransacked the entire place. Ten people were killed. What unexplainable craziness.

I visited a woman in deep depression today. The factory in which she had worked for 23 years was destroyed. "Where will I find work now?" she lamented. With all the violence, we are concerned about our newly completed $1.5 million seminary complex in the village of St. Vlash-Durres. We need to pray for angels to protect our seminary.

On Saturday, Archbishop Anastasios made an appeal on the state television's nightly news. He repeated the message on the official Italian and Greek stations (which many Albanians watch). The clergy read the appeal in all the Orthodox churches on Sunday as well.

An Agonized Appeal:
No One Can Play with God's Justice

During these tragic hours which Albania is undergoing, indefinable and uncontrolled dark powers are released from even the hearts of common citizens. When the smallest opportunity is given, there are many who will mercilessly steal from whoever it may be, even their own neighbor. They do not hesitate to plunder hospitals, orphanages, and religious institutions, injuring the sick, the elderly, and innocent children.

Enough! This hysteria must stop! It is unheard of for someone to protest against an injustice that was done to him by some in power, by doing injustice to others who are even weaker than he.

Those who act in this way do not seem to believe in anything at all. Nevertheless, especially to those who pretend to belong to some religious community, let them responsibly hear this: As much as they steal, they will not prosper. It is as if they invest in pyramid schemes. They are happy for a short time, but in the long run they will lose everything. No one can play with God's justice.

Those who are faithful must protect, in the name of the living God, the weak, all places of religious worship, schools, and the centers of social welfare and love. As decisively as possible, with faith and love, let us resist this inexcusable injustice, which is quickly spreading like an epidemic. Be without fear! "Perfect love casts outs fear" (1 John 4:18).

As archbishop, I will stay with you always, sharing—in prayer, word, and work—the pain and the efforts for a society that will be inspired by justice, freedom, love of God, and a sincere respect towards every person.

+ Anastasios,
Archbishop of Tirana and All Albania
Tirana, 15 March 1997

"THE SADDEST DAY OF MY LIFE"   MARCH 18

Problems continue as the president ignores all the chaos around him. Yesterday looters destroyed the Agriculture University, burning its library, which contained 150,000 books, and leaving its classrooms, laboratories, and computer rooms empty. It's hard to comprehend such destructive madness. After hearing about this, Fr. John Pelushi confessed, "This is one of the saddest days of my life. I can't understand this madness. I can understand stealing food, although even this isn't justifiable, but to simply destroy a library, a laboratory. Who profits from this?"

In Korça, whose people often boast it is the cultural capital of Albania, the death toll has reached eighteen. And the unanswerable question is how people could loot an orphanage—rob such defenseless children. I met a gas station attendant who was injured when robbers came to loot his station and a gunfight ensued. It's like the old Wild West. One friend told me that only two families in her apartment complex don't have guns.

The only hope we have is in our Lord. As the Great Compline hymn expresses, "Lord of the powers, be with us. For in times of distress, we have no other help but You. Lord of the powers, have mercy on us!"

I want to say that things are returning to normal, but I'm fooling myself. Each day we hear new reports of madness. Bandits looted a $10 million Italian wood factory in Elbasan, then burned it down. Others vandalized and demolished an Italian factory in Gjirokaster that employed 300 workers. The bank of Gjirokaster was robbed and set on fire. In Korça, people looted the Orthodox Chapel of St. Paraskevi, along with a mosque. Looters cleaned out a church warehouse outside of Tirana. Other schools, factories, and shops continue to be looted and destroyed. An attempt was made on the Cultural Museum of Korça, which used to be an Orthodox church and houses thousands of old icons, but guards repelled the attackers. Now a tank sits outside the museum protecting it.

The entire country has gone crazy. A dark spirit lies heavily on this whole nation, and everyone suffers. One can understand why so many long to flee this land. Senseless destruction everywhere. And once things calm down, then what? People will begin from ground zero. Or in reality, below zero. After such insane behavior, what foreign companies will risk investing here? Every factory destroyed means hundreds of people out of work. And we don't even know if we have seen the worst yet.

Forces in the south have set an ultimatum. If President Berisha won't step down by tomorrow, they threaten to advance toward Tirana and take it by force. Meanwhile, people from the northern region flood into Tirana, swearing to protect the president and fight against the south. One injured soldier told me that people from the north have filled his army barracks. Rumors? One of the great difficulties here is a plethora of misinformation.

Who is behind all this? No one seems to know. The mafia? The secret police? The 1700 criminals who have escaped prison? The government? Rebels? The common citizen? Or a combination of all the above?

In the midst of this, we continue to hope. This morning we celebrated a comforting Presanctified Liturgy. Following that, I visited a hospital with Penny and Aleksandra. What an interesting, yet depressing visit. We walk into the decrepit military hospital and see dirt everywhere. Plaster falls from the walls. Windows and doors are broken. Beds are rusty. Mattresses missing half the foam serve as beds. Medical attendants, doctors, nurses, and visitors smoking everywhere. Surgeons even smoke during operations!

We visited Eda, a seven-year-old girl with a bullet in her stomach. The bullet hit her as she played in her yard. After waiting for six days, doctors finally operated on her today. Doctors just took a bullet out of the back of Valbona, a 16-year-old girl. Fiqeri, a 35-year-old soldier, had a bullet go through his side. Shpetim, a 54-year-old man, had a bullet lodged in his shoulder. Faik, 32, has had a bullet in his stomach for seven days now. Flamur and Halil, 16 and 17, were injured by stray bullets. Dorean, 21, has six bullets in his leg. Fatmir, 23, described how he tried to warn a young boy to put down his machine gun, and out of fear the boy shot him.

I keep reflecting on Archbishop Anastasios's words: "Remember, satanic forces controlled this country for many years. Don't think that he is going to sit back while we try to bring the light of Christ into this land." Few would argue right now that Satan isn't alive and well.

THE ROOTS OF EVIL   MARCH 20

As of 5:00 PM, peace reigns in Tirana. The forces from the south have backed down from their ultimatum and agreed to replace the president through more dialogue.

I visited the hospital again, taking four students with me. As I entered, I noticed water dripping from the ceiling. The roof was in utter disrepair, and last night's rain had leaked through. I also noted a bullet hole in the doorway. A stray bullet must have come through the hallway window and into the door.

The patients appreciated our visit. They treated us like old friends. Seven-year-old Eda smiled when she saw us, showing us the bullet the doctors had successfully removed from her stomach. Her mother described how Eda had been hit. That same day, stray bullets killed three other children in her neighborhood. One bullet came through the window and hit a two-year-old child sleeping inside her home.

This crazy anarchy hit us full force as we listened to these stories. In every room we heard similar stories. The director of the hospital told me that so far, 309 people have come in with injuries from stray bullets. And how many have died? How many have gone to other hospitals in Tirana and throughout Albania?

Later I visited two students. I could sense fear, sadness, and depression.

In one visit, the parents told me they hadn't left their home for a week. People are afraid and don't know how to proceed. Unfortunately, too many people are blaming others instead of looking at themselves. "It's the Gypsies who are causing problems in Korça." "It's the people from the north who disturb the peace." "It's the president's fault." Obviously, this crisis didn't begin a week ago in Tirana, or even a month ago in Vlore. For months, the pyramid invest- ment schemes tempted countless people. Too many wanted to believe in quick money. They willingly invested in these firms, even though rumors said the companies made their money through drugs, prostitution, arms, and money laundering. Everyone wanted to believe they could receive a 300 percent return quickly.

All of us in Albania need to look at what role we played in this crisis. I question myself as well. Maybe as the Church, we needed to take a larger role in speaking against these investment firms half a year ago. In all the homes I visit, I try to tie in this season of Lent with our situation here. Lent is fore- most a time of self-evaluation and repentance, but also a time of hope. We fast and repent in order to better celebrate the victory of our Lord Jesus Christ's Resurrection. Albania as a country and Albanians as individuals need to fol- low this wisdom of Lent. Evaluate yourself, repent, but always have hope!

STATE OF EMERGENCY   MARCH 21

I hear spatterings of gunfire. Although the continuous gunfire stopped a week ago, the occasional outbursts instill more fear. Last week, we knew that much of the gunfire came from thrill-seekers shooting up in the air. Now, when I hear the guns, I wonder if a shop is being robbed or a person is being killed.

We remain in a state of emergency, with a forced curfew from 7:00 PM to 7:00 AM. Anyone found outside during these times puts their own life in danger. Police have permission to shoot on sight anyone seen with a gun. Yesterday, they killed two teenagers right outside my home.

A few hours ago, I heard yelling and gunfire. Was a person shot? Was someone killed? Was it another senseless death? Isn't every death senseless these days? Papa Jani told me that in the past week, the Orthodox church in Korça has buried 30 people. How many others, outside the church, died?

I keep wondering, what about all the other people throughout the world who face similar violent situations? How have the people in the former

Yugoslavia suffered this past decade? What about Chechnya? Rwanda's tragedy is unimaginable. I shudder every time I think of Afghanistan and its 27 years of violence. And what about Burma? The list can go on. Sometimes the evil throughout the world is overwhelming. I keep asking myself, how often have I prayed for these other peoples? Have I tried to empathize with my suffering brothers and sisters around the world?

The world's attention is focused on Albania today, but this country will quickly fade from people's memories. I've noticed that Albania isn't even making headline news anymore on CNN. Yet for all those families who lost loved ones, for those young men and women who face life paralyzed and permanently injured, and for the thousands who struggle to survive, their pain and suffering won't disappear so quickly.

I hope one positive consequence of this tragedy is that I become more sensitive to others around the world. I pray that I will grow in solidarity with the suffering and dying of others. Of course, I'm afraid that once this crisis passes, or once I move back to a comfortable life in America, I also will forget.

I've been reading through the Book of Genesis during these first two weeks of Lent, and one thing that has struck me has been the numerous times the patriarchs made monuments or altars at every point where God intervened in their lives. Whenever God acted, He wanted them to remember. Our modern mentality does the exact opposite, focusing on the future and ignoring the past. This represents a dangerous and unhealthy spiritual attitude. God calls us to remember!

I conclude with the words of St. Paul: "We were burdened beyond measure, above strength, so that we despaired even of life. Yes, we had the sentence of death in ourselves, that we should not trust in ourselves but in God who raises the dead, who delivered us from so great a death, and does deliver us; in whom we trust that He will still deliver us, you also helping together in prayer for us, that thanks may be given by many persons on our behalf for the gift granted to us through many" (2 Corinthians 1:8–11).

GOD IS WITH US   MARCH 24

The situation continues uneasy and uncertain. In Tirana, life is returning to normal. More shops have opened, although they won't display all their goods for fear of looting. People have returned to the streets. We can see villagers with their horses and carts traversing the city trying to sell their milk, yogurt, and other produce. This image, though, gives a false sense of normalcy. Students haven't returned to school. More police than usual roam the streets. And one can see a deep sadness, fear, and despair in people's faces.

Yesterday, George from Delvina came to Tirana and described the situation there. The southern third of Albania still lives in anarchy. Warlords and bandits control the area, with no police anywhere. The government has absolutely no control over the south. Imagine life with no police and everyone having guns. George described how people fear to leave their homes. At night, they hear constant gunfire and sleeplessly wait to see if someone will break into their home and rob or hurt them.

The people of the south have refused to lay down their arms as long as Berisha still holds the presidency, and he shows little sign of stepping down. In fact, Parliament, which the president's party controls, is acting as if the worst is over. They want life to continue as before and ignore the anarchy. We watch parliamentary sessions on TV and hear deputies denounce everyone else— from the mafia to the communists to the CIA—but accept no responsibility themselves.

Mihali explained that his village has formed a security council, which keeps constant watch over his village. He is one of the students who left his wife and children to stay at our seminary for a week to help protect it. Yesterday I visited our seminary, and thank God everything is undisturbed, although fear of an attack remains.

Yesterday, I traveled to Durres for the Divine Liturgy. I preached a sermon on the need to repent and take responsibility for the mistakes made, instead of blaming others. Ultimately, hope comes from sincere repentance. One old man came up to me after the service and pleaded, "Please tell the archbishop that the people of Durres have suffered too much, and we desperately need help—with food and whatever else the Church can offer."

Numerous international agencies have promised to send aid, but things remain quite dangerous. Imagine taking a truckload of food and supplies anywhere down south with no police and no protection. When to help and how to help is an urgent, yet difficult question.

Tomorrow is the Feast of the Annunciation. I will go to Durres again to celebrate the Divine Liturgy. I have been thinking about what message to offer to people in despair. What greater message than to know the Annunciation reminds us that God is with us? The Creator of the universe decided to humble Himself and live among His people, to experience life as they knew it, to suffer with them, to feel abandoned and alone as so many of us do, to feel rejected, to be tempted, yet in the end to offer the greatest gift of all—victory over evil and union with God. The celebration of the Annunciation is most appropriate at this time in Albania.

"SECRET INFORMATION"   MARCH 27

Yesterday, we witnessed a scene from the old communist days. The head of the SHIK (the secret police) addressed Parliament and told them about some "secret information" they just discovered. This "information" revealed that certain foreign elements had instigated all the recent violence and chaos, including the past years of pyramid investment schemes. Now, the SHIK has discovered these foreign elements are extremist groups from Greece. The SHIK head announced that Greece had planned this chaos so that it could annex the southern part of Albania. He even accused the Greek-American lobby, naming Nicholas Gage in the conspiracy.

Two Albanian co-workers told me it reminded them of the parliament sessions during the Hoxha era. Back then, the communist leaders were continually finding "secret information" against America, the Soviet Union, Greece, Serbia, or whichever other state was their prime enemy at the time, and then the government would incriminate some people within Albania. I commented that the international community wouldn't accept this farce, but a friend corrected me. "They're not trying to convince the international community. They want to convince the people up in the mountains. And unfortunately, some of them will believe them."

"What future do we have here?" people keep lamenting. "What foreign company will now invest in our country? What future will our children have?" One can see how the devil uses the vice of despair so well.

"IS THERE HOPE?"   MARCH 29

"Is there hope? I saw the destruction of Korça—the factories, the schools, the university, the orphanage, the shops, everything. What hope is left for our future?" one of my dear students, Pandi, lamented. He described the

chaos in Korça. One friend was killed and his body left in a bunker. His father had a dream the following night and found his son's body outside the city. Then at the funeral service, as they buried the boy, a woman began to scream. She suddenly put her hand to her neck and blood began dripping down. In the middle of the funeral, a bullet had come out of the sky and hit her. She was only five meters away from Pandi.

"What future do we have?" he asked, despairing. "The school where my father is the director was completely looted. The factory where my mother worked was utterly destroyed."

He even admitted taking a machine gun home to protect his family. At first, his mother adamantly did not want the gun in their home. After two nights of chaos and countless stories of robbery and rape, she agreed to keep it. His cousin brought home three boxes of explosives.

I keep asking myself, "What can the Church offer these people?" There are no easy answers. When I hear about the suffering, when I see the fear, when I feel the despair, I realize how little consolation words can be. So I listen. I pray. I sit with others. I try to comfort and encourage in whatever way I can.

During times like this, I've often thought about the words of the Prophet Habakkuk:

Though the fig tree may not blossom,
Nor fruit be on the vines;
Though the labor of the olive may fail,
And the fields yield no food;
Though the flock may be cut off from the fold,
And there be no herd in the stalls—
Yet I will rejoice in the LORD,
I will joy in the God of my salvation.
The LORD God is my strength;
He will make my feet like deer's feet,
And He will make me walk on my high hills.
(Habakkuk 3:17–19)

DEATH AT SEA   MARCH 30

Another tragedy as we mourn the death of scores of refugees drowned in the Adriatic Sea. An Italian naval ship sank a boat carrying possibly up to one hundred refugees. Authorities fear many women and children are dead. Some of the survivors claim that the Italian vessel purposely collided with the refugee boat as a warning for future Albanian boats. In fact, this accident occurred two days after an Italian leader in Parliament commented that all the Albanian refugees should be drowned in the sea.

Shock and distress are turning to indignation and anger. "What are we, animals?" one Albanian complained. "No country has a right to do such a thing."

WEEP WITH THOSE WHO WEEP   APRIL 1

I returned to the hospital today and visited the burn unit. We heard Bashkim, a twelve-year-old boy, screaming because of burns that covered his entire arm and side. He and a friend had been playing with some flares they'd found when his friend jokingly put the flare down his shirt. It unexpectedly went off.

Aleksandra was wonderful with Bashkim. She sat beside him, caressing his head and trying to make him forget his pain. As she was doing this, Bashkim had tears in his beautiful blue eyes and softly said, "Thank you for coming. Whenever you are here, I forget about my pain."

We then visited Albona, an eleven-year-old girl who had a bullet in her leg. The precious girl was obviously traumatized. She wanted no one to come close to her and kept her head under the covers.

Altin was a twelve-year-old boy with an amputated leg. He had been walking down the street with a group of friends when a man on a bicycle rode by. The cyclist was carrying a box of explosives, which accidentally fell as he passed the children. The bombs exploded. The man riding the bike lost both legs. Altin lost one leg. The other boys suffered serious burns.

In the last room we visited Sabri, a poor villager and father of seven. He comes from a small village in the mountains. While he was out with his sheep, a bullet came out of the sky and hit him. Yesterday, doctors amputated his leg. Today, he lamented about what he would do. How does a crippled villager survive in the mountains? Who will now take care of his children?

People keep asking me what we say in such situations. Really, I'm struggling to find answers myself. Now is not a time for many words. St. Paul advises to "weep with those who weep." Thus, we sit with those in pain, hold their hands, caress their heads, and offer a comforting presence in silence.

CHURCH DAMAGE   APRIL 5

Along with the tragic destruction, arson, and robbery committed against countless individuals, personal property, shops, businesses, factories, museums, libraries, governmental residences, hospitals, orphanages, old-age homes, and prisons, religious properties have also faced the bitter reality of such violence.

Up to this moment, no Orthodox church has been damaged, but much has been stolen. Masked men broke into the diocesan house of Gjirokaster, tied up the resident priest, and stole $10,000. Thieves took $20,000 worth of building materials for construction of the Ascension Church outside of Pogradec. Looters cleaned out a large warehouse full of equipment and aid in Tirana, the church's nursery school in Korça, and all the kitchen equipment in our youth camp at Skrofotina.

Thank God, armed villagers foiled an attempt by a gang to rob the monastery of Ardenica, with its priceless treasuries of Orthodox icons. The same scenario occurred at our newly built theological academy and monastery at St. Vlash in Durres. In Korça, the local clergy and faithful organized guards to protect the national museum (which was formerly a church) together with its thousands of priceless icons.

THE CHURCH RESPONDS   APRIL 10

Throughout this crisis, the Church has been among the first to reach out to the people and offer hope in a variety of ways. Through continuous prayer, combined with a concerted effort of concrete action, Archbishop Anastasios has acted as a voice of conscience, calling the country to peace and its leaders to truth and justice. Three times, he spoke on national television, calling a stop to the hysteria of violence, hatred, chaos, injustice, and blood.

Shortly after the crises began, Fr. Spyridon began quietly trucking emergency aid into the Saranda and Gjirokaster. When I asked him how he traveled in those dangerous areas, he told me his secret. He delivered the first truckload of aid to the village of one of the main warlords. After that, this warlord guaranteed his safety for other deliveries.

By the first week of April, more than 25 tons of food had been delivered from Greece to the local institutions (orphanages and hospitals), as well as to individual families in numerous villages. Another 150 tons of emergency aid will arrive from Greece over the next several weeks, and an additional 350 tons is expected during the next three months.

Diaconia Agapes, the Church's social and developmental office, under the capable leadership of Penny Deligiannis, has secured a further $350,000 in funding from the WCC, the ecumenical Action by Churches Together Network, and the International Orthodox Christian Charities. Diaconia Agapes will distribute 10,000 family food parcels, as well as medicines, during the next three months to especially vulnerable families in ten hard-hit areas.

EVACUATION CONFUSION   APRIL 25

Faith finally returned to Albania following her evacuation some five weeks ago, just in time to celebrate Pascha. We thank God for our reunion, and she is so happy to be back with our Albanian family. I think she is among the first of those evacuated to return. She felt terrible about leaving our Albanian friends in the midst of this crisis, but everything was so uncertain back then. No one knew how long the anarchy would last or how dangerous it would get.

Not all the evacuations went as smoothly as Faith's. Back in March, we had two missionaries staying in our home—Peter Gilbert, a PhD scholar from the United States, and Frank Garcia, an Orthodox Christian from England. Both wrestled with the thought of whether or not to evacuate.

Peter struggled with leaving for several days. He is quite the scholar and taught at our seminary for the past three years. When I asked him what his dilemma was about leaving, he responded in all seriousness, "We are allowed only one bag to take with us on the helicopter, and I just don't know what books to take." Well, he eventually figured out which were most essential and departed on the same flight as Faith.

As for Frank, I remember his 97-year-old grandmother calling him and asking, "Frank, don't you think it's time to come home?" as machine gun fire could be heard in the background. In the end both left with their respective embassies, but in very different fashion.

Frank evacuated under the British Embassy on March 14, a day prior to the US airlift. At the time, I questioned why the British, along with most other

Faith, OCMC missionary Peter Gilbert, and Presbyterian missionaries Art and Eloise Ware get ready for the US Marines to evacuate them by helicopter during the crisis of 1997.

embassies, were evacuating earlier than our own US Embassy. My doubts and frustration increased the following day, when I wasn't sure whether Faith's evacuation had succeeded due to machine gun fire on the US helicopters. Where was the supposedly superior US military intelligence? Why had other foreign embassies understood something better than our own US Embassy? I wrestled with these doubts.

Only later, after talking with both Faith and Frank, did I learn the truth. Faith and Peter had as smooth and safe an evacuation as possible. No complaints from them! Faith's only surprise came upon her arrival in the States, when she learned that evacuated US citizens would not be able to use their passports again until they paid the $400 evacuation fee required by the US government.

Meanwhile, Frank had an entirely different experience. The British Embassy chose to evacuate their citizens via ship. So on March 14, we dropped Frank off at the British Embassy, and his adventure began. First, all British citizens loaded up into cars and vans and headed in a caravan towards Durres, the port city forty minutes from Tirana. Frank's caravan had traveled only ten minutes out of the city when it encountered a roadblock with dozens of men shooting Kalashnikovs into the air. The caravan quickly turned around and took a longer route to the port. After an hour of fear and uncertainty, they arrived at the docks only to see utter chaos. Crowds of people roamed about shooting their guns.

Every time the British officers called their ships to come on shore, hundreds of Albanians with guns would flood the dock, trying to board the ship. After several attempts, the British authorities adjusted their evacuation plans. They informed Frank and the entire contingent that they would have to spend the night on the dock and wait until conditions changed. They suggested that they all gather in a circle, with the children in the middle, the women next, and the men on the outside. In this way, if any stray bullets came, the children would be the safest.

As Frank described his horror, he quietly told me, "I was feeling terrible about leaving Albania to begin with. And while sitting in the middle of the dock, I kept thinking, not only am I a coward, but a stupid coward for the way in which this evacuation evolved!" In the end, the group stayed together until the middle of the night, by which time most of the Albanians had gone home. This allowed the British to properly land and rescue all their citizens.

LOVE IN ACTION   AUGUST 18

During the past six months of national crisis, the Church has ministered to the physical needs of the suffering people, regardless of religion or race, by distributing bulk food commodities and medicines to hospitals, orphanages, homes for the elderly, and other state institutions, as well as to needy and desperate families. The Church's relief program was the first of any national or international agency to be implemented, when Fr. Spyridon began overseeing distribution of large quantities of food throughout the country on March 18. Over the past six months, at least 545 metric tons of bulk food commodities and medicines have been disbursed by the Orthodox Church to more than 60 villages and cities.

Along with aid coming from Greece, the International Orthodox Christian Charities (IOCC), in conjunction with the Action of Churches Together (ACT) Network of the World Council of Churches, offered another 225 tons of food parcels to the Orthodox Church. Penny and Diaconia Agapes completed delivery of this aid directly into the hands of 15,164 vulnerable families in ten different regions throughout the country. Working with dozens of local implementing partners at 52 distribution points, the DA/IOCC staff traveled more than 17,000 kilometers (10,000 miles) over a three-month period. Five tons of food parcels were delivered daily to poor families, regardless of their religion. In addition, medicines were delivered to the St. Luke Health Clinic in Tirana. Due to the ongoing security risk throughout Albania, the Church worked closely with the multinational military force, which provided escort and full protection during distribution. The DA/IOCC program was successfully completed on July 19.

One example of the danger in delivering relief aid in the midst of crisis occurred in Vlore. One hundred thirty Italian soldiers accompanied Penny and the Diaconia Agapes workers during their delivery. The program had been organized to deliver five tons of food parcels at the Orthodox Church of St. Theodore. Word spread that aid was being distributed to the neediest families. More than a thousand citizens showed up. The restless crowd started to panic. Pushing, shoving, and then fighting broke out within the crowd. Some people from nearby apartment buildings began shooting machine guns into the air.

The military force quickly took control of the situation by sending soldiers atop the apartment buildings. Quickly the shooting stopped. Still, the unsettled crowd panicked when they realized that not all would receive food. Some threw stones at the workers, which even hit the supervisor of the project. The military force helped the staff safely finish their distribution and depart without further mishap. The Diaconia Agape office was asked, however, not to come back to Vlore with more distributions because of threats made against the local priest, Fr. Ilia.

Prices have increased more than 17 percent in one month for staple foods, while inflation has greatly decreased the value of the currency. In January 1997, one could exchange the US dollar for 105 Albanian lek. By July, the exchange rate had reached 190 lek to the dollar.

RESUMING LIFE   SEPTEMBER 17

Albania has truly passed through another dark period of its history, with too much chaos, anarchy, madness, suffering, hopelessness, and pain.

Life is returning to normal, yet "normal" for Albania still implies a lack of continuous running water for most homes, insecurity throughout the countryside, corruption in every facet of life, teachers who receive a monthly salary of $50, and an overall hopelessness for the future. Too many people remain obsessed with leaving the country.

In the midst of such despair, we see rays of hope. The recent death of Mother Teresa, the most famous and beloved Albanian in the world, offered a moment of joyous reflection for all Albanians. The country took pride in the fact that the entire world was honoring one of their own children as one of the great figures of her generation.

On a personal note, Faith and I have resumed our various ministries. Faith has been active in the English language program, high school catechism, Tirana youth center, kindergarten teacher training and preparation, and the new children's magazine *Gezohu* ("Rejoice"). The university reopened in June, and I am focusing much attention on the students. In fact, we even ended the school year with the largest number of students ever taking part in our activities. We also created a group of ten students and graduates who are committed to working on evangelism and outreach within the university next fall. Our seminary reopened in August, and next week we will have our final exams to close out the 1996–97 school year. We'll only have a two-week break before we begin the new school year on October 15.

One of our most exciting recent activities has been two mini youth camps. One hundred and fifty youth from seventeen areas of Albania came together for these camps. Highlights of the camps were our visits to a local orphanage and handicapped school. The majority of the youth had never visited either of these state institutions, and they were deeply touched and enlightened about the conditions of these children of God. Lord willing, if security improves, next year we'll resume our normal summer camps.

CHAPTER 5

A MISSION RESUMED

(1998)

Due to a fire that engulfed our home in 1999, many of my journals from 1998 were lost. Thus, this chapter only details a few of our experiences and stories from that year.

THE BAPTISM OF
KRISTINA LULJETA   JANUARY 25

Today I celebrated a memorable baptism. A small group of 30 people, 25 of whom were Muslim, gathered in the church baptistery. It was the first time for most of these people to step inside a church. They came for the baptism of Luljeta, a 45-year-old Muslim woman with muscular dystrophy. For 23 years she has been unable to move anything but her head and hands. She has lived in a hospital room for the past seven years.

Two years ago she met Daniel, a second-year seminarian. Daniel spent hours talking about the hope he derived from his own Christian faith. He also came from a Muslim background. Through their friendship, Luljeta came to believe in Christ.

This baptism touched me because of the way she came to faith, and the witness she is offering to her mostly non-Christian friends. I carefully explained all that occurred throughout the service, and by the end, several of the Muslims expressed their gratitude for attending such a moving ceremony.

FAITH IS PREGNANT

We went to the clinic today and found out that Faith is pregnant! We sort of expected that over the past ten days. We're so excited, and truly thank God for this blessing once again. We continually pray for our little angel in heaven, and hope this time our Lord will allow our second child to work out his salvation here on earth. His will be done! But we are praying for our Lord's protection and blessing, asking Him to raise up a saint who will bring glory to His Name.

As soon as we found out, we told the archbishop and received his blessing. As always, he offered such gracious, loving, and kind words to us. We then called our parents, who were thrilled, our friends at the Mitropoli, and some of our youth.

We've received an interesting reaction from people. Some warned us not to tell anyone we're pregnant, because they don't want Faith to get the "evil eye." We told them we want our friends to pray for our baby, and we believe the prayers of faithful people are stronger than any curse of the evil eye.

ANOTHER MISCARRIAGE?   FEBRUARY

Faith felt crampy and saw some spotting, two signs of a possible miscarriage. All our thoughts went back to two years ago when the same thing happened. We're not sure of anything, but we're quite worried. We both say, "God's will be done." We will try to glorify God with whatever happens, but it will be hard if we lose another child.

This morning we woke up early and prayed the Paraclesis service. Right now, I'm at the seminary and had two hours free, so I went to the Church of St. Vlash and again prayed the Paraclesis service. These prayers brought me comfort, but I'm unsure how to pray. I say, "Lord, Your will be done. May everything occur for the glory of Your name. If You want another saint in heaven, interceding on behalf of the world, then take our child now. Your will be done. Yet You know our desire for a child. We humbly ask You to bless us with a child, to bless this child and keep him safe. Whatever happens, please keep us, especially Faith, in your loving and comforting hands. Amen!"

It's hard and confusing to pray "Your will be done" while also asking for something specific. "O Lord, please show me the way. Fill us with Your Holy Spirit, so that He may pray for us and guide us in a way that will glorify Your

Name." On the following day, we had a day of total fasting and prayer, dedicating the day to our child in the womb, to Faith, and to all the mothers who are pregnant and who have suffered miscarriages. We began the morning with a Paraclesis service, asking the Mother of God to embrace our child. I prayed the Hours at 9:00 AM, noon, 3:00 PM, the Vespers at 6:00 PM, and the Compline. It's been a peaceful and restful day, just staying with Faith. The doctors told her she must go on bed rest. She's learning from now how we all must sacrifice for our children. Spiro Lazarou often tells us that parenthood is a great teacher for the Christian journey. From this early beginning, I agree, and I hope I will understand even better later on.

RACISM

Although we enter a new life in Christ, we still have to wrestle with the fallen world all around us—including inside the Church. Our Gypsy friends Josif and Kristina continue to come to church regularly, even though they face the racist comments of others from time to time. After a recent visit, Kristina shared with me her anger at a doctor from our church clinic. Several weeks ago, an Albanian doctor initially ignored her, then made some racist comments to her. Although this happened several weeks ago, Kristina was still furious and told me she would never forgive him.

This discussion opened up a great opportunity to talk about the parable of the unforgiving servant and our need as Christians to forgive one another, even up to seventy times seven. We discussed how difficult it is to forgive those who have hurt us, and yet, how important it is for us to try to forgive. We forgive, not because others deserve it, or even because they have repented. We forgive because Christ has forgiven us and shows such great mercy to us!

By the end of my visit, both Kristina and Josif seemed at peace and ready to forgive. I truly felt the presence of the Holy Spirit in our midst during that visit.

ONGOING DANGER AND TERROR

Albania is still a land without security. A couple of weeks before Christmas, our Kenyan missionary friend Elekiah Kihali was walking around the seminary, near the Gypsy village of Shtula, when a young man riding a bike stopped him, pointed a gun at him, and demanded money. Elekiah insisted he had nothing. The man probably thought he was American. When Elekiah couldn't talk to him in Albanian, the robber shot his gun to one side of Elekiah, then to the other side, and then near his feet. Elekiah thought he was going to die. In the end, though, the man left him unharmed.

Taulant, a first-year seminarian, recently came to school a day late. Why? Robbers with machine guns had hijacked his bus. They robbed every person, taking their jewelry and whatever money they had. Unfortunately, this is a common event. The government is still weak. One friend told me, "Our government is worrying too much about Europe and their views on human rights, while forgetting about human rights for the common Albanian, who is being terrorized daily!"

In October, I experienced something similar on the bus going to Greece. We passed Tepelena, and a man with a Kalashnikov entered and demanded that we pay for his "protection." We gave him some money, and thankfully he left us in peace.

UNIVERSITY OUTREACH

Joana shared with our student group a recent terrible tragedy. Her cousin was in a car with two friends, one of whom was a policeman, and some mafia people gunned them down in broad daylight. Her cousin leaves behind a 30-year-old wife and two children.

At our weekly Thursday morning Divine Liturgy at the University of Tirana, we offered a memorial service for Joana's cousin. Fifty students were present. It's really amazing to see fifty or so students coming every Thursday at 6:30 AM to celebrate the Divine Liturgy. A couple of weeks prior, on a particularly cold morning when we could actually see our breath in the room, we celebrated an unforgettable Liturgy. At one point in the service, I turned to bless the people and quickly counted how many students had awakened so early to come. Then I thought to myself, "Why would 65 young people get up so early to worship God?" Eight years ago, students couldn't mention the name of God in this country. Now, at the heart of the intellectual center of Albania, we had 65 young people waking up on a cold, early morning to pray to God and be united with Him through Holy Communion. Truly amazing!

In addition to our weekly liturgies, we hold a weekly evening discussion group, and I run several Bible studies in the dormitories. I'm starting to train several of our student leaders to lead the Bible studies in the dorms as well.

REVENGE KILLING   MAY

Faith and I traveled to Shkoder, where I gave a lecture at the Roman Catholic seminary. When we arrived at the seminary, a large crowd had gathered 100 meters away. We learned that three young men had been killed in a fight over a soccer match. The rector of the seminary told us this was a common happening in Shkoder. Life seems so cheap. People don't value life and don't think about the consequences of their actions.

Several days later, after church on Sunday, we discovered another sad reality. Vjolca, a woman whom we have helped in the past, came to talk with us. It turns out that the boy responsible for killing the others in Shkoder was her husband's nephew. This nephew is 20 years old, and now that he has killed another person, the old canon of *lek dugjani* comes into play. This is a medieval custom that some northerners still follow. It says that if someone is killed, then the dead person's family can seek revenge by killing any adult male from the killer's family. This means that Vjolca's husband, along with all the males on his side of the family, now live in constant fear that they may become victims of this revenge killing. Vjolca begged me to help her husband leave the country for a period of time.

Sometimes, life here is like life in the Middle Ages. Old traditions prevail, and life can appear so cheap. Someone can kill another over a silly soccer game. And not only will this young boy suffer in prison, but his entire extended family will be imprisoned by the fear of revenge.

Here is where the Gospel must touch and transform lives, one by one. This idea of revenge is so engrained in the mentality here, yet if the Gospel can enter into the hearts and lives of people, forgiveness and mercy may prevail over revenge and killing.

THE BIRTH OF OUR
SON PAUL   SEPTEMBER 29

After four years of marriage and one miscarriage, Faith has given birth to our first son, Paul. We thank God for this special blessing and new joy in our lives. Faith had gone back to the States three months before her due date, and then I arrived a few weeks before the birth. Paul gave Faith a battle with a long, 36-hour labor, but thank God, he came out healthy!

Long before I was married, I always said I wanted to name my first son Paul, after the apostle Paul. He was the greatest missionary of our Church, and I love his story of conversion and transformation. Faith laughed when she first arrived in Albania because my students at the seminary were already telling her that they knew we would be having five kids, and the name of our first son would be Paul. When Faith and I actually discussed possible names for our children, we decided that if the first one was a boy, I would name him. If it was a girl, she would name her. In the end, we had a son and named him Paul, with the middle name Alexander, after my father. May he grow up to imitate his patron saint Paul, and take on the best of virtues from his grandfather Alexander!

FORCED ASCETICISM   DECEMBER

Life here can still be quite challenging. We have water only six hours a day. Electricity is typically out five hours at nighttime, and a few hours in the morning. Recently, a major cable burned out, and we had no electricity for eight days straight. No electricity means no hot water (and thus cold showers). At night we work by candlelight or gas lights. It is hard to read or work under such conditions.

Then we have our outdoor excursions. As soon as we walk out of our door, our shoes get full of mud. Tirana is sometimes like a village. When I drive to Durres, this one hour trip feels like a five-hour trip in America because of the bumpy roads. Sometimes I think people in America can never really understand life here!

Yet, as much as they can drive me crazy, I must admit that most of the time I like these conditions. I like the "forced asceticism" placed upon us, because it keeps us from the dangers and temptations of a comfortable life. Sure, I get tired of these conditions once in a while, especially after a long day when I have to walk home from where I park my car, and the cold creeps into my bones. Then I approach our apartment to realize that the entire neighborhood has no electricity, which means returning to a cold home. Most of the time I see this as a blessing, though, because it helps me relate to the way a majority of the world lives.

As I think of our future and of three-month-old Paul, part of me would love to raise Paul under these conditions. Maybe it would help him put life in a proper perspective—a perspective in which he wouldn't take such simple things as water and electricity for granted; a perspective in which he would appreciate the little blessings of life. Far from what people in America think, who say that we are depriving our children of the material advantages of life in America, I honestly believe that our children will have a much richer education in what life is truly about.

CHAPTER 6

THE KOSOVO WAR

(1999)

The long tension between Serbians and Albanians in the Kosovo region of former Yugoslavia reached a climax on March 22, 1999, when NATO forces began the bombing of Serbia, which lasted almost three months. Tragic events and atrocities committed by both Serbian and Albanian nationalists eventually led to more than a half-million refugees, mostly Albanian Muslims, flooding into Albania, with many more going into other countries. Albania, along with the Church, faced another crisis. How should we respond? This chapter offers a perspective on the suffering, as well as the unique opportunities to offer God's love.

FIRST IMPRESSION:
THE UNBEARABLE SUFFERING   APRIL 2

The numbers are so large, they become incomprehensible. A half-million people displaced from their homes. Over one hundred thousand refugees in Albania, a country that is struggling to take care of its own people. Possibly another hundred thousand arriving in the near future. When repeated often, such large numbers become meaningless.

It is the same with scenes from television. We see tragic images of refugees walking through the snow, fleeing their homeland. Mothers carrying their crying babies. People with looks of fear, despair, hopelessness. They make us angry, upset, sad. And then we turn the channel to a more entertaining program. Out of sight, often out of mind.

And what about the bombs? How easy it is for people in comfortable places to discuss and debate the pros and cons of bombing another people. We

speak so lightly about war, as long as it is far from us. It's so easy to say someone else deserves such forms of punishment. Some people even watch in awe
and wonder as jets take off through the air, forgetting that each mission causes
indescribable destruction, death, and suffering to real people—even innocent
civilians mistakenly killed or permanently injured by such bombs.

Do we stop to think about such people as individuals—individuals with
families, histories, dreams, and hopes? The last few days I have been visiting
the refugee camps and have seen this tragedy up close. Too many numbers and
images overwhelm us. Personal contact with real people leaves unforgettable
imprints on one's soul.

In the Tirana Sports Complex Tuesday night, I wondered what the hundreds of refugees streaming into the building were thinking. So many people huddled together—dirty, hungry, in shock, with a lost look in their eyes.
Numerous children sat all over the place. In one corner a mother was comforting her two-week-old baby. What was she thinking? What concerns and fears
did she have? Will her baby even survive the upcoming weeks?

Our son Paul is only six months old. What care we took of him during his
first few weeks of life! How we still shelter him from any stray germ or sick-
ness! It's hard to even imagine the concerns of this mother with her two-week-
old baby after traveling several hundred miles by foot, then in the back of a
truck, or a crowded bus, or in whatever vehicle she could find. And now this
infant will live in an army tent along with ten other people.

I thought of this little boy the last two nights when it rained. The army
tents have nothing on the floor, so surely the ground was wet and muddy. A
two-week-old baby sleeping in a damp tent throughout the night. Not for only
one night. Not two. Who knows for how long? It's hard to imagine.

Faith had a similar experience at the maternity hospital. Seven refugee
women just gave birth. Five of the women don't know where their husbands are.
They have nothing. No baby clothes. No diapers. No baby food. Nothing. Not
even husbands to comfort them and offer security and hope for their future.

Things in Tirana seem under control. Only about 8,000 of the 100,000 refugees have arrived in the capital. The Albanians, even though they are among
the poorest people in Europe, have responded with incredible compassion
and love. Two neighbors in our apartment building have taken families of six
and four into their homes, even though they live in small apartments. One

family, living in a three-room apartment, agreed to take a family of nine into their house. And the international community promises to respond. Today, the first relief plane with 40 metric tons of food and materials arrived, bringing emergency aid that will be distributed to refugees through our Church's Diaconia Office.

Yet how long will such hospitality and aid last? How long will these refugees stay? What will happen after another week or another month, when the world's attention turns to the next international crisis?

AND THE RAIN CONTINUES   APRIL 13

It's pouring down rain and has been damp and cold the last few days. I keep thinking about the refugees and how they endure such conditions. How do the children and infants survive? Obviously, some don't.

Yesterday we visited the main refugee camp in Tirana with Archbishop Anastasios. The Orthodox Church was delivering several tons of bread and children's milk to the camp. This was only a small part of the more than 200 metric tons that have been delivered so far by our Church to various camps and cities. What a joy to deliver aid, but I must admit that the visit depressed me. The camp is a city of mud. Everywhere you walk, you risk slipping on the slick mud. And the tents have no floors. Imagine, sleeping in army tents with eight to fifteen people inside, and only pieces of cardboard boxes as a makeshift floor.

This refugee camp houses approximately 2000 people, and they have only eight showers. The camp administration is in the process of building more, but many of these people have already passed two weeks without a shower. Two weeks under filthy conditions without showers. Mud everywhere and eight to fifteen people in a tent.

And the rain continues.

I'm not sure if this is the worst situation. We've developed a friendship with one Kosovar family. Zef and Violtsa have two sons, Emanuel and Mihal. Mihal was two days old when they fled Kosovo. They walked four hours by foot across the border, then caught a bus down to Tirana. Violtsa didn't eat for two days, and no longer has milk to give Mihal. When they finally arrived in Tirana, they went straight to the hospital. Mihal was four days old. Faith met Vjoltsa while delivering clothing to the Kosovar women who recently gave birth. (The hospitals now call up Faith every time a Kosovar woman gives birth, and our Church provides clothing and supplies to the babies and women. They've delivered 32 care packages thus far.) We, together with our friends and co-missionaries Lynette and Nathan Hoppe, have developed a nice relationship with this family.

When we took them to their refugee camp on the outskirts of Tirana, we discovered that they were housed in an old army barrack together with 117 other people. Fifty or so bunk beds were lined up side by side all in one room. They slept on old Albanian army mattresses. Just imagine the sanitary conditions. They even had the added concern of finding two snakes in the barracks the first night. Although the Hoppes offered to keep Violtsa and her family in their home, they preferred to keep their extended family intact. Too many families are separated and then have difficulty finding one another.

And the rain continues.

Tonight I visited Violtsa in the hospital. She returned last night because her ten-day-old Mihal has caught a serious cold from the dampness of the camp. She told me that the roof was leaking, and everything has become so filthy inside the barracks. Imagine 117 people in one room. Children are always the ones to suffer the most in any war. They are the most helpless and yet the most innocent.

And the rain continues.

THE REFUGEES   APRIL 25

Many refugees' stories sound the same. Everything is calm in their village, and no one believes in the atrocities they hear about. Then they hear rumors about tragedies and forced exodus in neighboring villages. People start to get nervous and anxious. The following day, soldiers or police or the militia come to their home, force open their door, and tell the family they have 30 minutes to leave or they will be massacred. Immediately, the families gather the children and leave, taking barely anything with them. Some leave with their slippers still on. They walk out of their village, and as they look back, their homes are ablaze. In some areas, they say the entire village is in flames.

Mehet and his two brothers tell us their story. It varies little from the general picture many of the refugees share. They talk about the massacre of a 70-year-old man who was unwilling to leave his home. "This is not human," they cry. "I can understand if someone kills men in war, but children? Women? Old men and women? This is savagery."

They have rented an apartment in town. They brought some money with them and are a little better off than those in the camps. In all, eighteen people stay in a three-room apartment. Eight people sleeping on the floor of a room 12 x 14 feet. They're grateful for the food and mattresses the Orthodox Church gave them. They tell us their story of suffering.

Bekim and his neighbor stay together. They have thirteen people in their three-room apartment. An Albanian family who are now in America allow this Kosovar family to stay in their house for free. Bekim's wife is eight and a half months pregnant. I told her that when she gives birth, Faith will meet her at the maternity ward. This family left Kucova with half an hour warning. They saw their house destroyed. They heard about the massacre of seventy children in the city stadium. They walked twelve hours to get to Albania.

When Violtsa gave birth to Mihal, she walked 15 minutes to the hospital. Her husband Zef was hiding in the mountains with their four-year-old son, Emanuel. The day after the birth, all the windows of the hospital were shattered by NATO bombs that landed on a nearby military depot. Violtsa decided not to stay in the hospital another night. Zef came down from the mountains and took his family on the four-hour trek by foot into Albania. The baby was only two days old.

Now Zef and his family are tired of being in the camp. Three weeks have passed, and they are tired of bread and cheese every day. Camp life is monotonous. It is unclean. Tempers are flaring as things become overcrowded. They were grateful when they first arrived, but already they are getting anxious. When will it all end?

Violtsa is thankful for the health of her two-week-old son. He is out of the hospital now and doing well. But she has other worries as well. Are her two brothers in Kosovo still alive?

I asked when all the trouble began, and they say when NATO began bombing. They are grateful for NATO, but they admit that the worst began with the bombs.

HEARTRENDING AND UNENDING   MAY 21

Across the street, we have Mimosa and her extended family of 45 refugees living in two rooms, neither of which is larger than 20 x 15 feet. Two of the matriarch's sons and two grandsons are still in Kosovo—whether dead or alive, no one knows. Each day this family struggles to find enough food for all their children, including five infants under the age of 12 months. Their two rooms are simply unbearable, especially as the hot Tirana summer approaches.

In our apartment building, Violtsa and her family are doing fine, staying with the Hoppes. But emotionally they struggle. They think their home has been burned down by Serbian militia. Violtsa's two brothers are still in Kosovo. Their future is uncertain. And several days ago, her sister-in-law's nine-year-old niece died. How? Violtsa explained that she fell into a coma from the constant stress and fear of NATO bombing and never recovered.

In the refugee camps, stories of death and loss are commonplace. As we took some clothing and supplies for a woman who had just given birth to a baby girl, we heard another woman outside her tent lamenting the death of her two brothers in Kosovo. They were only 27 and 29 years old.

In Tirana's two maternity hospitals, Faith hears countless tragic stories. Almost half the women have husbands still in Kosovo and are unsure whether they're dead or alive. Some women have given birth in the mountains on their way to Albania. One woman recently gave birth to her child in the taxi on the way to the hospital.

Mira and her two-month-old baby were told by the nurses that they must leave the hospital within three days. She is worried because they stay in a small, empty room with only two blankets on the floor. Nowhere to sleep or keep the baby.

Faith has witnessed numerous miscarriages, several stillbirths, and other babies who died in the initial days of life. Three days ago, a set of twins died. The probable cause is the constant stress the women have endured—pregnant mothers fleeing their homes, walking hours or even days under harsh circumstances, worrying about their husbands, and then staying in unhygienic conditions.

The stories are heartrending. The pain is unimaginable. The need is unending. And we only hear a few of the stories—how many other tragedies there are here, in Kosovo, and in Serbia.

The only bright spot is that so many people are reaching out to help. Although Albania is the poorest country in Europe and probably the least fit to assist 400,000 refugees (equivalent to approximately 12 percent of her population; that would be like the US taking in 30 million refugees), Albanians have responded in a Herculean manner. Elderly couples living with a $50 per month pension willingly take in a family of four. Numerous people open their newly built homes for families of 30, 45, and even 55 refugees. In the case of the family of 45 that lives across the street, the surrounding neighbors share what little food they have, while others allow the refugees to take baths in their homes.

We also are trying to offer help in whatever way we can. Faith continues in her outreach to pregnant mothers and newborns. She has now delivered supplies to 140 women. And through her initial contact, she has helped arrange for whatever needs these women have—buying medicines, arranging post-hospital care, paying funeral costs, transporting them to their homes or camps, and delivering food, mattresses, and supplies to their homes.

I've been organizing volunteers to work at the camp sponsored by the Action by Churches Together/Orthodox Church's Diaconia Agapes. Our seminarians go three times a week to set up tents, sort and distribute clothing, load and unload trucks, and simply interact with the Kosovars. It's been a blessed and educational experience for our students and for the refugees. Also, a group of 25 students from our Orthodox University Group go regularly to play with the children and offer a loving witness among the people.

In another effort, our seminarians prepared and distributed 25-kilogram food and supply packages for more than 150 families (approximately 1700 persons) living in the village surrounding our seminary. Next week, we plan to deliver mattresses, clothing, and baby food to these same families. And whenever we find time, we visit homes and deliver food packages, mattresses, and blankets to the countless refugees throughout Tirana. Tonight, for example, we visited five houses where a total of 124 refugees live. Each home has a unique and depressing story. Their needs seem overwhelming and unending.

Our help is limited. And yet we offer whatever we can. I've come to a new understanding of Christ's words, "It is more blessed to give than to receive." How blessed we truly are to be able to give, as opposed to being among those who wait, often in hunger and suffering, to receive.

JOYFUL SORROW   JUNE 21

Life in the camps these days is quite lively. Two weeks ago people were tired. The food was monotonous. The days passed slowly. And so many people were uncertain about where all their family members were.

Today things have changed. Excitement is everywhere as all talk about returning home. A few brave ones left last week, and news has trickled back into the camps. Although NATO and camp officials are telling the refugees to stay put until things are safer, few people are listening. They're anxious to return and begin rebuilding their lives. Many don't know the status of family members or of their homes, and they want to return and discover the reality of their lives.

In the Ndroq camp, I made a nice friendship with Ramadan. Several times we had long conversations about why this tragedy happened, how we must all forgive one another, how he himself had many Serb friends and still looks forward to seeing them again, even though he admits it will be extremely difficult now to continue an open friendship between Albanian and Serb. He knew of Fr. Sava of the Decani monastery and had only good words for him and his loving spirit, which transcends ethnicity. This past week, our talk was only about his plans to return. He will leave on Wednesday with a group of other families. Ramadan is anxious to find out whether his house is still standing. He knows that his business was burned down, but he hopes to make a new beginning. He worries, because the future is so uncertain. Yet he hopes.

Others have more concrete news. Three days ago our dear friends, Zef and Violtsa, heard news from their cousin that their house is still intact. More importantly, their parents are alive. They never left Djakova the entire time. They were frightened—their house was robbed, and soldiers came numerous times asking for any young men. But in the end they stayed and survived. Tomorrow, Zef and Violtsa, together with his brother's family, are returning. Two days ago they had an even bigger surprise when their father actually arrived in Tirana and showed up at their doorstep. He was too anxious to wait for them to come to Kosovo, so he decided to surprise them here.

What joy and happiness! For three months neither knew if the other was alive, and now they are reunited.

Yet not all are happy. Violtsa and Sevdi came by with their news. Their home was burned to the ground. Nothing left. They have four daughters, ages five to fourteen. What to do now? Where to go? How to begin rebuilding their lives? How can they take four daughters back to nothing?

At the Mullet camp, we helped Anu and Mira pack up their bags and prepare for their return. The camp was abuzz. As some families packed their vans, others just watched, knowing they couldn't return yet. Their homes had been burned down. They had nothing to return to. And they were afraid to leave the security of camp life for the unknown.

As the day went on, Fatmir came by our house. He said goodbye and thanked us for the help our church gave his family and their newborn twins. He was anxious about how he would take care of his two-month-old twins back in Kosovo, but somehow they would manage. When we gave him some final food and supplies for their babies, as well as help to pay for the transport home, he cried. He said he would never forget what the Church had done for him. He was grateful and only hoped that one day in the future we would come to Kosovo to visit him.

The day went on with both mounting joy and growing sadness. We really have become good friends with a number of these families and are going to miss them. Zef and Violtsa, who lived with Nathan and Lynette Hoppe for two months, recently moved into the apartment next door to us. For several weeks we went in and out of each other's homes each day. Their four-year-old son Emanuel would barge into our home at any moment of the day, wanting to play with Paul, looking for a snack, or simply wanting to run around our house.

Of course, their excitement at leaving tomorrow morning is tempered by the realities of war. As we were packing the minibus in which they would return, Zef's sister-in-law Mira came out of the Hoppes' house with a shocked look. A moment before, we had all been gathered eating our last meal together, but something had obviously happened. She had just received a phone call and heard that her two male cousins, aged 20 and 22, were killed in the war. Her sister's sons—dead.

The return home will bring many more moments of joy mixed with sadness. All sides will struggle with the fruit of this tragedy. We must continue to pray and not forget those in need, regardless of who they are. My fear is that, as many refugees leave Albania, the world will forget those who stay behind. Soon another world crisis may arise, and the realities of rebuilding Kosovo and Serbia will be forgotten.

ANTIDOTE TO THE
RADIOACTIVITY OF HATRED

Special Appeal from Archbishop Anastasios
(JUNE 24)

With sincerity and pain, by word and action, the Orthodox Autocephalous Church of Albania has repeatedly expressed her full assistance to our Kosovo refugee brothers and sisters. At the same time, she has persistently proclaimed that the oil of religion must never be used to increase conflicts, but instead must be used to heal wounds and calm hearts.

Now, after the cessation of armed conflict, all religions are called to work together for peace and reconciliation. Particular respect should be shown to every religious symbol and monument (be it a mosque, church, teke, or monastery). A basic presupposition for peace and justice, which all of us are seeking in our region, is first of all respect for whatever is consecrated to the God of peace and justice. When monuments of worship are destroyed, then whatever has been most precious and hopeful throughout the centuries is hurt.

After the return of democracy in Albania, all religious communities have tried to cultivate not only tolerance and respect for one another, but even something greater—a harmonious cooperation for the good of the entire society, for those who believe in God as well as those who do not believe in Him.

In all the Balkans, and especially now in Kosovo, the different religious communities must draw from the deepest and most genuine layers of our teachings and tradition and become inspired workers of reconciliation and peace. We should take the initiative in building a free and just society that will respect the religious freedom and particularity of the other—one who does not cease to be God's creation and our brother or sister, no matter what he or she believes.

Blessed are those in this historic time who boldly and self-sacrificially offer sincere love, which is the only antidote against the unhesitating hatred that has been sown in our region and threatens it immediately, and in the long term, as dangerous radioactivity.

GRATITUDE   JULY 6

A week after he left, I received a phone call from Ramadan, the man I had become friends with during our weekly trips to the camp in Ndroq. He told me that he's back in Tirana, buying needed supplies that are hard to find in Kosovo. While in Tirana, he wanted to meet with me. He came into my office with a neighbor from Djakova and told me about his situation back home. Ramadan's house was totally looted, but at least the structure remained intact. In general, his family was well, except for two nephews, whose whereabouts were unknown. He was hoping they were in prison in Serbia, but this was unconfirmed.

His neighbor shared a more gruesome tale. His house was spared, but his sister and brother-in-law were burned alive in their home. He saw the skeletons himself. As we talked, Ramadan said he still believed Kosovo could be a multiethnic country, with Albanians and Serbs living together. His friend disagreed. He bluntly said he could never live with a Serb as a neighbor.

An awkward moment followed, but since I had a relationship with Ramadan, I felt that I could express my hope in the future. From a human perspective, I understood this man's anger and hatred. I cringed when I heard him describe the skeletons of his sister and her husband. Yet I softly told him that such human anger and hatred would only perpetuate other acts of violence in the future. What Kosovo and the entire Balkan region need more than ever is not human anger and revenge, but divine mercy and forgiveness. He looked at me, not fully understanding, but he politely listened as I told him that only through the grace and power of God can hatred be turned into mercy and love for our enemies.

Surprisingly, Ramadan nodded his head in agreement. "It will be extremely difficult, seemingly impossible," he reflected, "but I still have hope." As he got up to leave my office, he handed me a large oil painting. He apologized that it wasn't the most beautiful painting, but said it was all he could find in Djakova. He told me it was a small token of his gratitude for all the Orthodox Church had done for him and his family. Through the concrete and loving actions of the Church and her people, he still had hope in humanity despite the atrocities he had witnessed. He ended by saying, "I have seen what true Christianity is all about."

ONGOING REFUGEE CAMPS   JULY 20

Life is quiet in the refugee camps these days. Several weeks ago, people were tired of life there as days monotonously passed by. Today things have changed. Hundreds of thousands of refugees have returned home, despite warnings from NATO and camp officials that safety and stability are still uncertain. Most families staying in rented flats or with host families have left.

Two of the three largest refugee camps in Kukes have consolidated into a transit camp, while others seem to be following the same path. Yet our Church, in cooperation with the ecumenical cluster of church agencies called Action by Churches Together (ACT) and overseen by our missionary Penny Deligiannis, continues to run its refugee camp with a capacity of 1300 persons right outside of Tirana, and is ready to open two more in the nearby village of Kavaja. As most refugee camps close, the Orthodox Church and ACT are discussing with local officials about preparing their three camps as places for refugees who are unable to return at the present time. Specialists believe a number of refugees will still be here by wintertime, and these camps could be winterized in order to house refugees into the coming year.

Three representatives of our Church have gone into Kosovo over the past weeks. Penny and Artan Kosti traveled with a delegation from the World Council of Churches to evaluate the situation there. Nathan twice traveled with refugee families to various cities and villages in the southern part of Kosovo, helping them relocate and assessing ways the Church could aid in the reconstruction of their homes.

I CAN'T STAY WHERE THEY MAKE
THE SIGN OF THE CROSS   JULY 30

Since Sevdi and Vjolca's home was destroyed in Kosovo, they chose to stay in Tirana, hoping they could find a way to emigrate to Canada. As they waited day after day in the sweltering heat of Tirana, I suggested that maybe we could take their teenage girls up to our summer camp for a little break. I explained to the parents that this camp was a church camp, with quite a bit of worship, Bible study, and religious activity. Although they were Muslims in name, I told them their girls could come to the camp and participate in whatever they felt comfortable with. Along with the religious part, they would experience a lot of fun and great fellowship.

Since the parents trusted me, they allowed their fourteen- and fifteen-year-old girls to go. Before they came to the camp, Faith and I instructed our camp staff in how to treat these Muslim refugee girls—with loving Christian hospitality, but also with the freedom to participate in whatever they felt comfortable with. Our visitors planned to stay only for two or three nights.

On the first day of their visit, a somewhat serious incident occurred. After a day of activities and fun, time came for our evening Vespers. All the girls of the camp came to the church, including Drita and Alba, our Kosovar visitors. When the fifteen-year-old Alba saw everyone making the sign of the cross, she immediately left the church. When one of the counselors walked out with her and asked her if she was okay, she simply responded, "Where I come from, the cross is associated with violence and death. I can't stay anywhere people make the sign of the cross!"

After the service I talked with Alba. I told her I would take her back to Tirana immediately, if she wanted, or she could stay and participate in whatever she felt comfortable with. Alba chose to stay, but emphasized that she wouldn't go into the church again.

Our camp girls overwhelmed Drita and Alba with such love. After the three days, Drita and Alba asked if they could stay until the end of the camp. Their parents consented. By the final days of the camp, not only were both Kosovar girls attending every activity, including the church service, they even were reading psalms in church! On the final night of camp, Alba got up in front of all the campers and said, "I have never experienced such love as I did at this camp. I will never forget this experience! It has given me an entirely new understanding of Christianity."

Before I took them back to their parents, they asked our camp leader for a packet such as all the other campers had received. The packet included a Bible, stories of the saints, icons, and other religious material. Both girls even put crosses around their necks. When I saw them wearing crosses and carrying these packets of materials, I asked them to please be very careful when they returned home. I told them not to wear the crosses, but to show all the things they had received to their parents, and ask permission from their parents about whether to keep the materials or not. I didn't want the parents to think we had brainwashed their children. In the end, though, I explained to them, "You have experienced a taste of God's Kingdom at this camp. Cherish this memory in your hearts. Seek out God, try to learn more about His teachings, and cultivate His Spirit within your hearts."

Through the Eyes of a Mother
by Faith Veronis

One could view the recent war in Kosovo from many perspectives—that of the Albanian refugees, the Serbian victims of the bombing, the NATO soldiers, the hosts to refugees, the humanitarian workers, and the list could go on. I experienced the war as a mother.

I am a mother who lost her first child in a miscarriage, who has an active eleven-month-old son, and who is now five months pregnant. As a mother, I felt a special bond with other mothers, and thus became directly involved in the crisis through the mothers who fled Kosovo. I also thought about the Serbian mothers who faced traumatic fears and concerns within their chaotic context.

Following is what I saw and heard, and through generous aid from abroad, we alleviated some of the anxiety of the mothers. My visits were often short, and I did not develop intimate relationships with all the

Faith, with six-month-old son Paul, visits some of the Kosovar refugees during the Kosovo war in 1999.

mothers as I wished, but for the moments we spent together, we formed a caring bond of friendship.

Through the eyes of a mother, it was difficult to witness a woman giving birth without basic necessities, and more significantly, without the presence of loved ones. For three months, I visited the two maternity hospitals in Tirana daily. In the end, I distributed care packages containing infant outfits, mother's clothing, a blanket, and necessary baby supplies to more than 300 women. More than half the women had nothing when they came to the hospital. The majority of them didn't have their husbands to comfort them. Together with the social workers of the hospital, with whom I worked closely, we delivered packages as well as caring for a variety of needs—medicines, transportation, additional clothing, formula, and supplies. It felt satisfying to enter the hospital and hear the personnel greet me saying, "Thank God for the Orthodox Church."

It was difficult to hear these women tell their stories. I suppose God grants people strength in times of need. I met some women who traveled long distances in their final days of pregnancy, and others who had just given birth and were forced to flee on foot to Albania. Most of these women had nothing to eat or drink for days, which then affected their breast milk. I met women who delivered in the mountains and later came on foot to Albania. Many of these women were anemic because of blood loss, and their newborns had infections. One woman gave birth in a taxi en route to the hospital. A few arrived by helicopter. For me, who was blessed to have my family surrounding me in a beautiful birthing room, it was so hard to imagine these harsh conditions at such a joyful time.

I shed tears for many women during their times of loss. Although most newborns survived, some tragic losses occurred as a result of the crisis. Some women gave premature birth in their final months, and Albania's prenatal care was unable to save the babies. Some had miscarriages due to the stress and difficult exodus into Albania. Our church paid for funeral costs for those that wanted to bury their newborns. I felt an extra sorrow because most of these women bore their grief alone, without husband or family nearby to comfort them.

The crisis brought other tragedies. Some women delivered healthy babies, but mourned the death of their husbands or other close relatives.

There were rape victims who aborted or abandoned their babies in the hospital. Some had nervous breakdowns and needed psychiatric help. One child born with spina bifida survived an operation in Albania only to lose his mother in Kosovo from a landmine accident.

As a mother, I thanked God for the moments we forgot the crisis and rejoiced in the birth of a newborn. First-time mothers were always the most precious. I remember when I delivered the one-hundredth care package to a mother who had given birth to her tenth child. My last delivery was to a mother of triplets, who all survived. It felt satisfying when mothers would excitedly dress their newborns with the clothing donated by the Church. But most meaningful to me was when we were able to develop a special relationship with some families after their hospital stay.

Most Kosovars have returned home, and I have not made a hospital delivery in over a month. However, I still think about the mothers and wonder how their newborns are doing. And for those mothers in both Kosovo and Serbia who are waiting to deliver, I wonder how their conditions are. As Luke and I await the birth of another child, I pray that we always remember the brave women I met during the crisis, and thank God for all our abundant blessings.

IF YOU DON'T BELIEVE IN MIRACLES, COME TO ALBANIA

Historic Visit by Ecumenical Patriarch Bartholomew
(NOVEMBER 1999)

The Ecumenical Patriarch, His All Holiness Bartholomew, made an historic visit to Albania on November 2–9, 1999. Thousands of Orthodox and non-Orthodox believers alike welcomed him in all the cities he visited. The government officials received him with head-of-state honors, welcoming him at the airport and inviting him to private meetings with the president of the republic, the speaker of the Parliament, the prime minister, the former president, as well as with local officials in every place he visited.

In his whirlwind seven-day tour, Patriarch Bartholomew traveled to all four dioceses of the Albanian Church. During his first three days, he visited a variety of projects within the diocese of Tirana. He praised the colossal work

Fr. Luke welcomes His All Holiness, Ecumenical Patriarch Bartholomew, to the Resurrection of Christ Theological Academy in November, 1999.

of resurrection Archbishop Anastasios has led. When I met him during an official luncheon and told him my name, I was shocked to hear him say, "Oh, your father has been the one so active in missions in the United States." When he visited our seminary, I offered an official welcome. The patriarch blessed me by giving me the honorary title of *stavrofore* (cross-bearer) and a cross.

On Sunday, a majestic, nationally televised hierarchical Divine Liturgy was concelebrated in the Annunciation Cathedral of Tirana by Patriarch Bartholomew, Archbishop Anastasios, and four other bishops, attended by hundreds of believers. During this climactic moment, His All Holiness summarized all that he had witnessed by saying, "For all who do not believe in miracles at the end of the twentieth century, let them come to Albania and see for themselves what has been done here. Our admiration for the work done by the Church is great. As we have said other times, we attribute this fact, first, to the blessing of God; second, to the esteemed government which has legally allowed tolerance of faith and to the Albanian people who tradition-ally respect this tolerance; third, to Archbishop Anastasios, who is a rare and

incomparable personality, greatly talented, with vast experience, a world trav-
eler, multilingual, very loving and wise, a good organizer, zealous, internation-
ally renowned and prestigious; and finally, to his coworkers and the faithful
believers of the Orthodox Church."

CHAPTER 7

A MATURING MISSION

(2000–2004)

OUR GIFT FROM GOD   JANUARY 30, 2000

We're back in the United States for the birth of our second child. I began the day with a pro-life gathering in downtown Lancaster. Then I went to church for a small, private wedding of an old high school classmate of mine. After checking in on Faith, my parents and I went to the home of a new Albanian family that just moved to the area. During our lunch, Faith called to let me know she was having contractions, but I thought it would be a long labor like she had with Paul, so I didn't rush home. The typical Albanian meal is a five-course meal, but Faith called again to let me know I wouldn't be able to stay for dessert.

We went to the hospital, and everything happened so fast that Faith wasn't even able to take an epidural. When I tried to remind her of the strong Kosovar women she had met during last year's crisis, she wasn't interested in hearing about them at that moment! Within half an hour, the baby was ready to come out, and the doctor still hadn't arrived because of traffic. I kept wondering why we'd come back to the States to deliver our baby if we were going to have it without a doctor. Well, the doctor finally arrived, and our Gift from God, Theodora Nicole, came five minutes later. It was January 22, 2000. We named her after Faith's mom. A precious girl to go along with our son! *Thank You, Lord!*

A week after her birth, I returned to Albania. Faith would come back with the kids two months later. Every time I return from a trip to America, I think about how I am not so eager to go back to the States. Sometimes life there seems so superficial. How many of our friends' and family's lives are caught up in meaningless or superficial things—whether it's sports, entertainment, or even their children's activities. So much of their lives centers solely around the family. Of course, family is a good thing, but if life is only about that, it can become very egocentric. A Christian life can't just be about family, but must focus on the world around us as well.

While I was home, my father told me about a funeral he recently attended where the clergyman said in his eulogy, "When we come before the Lord in heaven, he is going to ask us only one question: 'Did you enjoy life?' If yes, then he will say, 'Come in and enjoy life here.' If you say no, then he will say that this is no place for you here." How sad that there are clergy that promote this superficiality in life! Psalm 4 summarizes this spirit when it says, "How long will you people mock My honor, love what is worthless, and chase after lies?"

Well, it's back to the reality of life in Albania. The municipality began repairing the road in front of our house before Christmas, and it's still not done two months later. This means that our road is total mud. We can't walk out or come in without mud everywhere.

EMERGENCY SURGERY   APRIL 25, 2000

Since my return from America, the electricity has become much worse. We were losing electricity only an hour here or there before Christmas, but we heard that our power line is no longer aligned with the university dormitory line, and thus, we have no electricity for four hours in the morning, several hours in the evening, and then nothing from 11:00 PM until 5:00 AM. We probably have no electricity fifteen hours a day. All the news reports say that it can get worse. We may lose our electricity for a week straight.

My main concern is for Faith and the kids. They returned a few weeks ago, and the lack of electricity can get you down. We thought about getting a generator, but I think that would be a bit scandalous to the average Albanian—another sign of how the foreigners live so differently from the indigenous people. I guess we will simply endure with many prayers.

Of course, whenever I think of our own problems, I then think of the reality for the Albanians. It has now been nine years since the fall of communism, and this European country still struggles with such fundamental issues as electricity. And no one believes things will get better next winter. They may get worse!

Things took a turn for the worse for us on April 17. Faith needed emergency surgery—an appendectomy. All day long she had a pain in her stomach, and we finally went to the hospital at 9:00 PM. Our greatest fear living in Albania has been that we would sometime need to have emergency surgery, and that day had come! The archbishop visited us at 11:00 that evening, bringing with him clean sheets, blankets, and a pillow. He understood the conditions of the hospital. Thank God, Faith's condition stabilized during the night, and there was an Olympic Airlines flight leaving the next morning at 6:00. We took the first flight to Athens, where our *koumbaro* Dr. Spiro Lazarou arranged for surgery at Hygeia Hospital. All went well with the surgery, but we learned afterwards that Faith has a form of cancer called carcenoid. The treatment for this cancer, though, was to take out her appendix, and that's exactly what we did. The cancer had not spread, thank God!

The whole scare of having an operation in Albania and facing cancer reminded us of the difficult situation so many people in the world face with health care. Our ability to leave the country immediately, along with the love and care we received from the archbishop and the doctors in Greece, reminded us of how privileged we are.

STREET EVANGELISM   JUNE 2000

I have rarely seen our students and youth so excited. Fr. Martin, now the director of the OCMC, and Fr. Peter Gillquist came up with the idea of doing a "cold turkey evangelism" mission team. We planned an evangelistic outreach into several areas where we have little or no Orthodox presence. We hoped this could be the start of a vibrant Orthodox community, so Nathan and I came up with an exciting three-week program.

First, we held a five-day evangelism seminar for all our students and catechists. Fr. Peter was the main event, along with Fr. Stephen Close, a passionate former evangelical who now works as a chaplain for the Air Force; Hector Firoglanis, a smart, humble, bold seminarian who will do great things for God; Panteli Daliganis, a senior seminarian who is a possible future missionary; and David Haag, an extremely shy kid who became an enthusiastic evangelist during our outreach.

Our seminar caused some of our catechists difficulty with its seemingly "Protestant" flavor of street evangelism. Fr. Peter, however, gave solid responses to all their questions. "Why is it Protestant to go out on the streets and share the word of God? Were the first apostles Protestant? Was St. Paul?" Fr. Peter asked. "How do you start a church in an area that has no church and no Orthodox Christians?"

Following our seminar, we began in Student City at the University of Tirana by passing out 4000 invitations to our two meetings on Saturday and Sunday. Our timing couldn't have been worse, since it fell during final exams, yet our team remained hopeful. Twenty-five students joined our team of five Americans. Fr. Peter offered a prayer asking the Holy Spirit to inspire and embolden them, and then sent them out into the streets with the Peace of God. Almost all came back so enthused, with only a few having a negative experience. Some had very in-depth interactions. For me, the project was a success, if only from the point of view that all these students began talking to total strangers about Christ.

I was praying that our students wouldn't be too disappointed if the turnout was small. About 150 students attended each meeting. This was fantastic for the month of June.

We next went to the northern city of Shkoder. Throughout the streets of Shkoder, and then Lezhe, our students went out two by two—on the streets, in cafes and bars, in parks, at the university, and even in the billiard halls. They invited total strangers to our general meeting, talking about "Hope in a Hopeless World." Many people politely listened, others asked questions, a few actually entered into deeper discussions, while some rejected the messengers with abruptness and rudeness. The words of Jesus—"I'm sending you out as lambs among wolves"—seemed so relevant to us!

Fr. Peter and I, along with Joan Lena and Fr. Aleksander of Shkoder, went to the two main TV stations in the city, not knowing what to expect. After we talked with their directors and paid $70 for TV time, both stations televised a 25-minute interview with Fr. Peter, in which he invited the people of Shkoder to hear a message of hope from the Orthodox Church. The stations broadcast each interview twice.

I myself learned quite a bit from this simple act of going to the TV stations. I would never have thought about going there. When I commented about it to Fr. Peter, he simply responded, "'Ask and you will receive.' Too often, we limit

God by limiting our own expectations. We must boldly ask God, and take some risks, believing that God is capable of doing everything."

Each evening the students returned with such enthusiasm. "Listen to what happened at the school we visited . . ." "No, listen to what happened when we went into the pool hall . . ." "But we met this devout Muslim who challenged us, and we invited him to come to our meeting . . ." "Several offended us, but thank God, we stayed peaceful throughout it all . . ." It all reminded me so much of the disciples coming back to Christ full of enthusiasm, and Jesus saying, "Don't rejoice in this, but rejoice because your names are written in heaven."

We witnessed our students filled with the zeal and fire of the Holy Spirit. Archbishop Anastasios has written that "missionary outreach does not only benefit the people who hear the good news, but it also strengthens, invigorates, and often renews the sending church and her people." A church concerned only with herself and her people becomes a "spiritual ghetto"—a dead branch in need of pruning. A body of believers, though, who share with others the great treasure will never lose that treasure, but will increase it with the passing of time.

Students who seemed unsure, fearful, or even scared about this whole process of street evangelism discovered an enthusiasm and boldness in trusting in the Holy Spirit. Even the critics who questioned these methods during the first days became strong believers in this type of outreach.

Missionary Mom
by Faith Veronis

Six years have passed since Fr. Luke and I were married. At our marriage, he promised me that our lives would be challenging, adventuresome, and filled with the Holy Spirit. He fulfilled this promise swiftly and faithfully.

In a matter of weeks, life changed drastically—marriage, Luke's ordination to the diaconate, our tearful departure from our loved ones, arrival in Albania, and Luke's ordination to the priesthood. With all these changes, new roles and responsibilities simultaneously followed—wife, presbytera, foreigner, and missionary. Fr. Luke often jokes that he took me to Albania on our honeymoon, and six years later, we're still here.

I have fond memories of our early years visiting the homes of priests and seminarians in many beautiful villages of Albania. With the freedom and time necessary to participate in ministries, I worked with the Church's preschool program, catechism department, English language program, and youth ministries, together with Fr. Luke. We grew as a couple.

Wherever we went, however, people began raising the question, "When will you have children?" I was 32, and married for a little over a year. It was untraditional to wait so long in Albania. Nevertheless, after a year and a half, God blessed us with the exciting news of our pregnancy. Local custom told us to wait until the baby moves to announce your pregnancy, but we immediately shared the news that another little missionary would be joining us in nine months. All rejoiced with us, especially our archbishop, who warmly embraced us and reminded us that he would be the spiritual grandfather.

Unfortunately, an ultrasound confirmed that I had miscarried, and the doctor recommended that I allow the miscarriage to run its natural course. For ten hours in our home, I experienced what felt like a birth. My husband, together with my spiritual sister Presbytera Renee, stood by my side. A very emotional period followed. Although Albanians do not talk about miscarriages, we received sympathy and encouragement. This experience itself made us more compassionate and aware of others who suffer miscarriages. We buried our little angel under a tree at St. Prokopi Church.

I remained active with various ministries over the following year and a half. Two traumatic events, however, greatly affected our lives. First, my beloved father died from a form of leukemia, and I was not home with him during his final days. This has been the most difficult cross I have carried as a missionary. I miss my father very much, yet find comfort knowing that he was a man of prayer. He is, Lord willing, with our little angel praying for us.

Then in March 1997, Albania made headline news when the country fell into anarchy. With 400 other Americans, the U.S. Marines airlifted me by helicopter out of the country, while Fr. Luke chose to stay behind. I felt much guilt during this time, realizing the privileges of my American citizenship and the tragic realities of the Albanian situation. I returned to the country five weeks later and worked with the Church in offering hope to the people.

I became pregnant again in January 1998. Again, we could not conceal our joy, although others cautioned us to be careful. After a short period, I experienced spotting and was advised to stay put in our fifth-floor apartment. Many friends came to visit and pray for us. We rejoiced when we finally heard our baby's heartbeat and I received the "OK" to resume my activities. I left for the States three months before the due date. On September 29, 1998, God blessed us with Paul Alexander. We baptized Paul, spent Christmas with our families, and shed tears when we departed, although we knew that our other family awaited us in Albania.

We received a warm welcome from our many friends upon arrival, but then experienced three extremely difficult months. I felt enclosed. That winter was one of the worst. The electricity was out six to eight hours a day. Our gas heater went on the blink. Fr. Luke was making up for lost time at the seminary, which meant less time at home. I often sat by candlelight in our cold apartment wrapped in blankets. I loved motherhood, but I felt the January blues. God, however, did not allow me to dwell in self-pity too long. The Kosovo war broke out in our own backyard in 1999, again putting Albania in the headlines.

I was horrified at the mass exodus of people, which made me especially think of the many fleeing mothers. At that time I was involved in an abandoned babies program at the local maternity hospital, and I began to see firsthand the plight of pregnant refugees and their newborns. These women had nothing when they arrived at the hospitals. Thus, I responded by gathering clothing from friends, and mobilizing our Church to offer supplies and whatever necessary medical and emergency assistance was needed. By the end, we helped more than 300 women and babies. Some of my visits turned into special friendships that continue today. From these women, I witnessed another side of motherhood— painful and uncertain, yet courageous.

During this time, I learned that I was pregnant again. Our work among the refugees kept us so busy that we did not share the news with others until after the war. Following the war, Fr. Luke and I began preparing to lead the church summer camps, an effort Archbishop

Anastasios has wholeheartedly supported since 1995. Although thoroughly exhausted from the refugee work and our preparations, we cherished six weeks at camp. God touched the lives of so many girls through this experience. Moreover, our nine-month-old Paul loved the outdoors—with roaming sheep and countless fruit trees.

That winter, we returned to the States one month before the birth of our "gift from God"—Theodora Nicole. On January 22, 2000, our baby came so quickly that there was no chance for an epidural. Throughout this natural birth, I thought of the Kosovar women. A few days later, Fr. Luke returned to Albania while the children and I stayed with our families. We returned to Albania after two months, and our schedules became quite busy as seminary ended and preparations for camp began. Again, we enjoyed a wonderful camp experience. We took delight in watching Paul interact with camp girls and village children. Paul understands both English and Albanian fluently. Theodora, the youngest girl at camp, received an abundance of love from her older spiritual sisters.

It is hard to believe that I am beginning my seventh year in the mission field. For me, these years have been life-changing. At times, I miss the activity of my first years in the field, but my husband often reminds me that one of our most important ministries is offering a strong witness of a Christian family. This new role of motherhood has strengthened my bonds with many women from our church. I have great respect for the Albanian mother. She is strong, sacrificial, protective, loving, and caring.

We now have two homes—America with our close-knit families and friends, along with our adopted homeland of Albania and our spiritual family there. Being far from our extended families, especially now with children, is the hardest aspect of being a missionary. Yet I remind myself that such sacrifices can never compare with the crosses of the early missionaries. And through such crosses, I have learned the importance of being bonded through prayer, as well as appreciating every moment we do have together.

I also thank God for our large spiritual family. We have received, as well as given, much joy and encouragement, and have grown closer to others through these experiences. Our ministries have been fulfilling and our home full. Our lives revolve around the Church and the church calendar. Our children have also been blessed with unique missionary *friends, as well as priceless Albanian friends. It's a special joy for us to see Paul excitedly jump up and down when his best friend Petro, who is Albanian, comes over to the house.*

Some people think that we sacrifice our children's welfare by living in Albania. True, our children may not have all the material possessions that American children have, but they live in a unique setting, surrounded by an abundance of love. I appreciate the simplicity of life here. It reminds me of my mother's stories of village life in Greece. Such forced asceticism makes it easier to lead a spiritual life with fewer distractions and temptations.

As a fairly new missionary mother, my hope and prayer for my children is that they love God and love their neighbor with all their heart, soul, and mind. Right now, Albania is offering our family very concrete and unique ways of understanding and living these two great commandments. Our more than six years as missionaries have included many struggles and challenges, unexpected adventures, and some crises. Yet we continue to witness the power of the Holy Spirit in the midst of the resurrected Church of Albania, our missionary outreach, and our relationships.

We give glory to God for all these things. And we thank Him as our honeymoon continues!

FACING DEATH   OCTOBER 2000

Kristaq's father was dying. When I visited him, I began by praying the Supplication Service to the Virgin Mary with the entire family. I then asked to be alone with the dying man, Zoi. I asked him if he was ready to die, and he said that he was afraid. I tried to offer words of comfort and strength, focusing on our Lord's promises. I asked him if he was at peace with all people, and thank God, just the day before, a nephew with whom he hadn't spoken in many years had come by. They talked and forgave one another. But Zoi seemed scared.

I called in Kristaq, along with his sister and mother, and openly talked about the possibility of death. I knew that this was something quite unusual for an Albanian family, but I thought it necessary. We prayed for a recovery, but we prepared for the reality before us. Zoi may die soon, I told them, and they needed to deal with this reality all together. I reassured Zoi that it was okay he was afraid, and he could express his fears to his family. Likewise, I encouraged the family to share their love with their father, along with their sadness and sense of loss. When I got up to leave, Zoi smiled. "Thank you. I really am happy. I am finally at peace." I think these last days will be more fruitful because of this conversation.

This visit reminded me of a similar experience I had a while back with another dear friend. Georgia's father had esophageal cancer. Georgia had told me about her father's condition two years before. She explained to me the dilemma of whether to tell her father the truth or keep it a secret. It was unthinkable for an Albanian family to tell someone they had cancer or some other terminal illness. In fact, the patient would slowly deteriorate from an illness, and the family would never openly discuss the truth or gravity of the matter.

Georgia, however, was a special girl. I met her through our University Ministry outreach in 1996. I remember meeting three gifted young women, each of whom came from a different background—Evis from an Orthodox family, Enkelejda from a Roman Catholic family, and Aida from a Muslim family. All three friends had come to faith through the evangelical missionary organization Campus Crusade for Christ. When it came time for baptism, though, we met because Evis wanted to be baptized as an Orthodox Christian. Eventually, I baptized all three women, and they became central members of our Orthodox college fellowship. Evis took the baptismal name of Georgia.

Georgia sincerely loved the Lord and longed to follow His ways. She had such a sensitive heart, always reaching out to others. I watched her grow spiritually and realized her potential. That is why, after graduation, she became our university ministry coordinator. She even began leading three Bible studies a week in the university dormitories.

Her newfound faith helped Georgia face her father's illness. She had the privilege of taking him to Thessalonika monthly for treatments. During this time, I encouraged her to talk with her father openly about his illness, and even about the possibility of death. Although she thought such a discussion would be impossible, she understood that death shouldn't be something fearful for Christians. Christ's victory over death is central to our faith, and He promises life for all who believe. Since she believed this, she overcame her doubts and hesitations.

She began to share her faith openly with her father and even broached the subject of cancer and death. Her father Grigor believed in God, but had lived much of his life under militant atheistic propaganda. Like numerous parents in Albania today, he learned much of his faith from his daughter.

Faith and I visited Grigor right before Christmas. We heard his situation was critical. He could no longer swallow, and received food through a tube in his stomach. His days were numbered. So we went to encourage and comfort Grigor, Georgia, and their family—to anoint him with holy oil in hopes of a miraculous healing, but also to hear his confession in preparation for death.

We arrived at his home with the entire extended family present. We spoke softly yet openly about the reality they faced. Some were uncomfortable with talking so openly about death, yet Grigor himself was peaceful. I spoke with him for an hour, listening to his life story—a story of much persecution, injustice, imprisonment for seven years, and discrimination against his entire family—and hearing his confession.

Throughout his story I sensed no bitterness. He confirmed that the past two years with cancer and continuous treatment had blessed him, because during this time he had grown in his faith. He saw life from a different perspective and even accepted his impending death with hope and peace. He was prepared to meet his Creator.

Faith and I left Georgia's home inspired, yet humbled. Grigor died three months later, but that visit helped him and his family prepare for his final journey—not a journey of fear or deceptive silence, but a journey of faith into the kingdom of heaven.

THEFT, FIRE, AND A MISCARRIAGE   MARCH 2001

We had quite a week from March 22–29, 2001. It began with Faith spotting and us fearing another miscarriage. Then I went to take Paul, Theodora, and two Albanian kids for some rides, and realized that someone had picked my pocket and stolen $600 which I was going to change into Albanian money.

As if things couldn't get worse, the next day I took Faith and her little day school with eight neighborhood children for an excursion to the park. I had forgotten Jim Forest's airline ticket, which I was planning to get changed, so I returned home, only to see smoke bellowing out of the window. Our house was on fire!

I tried to open the front door, only to see the entire house, from knee-height up, covered with black smoke. I didn't know what to do, so I shouted to some neighbors to call the fire department. I wasn't even sure if there was a fire department in Albania! I learned, though, that the fire department was actually only 200 meters away on another side street. The firemen came within five minutes, by which time flames were coming out of every window. The firemen pumped water into our house, and after five minutes, one of them put on a smoke mask and tried to enter the house. It was too difficult. After another five minutes, they entered and shot water from the inside.

The damage was severe. The fire destroyed everything in our office/children's room, while blackening the entire house. We lost our two computers, all my books and files, all the children's clothing, books, and toys. Faith's first question after seeing the house was, "Did the birds die?" She was a bit upset about their loss. We had two parakeets, Gezim and Shpresa, that she had given me for my birthday. Jonah, our fish, survived.

We think the fire started from a new voltage regulator I had bought the week before. We couldn't imagine what would have happened if the fire had started in the middle of the night.

Fr. Luke and Faith looking over the fire damage in their children's room and office.

As we reflected on the incident two weeks later, Faith and I thanked God for the love we received following this crisis. We had offers to stay in eight homes, including the French Embassy, whose ambassador happens to be Orthodox. We stayed with the Hoppes. Too often all the missionaries are too busy and we don't spend enough time together, except for our weekly Saturday evening Vespers service and an occasional birthday or special event. So we enjoyed eating breakfast daily with the Hoppes, sitting at night and talking, and watching our kids enjoy one another. The Hoppes are used to a quieter lifestyle, and our presence in their home brought numerous people and continuous phone calls. But I think they enjoyed us as well.

Since the kids lost everything, we had people bringing us clothing. One of the poorer people in our church was the first to bring a bag of clothes. Others, like Tefta, Natasha, Ana's parents, as well as our fellow missionaries, offered clothing and toys. And just a couple days ago, we received our first of what I'm sure will be several packages of clothing and books from my sister Rebecca.

Nathan, Charles Linderman, Pieter Dykorst, and the entire mission team have come over to clean up our house. Ana Kruja came over four or five times ready to work. Marinella came over numerous times. Petraq worked hard daily. And others kept showing up.

The archbishop told us he would take care of whatever financial losses we faced, and offered the Church's technical service office to take care of all the repairs on the house. Fr. Martin said the OCMC would also take care of any of the important things I lost. Mom and Dad sent $3000 to take care of any immediate needs, and our Annunciation family in Lancaster have begun sending many letters of support.

We feel like Jimmy Stewart in *It's a Wonderful Life* because of the concrete love of so many people. We even feel a little guilty because we ended up in a better state than we began. My only great loss is that of a year's work on my computer. Thank God, though, one of my backup CDs, which was in the midst of my books, was spared, so I was able to recover my work from 1992–1998.

This difficult week ended with Dr. Kosova telling us that our little baby had definitely died, and that Faith needed an immediate D&C. We went to the newly renovated maternity hospital, where the procedure took only ten minutes. We were out of the hospital after an hour with no complications. Well, I always wanted four or five children, and Faith and I have four now. Two of our little angels, Evangelia (since she was conceived around the Annunciation) and Lukie (since his due date was to be on the feastday of St. Luke on October 18), are with our Lord Jesus in heaven.

Faith handled this miscarriage much better than the first. I'm sure it's because we have Paul and Theodora, as well as because we have been facing other crises. We want to go up to St. Prokopi Church and say a little trisagion for our two little angels.

With all that happened this past week, all I can say is, "Thank you, Lord, for all things!" Really, all the struggles helped remind us about what is most important in life—our faith, which can never be taken away from us, and our family. We realize how blessed we are with the amazing love in our lives. A deep love from our close, intimate family, but also a special and deep love from our spiritual family here in Albania and around the world.

I pray that we may always remember these experiences and keep their lessons close to our hearts.

CAMP GOOD SHEPHERD   JULY 2001

Faith has been overseeing Camp Good Shepherd since 1997. We have created an experience similar to Camp Nazareth, the Pittsburgh church camp that influenced both of us as we grew up. In other words, we have created an atmosphere where God's power and grace are touching the lives of hundreds of girls. We run three two-week camp programs for girls from ages 8–12, 13–17, and 18–24. A camp for boys is run in Svernec by Fr. Theologos, a monk from Mt. Athos.

This two-week camp experience is a highlight of the year for many of these girls. Faith works with a dynamic group of women—Gabriela, Ana B., Ana K., Sonila, Jezuela, Georgia, and others—who graduated from our seminary and from the university. They put together such a fantastic program! She has trained these women leaders so well that they now run most of the program on their own.

This past year, one visitor from Greece told our girls, "We have been involved in camps for many years, and this is one of the best camps I've ever seen. Don't be jealous of any camp in Greece, because what you have here is just as good." Our co-missionary Lara Callas experienced a church camp for the first time in her life and raved about the experience.

This year's theme was "Christ Knocking on the Door of Your Heart" from

Girls at the Good Shepherd Summer Camp gather around Archbishop Anastasios as he visits the camp in 2000.

Revelation 3:20. Faith prepared a meditation book for our daily quiet time on the Beatitudes, and I wrote out the daily Bible studies. Along with our daily worship, quiet time, Bible studies, and spiritual talks, we offer a good dose of sports, activities, arts and crafts, and times of fellowship. Our Olympics are always a hit, as well as some special evening activities. This year we offered an International Night when the girls prepared foods from around the world, along with dances, skits, and presentations from different countries.

I also spent a week at the boys' camp in Svernec. When I was there, we baptized twenty boys. At this camp I met Kristo and Aristani, two kids from the same village who hadn't spoken to each other for three years. Although they saw each other daily in their small village, they had vowed years ago never to speak to one another after an insignificant fight at a soccer match. Such hardheadedness is a common trait the children learn from their parents. During one morning liturgy, Kristo wanted to receive Holy Communion, but his cabin leader knew about the ongoing feud, and after talking with me, told the boy that he couldn't receive the Eucharist until he reconciled with Aristani. At first,

Kristo was angry. But slowly the Holy Spirit touched his heart and led him to repentance. He approached his old friend, and after an awkward moment, both boys asked each other for forgiveness. Three years of pride and stubbornness finally ended. Thank God, these actions are the fruit of our camps.

SEPARATIONS   AUGUST 2001

During our first seven years of marriage, Faith and I have lived apart from one another for 51 weeks, almost one entire year. Although neither of us ever imagined that our married life would include so many separations, we now realize that this is part of our missionary life. Some of our separations came from unexpected crises—the death of her father on July 22, 1996, a family crisis, the national chaos of 1997, and the Kosovo war of 1999. Other times were moments of deep joy, like the birth of our first two children. Faith returned to the States to give birth to each of our children and share our joy with our extended families. Each time, she would leave for the States two or three months before the birth and stay for two or three months after. I usually came only a week or two before the birth and stayed for a couple of weeks after. Other separations included my travels with the archbishop, as well as my representing the Church of Albania at various conferences in Germany, Poland, and Syria. On one or two occasions, Faith returned home not in response to any crisis, but simply to be with her mother and sister and nephew.

The greatest sacrifice for us as missionaries is being far away from family, especially during times of crisis and need. Therefore, we understood beforehand that this call would mean certain sacrifices in our marriage. Thank God, we have dealt well with our separations.

SEPTEMBER 11, 2001

Two days ago occurred one of the greatest tragedies in our generation—the terrorist destruction of the World Trade Center and bombing of the Pentagon with four hijacked planes. It seems unbelievable. As we watch continuous footage of the planes slamming into the Twin Towers and see the buildings leveled, it appears like some Hollywood B movie. Who could have ever believed that the Twin Towers would be leveled and the Pentagon itself attacked? Surely this is a turning point in modern history.

What hatred and darkness committed in the name of Allah! Unfortunately, Christians have committed atrocities in the name of God also, but it's impossible to justify such violence based on the life of Christ and the New Testament. Our faith is a faith of love, by a leader and His followers who shed their own blood rather than take the blood of others. The first three centuries of Christianity clearly reveal how the Gospel was spread by the blood of the martyrs—not by their shedding of someone else's blood. Here lies the essence of Christ's Good News! We must be ready to sacrifice out of love for the other, to serve the other, even to die for the other. We pray daily in our Compline service "for those who hate us and those who love us." Christ taught that we must love our enemy. Authentic Christianity has no room for hatred and violence!

Islam, on the other hand, cannot deny that it justifies violence and war. It promotes jihad, which many interpret as holy war. The Koran talks about violence. Muhammad himself was a warrior who fought and killed and advocated violence in the name of Allah. Muhammad saw himself in the line of the Old Testament warriors like Joshua, Gideon, and David. One sees quite a different picture in the person of Jesus Christ.

We do not know how many thousands of people were killed in these attacks, but I am afraid of how America will respond. They are looking for the perpetrators and are ready to attack any people and country that has helped these terrorists. This event marks a sad day in world history. Violence breeds violence. Hatred breeds hatred. Sure, we have to send a strong message to those who perpetrate violence and terrorism, but I pray that our country can take care not to inflict senseless harm and death on the innocent civilians of other countries.

I often think of some of these fanatics being like the apostle Paul. Before his conversion, St. Paul authorized killing in the name of God. He fervently traveled from house to house and even to faraway cities to root out the Christian "heretics," all in the name of serving God. Yet look at the way God transformed Paul from one of the most misguided zealots to the greatest apostle, someone who willingly suffered everything for the sake of Christ! May the same conversion come upon these contemporary fanatics.

Yesterday, I met the archbishop and saw how shaken he was by all these events. He kept saying this was a turning point in world history. He also mentioned that America has to use this as an opportunity for self-criticism. At first I thought he was implying that America has been too violent in Serbia and in other countries. He was talking, though, about how America and the West have readily supported Islamic countries without fully understanding Islam. The West has become too secular and doesn't understand the religious mindset of Muslims. The West thinks that moderate Muslims will determine the path of Islamic countries, when in reality, fundamentalism is on the rise everywhere.

He said to me, "Those pilots were probably happy when they ran into the towers. They thought they were on their way to paradise. I must say that any paradise based on hatred must be a terribly dark and hellish paradise!"

He pointed out the irony that so many people in Greece and America think it is so dangerous for us to live in Albania, and yet, look at New York. The only safe place is in the hands of God, whether in America, Albania, or anywhere else. I hope this terrible tragedy will help us reevaluate life itself. Life is meaningless if we solely pursue wealth, pleasure, and power. Life makes no sense if we allow violence and hatred to control our worldview.

I don't know how I would have reacted if I had been on the hundredth floor of the Twin Towers, but Faith jokingly said to me, "You would have called me on the cellular, and probably said, 'Well, I'm about to die, but don't worry for me. I pray that I will be with our Lord, and when I am there, I will be praying for you and the kids.'" To be honest, I don't know how I would have responded, but I pray that I would respond in such a way.

MISSION TEAM RETREAT   MAY 2002

Fr. Martin, now the director for the OCMC, came and led a fantastic missionaries' retreat. It was our first one, attended by the ten OCMC missionaries to Albania (the Hoppes, the Lindermans, the Callases, Pieter Dykorst, Jen Maple, and ourselves), and four from Romania (with four of their children). We spent four days and three nights at a resort in Durres. We enjoyed just relaxing, talking to one another, hearing one another's testimonies and ministries, and being nourished by three Bible studies. Fr. Martin led the first one on John 17. I led the second Bible study on Ephesians 3:14–21—St. Paul's prayer asking for the Christians to be united more closely to Christ, and then to receive His blessing of abundance. The passage ends by saying, "God is able to do abundantly far more than anything we ask for, and more than we can even imagine." Fr. David Hudson, one of our missionaries to Romania, led a Bible study on the September 11 tragedy and our security in God's hands.

What a special group of missionaries we have! We truly love one another, and each person has something special to offer. One of the results of this retreat was a commitment by all to begin holding a weekly missionaries' Bible study. We want to keep the momentum going.

DID JESUS REALLY RISE?

Before Pascha, Faith and the Children's Office organized retreats for more than 450 children in five areas of Albania. The retreat focused on Pascha. At the conclusion of one retreat, Faith rode home on the bus with 50 children. Little eight-year-old Joana seemed a bit embarrassed, but posed a serious question to her. "Tell me, is the story of Jesus rising from the dead really true?"

What an honest question from children who have never had any religious upbringing within their families. A few months later, the Children's Office held seven week-long day camps for more than 550 children. During our camp in Tirana, Faith saw little Joana once again. Joana excitedly told Faith about her recent baptism and how she continues to learn more about the faith. Thank God for the seeds we're planting for the future generation!

REMEMBERING 9/11   SEPTEMBER 11, 2002

The US Embassy prepared a night of remembrance for the tragedy of September 11. They invited all the diplomats, Albanian politicians, and the leaders of the religious communities. The entire ceremony was nationally tele-vised. I represented the Orthodox community since Archbishop Anastasios was out of the country. I sat in the front row with Archbishop Rok Merdita of the Roman Catholic Church; Sabri Koci, the head of the Islamic community; Baba Reshat, the head of the Bektashi community; and a representative of the evangelical community. The president of Albania, its prime minister, and the US Embassy chargé d'affaires sat in the front row as well.

The entire night was quite a religious experience. They held the event in the National Gallery of Art, which providentially was showing an exhibit on the treasure of icons Albania possesses. Thus, beautiful icons adorned the walls of the entire hall, and the backdrop behind the speakers was a magnificently carved wooden icon screen. The entire setting looked like an ancient Orthodox Church. Although the embassy chose the Academy of Art as a neutral place, it looked just like an Orthodox church!

Each speaker offered a five-minute reflection, with musical renditions between the talks. The prime minister and then the president opened with a few words, then each of the religious leaders spoke. I offered the first meditation of the religious leaders. Afterwards, the Egyptian ambassador said to me, "Where did you learn to speak English so well? Your talk was very moving."

Here is the talk I offered:

"Love your enemies, and pray for those who persecute you, that you may be children of your heavenly Father." The call to "love your enemies and pray for those who persecute you" is one of the most radical teachings of Jesus Christ, and yet it is one upon which we can reflect tonight.

As we commemorate the events of September 11, we pause to look back and remember: to remember our beloved brothers and sisters who died in the tragedy; to remember the heroic men and women who risked, and even sacrificed, their lives trying to save the victims; to remember the countless families whose lives were drastically and forever changed by this disaster; and to remember the response of love and compassion from the worldwide community.

While remembering, though, we also need to forge ahead. Maybe the most important reflections tonight will not be about the past, but about the future. How do we face our post-September 11 reality? With what attitudes and with what hopes? Is our hope only to punish the perpetrators and to protect ourselves against any future evil, or can we seek for something more positive, creative, and beneficial for the world?

The great American prophet, the Rev. Dr. Martin Luther King, Jr., preached, "Hate cannot drive out hate. Only love can do that. Hate multiplies hate, and violence multiplies violence in a descending spiral of destruction. . . . Love is the only force capable of transforming an enemy into a friend."

As we forge ahead, we need inspired thinking that will risk striving to transform our enemies into friends. We need to use the greatest arsenal in the history of the world—not the military power of techno-

logically advanced weapons of mass destruction, but the oldest and only eternal power, the weapon of divine love.

"Love is the only force capable of transforming an enemy into a friend."

How can we cultivate such divine love among all peoples throughout the world, especially among those who feel marginalized and rejected? Only through critical self-evaluation and a readiness to sacrifice for the other—to follow the Golden Rule of the Bible, which says, "Do unto others as you want them to do unto you"—only with such a spirit can we reach our goal of peace and love.

As the Orthodox Church community in Albania, cultivation of divine love is at the center of our identity. We are called to accept the freely given love of God into our lives, and then share that love with others, even our enemies. The head of our Church, His Beatitude Archbishop Anastasios, who unfortunately is out of the country tonight, and thus unable to attend this ceremony, has often emphasized how the religious communities need to nurture this type of love in society. He often says, "The oil of religion should never be used to ignite the fires of hatred, but should be used to soothe and heal the wounds of others."

America is a great nation built on such Christian foundations and principles, the greatest of which, according to Jesus Christ, is love—even love for your enemy, even love for those who hate you and persecute you. Tonight, as we commemorate the victims of September 11, let each of us meditate on how we can build a lasting memorial for those who died—not simply a beautiful edifice of stone, but a living memorial of divine love; an eternal memorial of concrete actions that help all people throughout the world live in peace, security, harmony, and with respect for one another.

Such a living memorial of divine love would truly honor all those who died by transforming their senseless deaths into the seeds of a new vision for the future.

PANAYIOTA'S BIRTH   JANUARY 2003

We returned to the States after Christmas 2002 for a six-month sabbatical. We decided to combine the birth of our third child with a missionary furlough, staying at Holy Cross Greek Orthodox School of Theology, where I would offer a class on missions. Several days before we left for America, four-year-old Paul was in the little shop that sits in front of our house. Our kids go into this shop every day to buy our milk, bread, and other daily necessities. The shop is no bigger than 12 x 12 feet. On this particular day, as Paul was getting our fresh bread, he looked at Faith and asked, "In America, will there be any supermarkets as big as Uncle Syri's?"

At the airport, a group of 25 friends came to say goodbye. Many shed tears. Paul looked at all the people crying and whispered something in Faith's ear. She didn't quite hear him, and told everyone that Paul said, "God bless you." When we got on the plane, Faith asked him again what he had said. Paul told her, "God will wipe away every tear from their eyes." That was a Bible verse Faith had taught him months ago.

When we arrived in Boston and moved onto campus, into a little four-room apartment, we bought a small TV for the kids to watch some videos. Our first night there, Paul asked, "If there is electricity, and if its voltage is high enough, can I watch a video?" He has a few lessons to learn about living in America!

On Thursday, January 30, Faith's water broke and we rushed off to the hospital. She didn't want to imitate the tough Kosovar women this time around and took an epidural. Our little Panayiota Maria Veronis was born at 1:52 AM on January 31, 2003, the feastday of the Unmercenary Saints John and Cyril. She weighed 6 pounds 7 ounces and was 19½ inches long. She fractured her collarbone when she came out, but otherwise was healthy. She came out rosy pink with black hair. Paul and Theodora were so excited to meet their little sister. We thank God for another special blessing from our Lord! May little Panayiota imitate her namesake, the Panayia, and her grandmother, Panayiota Pearl.

PARADE MAGAZINE   JULY 2003

On Sunday, July 27, 2003, Archbishop Anastasios was on the front cover of *Parade* magazine. "He Gave His Country Hope: The Story of Archbishop Anastasios Yannoulatos of Albania," written by the noted Greek-American author Nicholas Gage, details the story of this holy man and God's miraculous work in Albania. The distribution of this magazine in America's Sunday newspapers has now exposed this story to an estimated 70 million people. Thank

God, the story contained an inspirational message of love, tolerance, and the blessing of reaching out and helping others—a message that we all need to hear again and again.

BEGINNING A NEW LIFE   SEPTEMBER 2003

Today we did a very special baptism. Our co-missionary Lara Callas, through the OSCE (Organization of Security Councils in Europe), has been working on a witness protection case for the past several months. There is a girl who was raped and beaten by a high-profile criminal. It's a long and sad story of how this man abused this young nurse, then threatened to kill her and/or members of her family if she reported it to the police. He also demanded not only that she stay silent, but whenever he would call her, she would have to come. Several weeks after the initial encounter, he called her, and she didn't agree to go. One of his thugs picked her up while she was walking home and took her to a hotel. There he raped and beat her, even breaking some of her ribs.

This is when Lara and the OSCE entered the picture. They promised to give the girl witness protection if she would testify against this criminal. The criminal threatened her and her family. She went through with the testimony, though, and has been in hiding for the past three months.

Lara became close friends with this girl. The girl comes from an Orthodox background, although she has never been baptized. Lara talked with her about faith issues, and eventually she expressed an interest in being baptized. Lara introduced the girl to me, and I catechized her. Two days before she departed to begin a new life in some unknown country, we baptized her in her apartment. Lara, her husband Anthony, and Faith acted as witnesses. The girl attentively participated, and expressed such gratitude at the end. I kept emphasizing that just as she was beginning a new life in two days, she has already begun a new life in Christ, through her death and rebirth in baptism. Her name is now Maria, and Lara is her godparent.

YOUTH LEADERS RETREAT   OCTOBER 2003

Faith and I took our youth leaders—Ana B., Ana K., Gabriela, and Sonila—on an overnight retreat on Mt. Djati. It was a beautiful and renewing experience for all of us. We stayed in rustic cabins, enjoyed nature, relaxed with the kids, while enjoying a spiritually renewing time. Our goal was to nourish these youth leaders in their spiritual life and create a closer bond with them.

We had two Bible studies, quiet time for reflection, and time for prayer. We then planned out our personal and ministry goals for the upcoming year. Everyone enjoyed the fellowship and time together, and we agreed that this would become a regular type of retreat.

PILGRIMAGE WITH METROPOLITAN JOHN OF KORÇA   MAY 2004

Metropolitan John shared with us that as a young man, he used to take pilgrimages to different holy sites and old, ruined churches, spending the night in prayer. He would walk from Tirana to St. Vlash (a walk of several hours), from Tirana to Lezha (a 12- to 15-hour walk), from Korça to Permeti or Gjirokaster, and other such places. He shared how beautiful it was to walk without being in a rush, stopping along the way, thinking, enjoying nature, praying, and then arriving at a church, where he would sit to rest and read the psalms. "You get a different perspective on the psalms, or prayer, or resting in the Lord after a long walk. It speaks to you in a different, unexplainable way. Those were days when I really felt God's presence," he shared with us.

Over the years, we have talked about doing such a pilgrimage together. Finally, a month before we left Albania, the metropolitan took his chancellor, Fr. Vasili, along with me, Nathan Hoppe, George Russell, and Panayiotis Sakelleriou on a pilgrimage. We began by walking from Korça to the monastery of St. John the Forerunner in Voskopoja. We began at 10:00 AM and walked for about three or four hours. It drizzled throughout the day. Twice we stopped to rest, read a psalm, and meditate on God's beauty. The metropolitan shared with us stories about his past pilgrimages during the time of communism. Each of us enjoyed walking side by side with the metropolitan, and then with one another, cherishing each person and every moment. Most of our conversations revolved around the Church and the spiritual life.

At the monastery, we rested in the church, sang hymns, then had a nice lunch—bread, cheese, and a piece of lamb given us by the local priest. After an afternoon rest, we prayed Vespers, had a simple dinner, made a fire, and talked late into the evening. It was quite cold for June, so we slept under two blankets.

Metropolitan John of Korça is surrounded by his chancellor, Fr. Vasili, OCMC missionary Panayiotis Sakalleriou, Fr. Luke, Fr. Konstandin, and OCMC missionary George Russell as they go on a two-day walking pilgrimage from Voskopoja to Vithkuq in May 2004.

The next morning, I woke up at 5:00 AM and had my quiet time. By 6:00 AM, everyone else awoke, and we had coffee. We then began our half-hour walk into the town of Voskopoja. This ancient town has thirteen churches. We stopped in the church of St. Nicholas and prayed Matins. We then began our walk to Vithkuq with a donkey carrying our bags. We walked for five hours, with a stop or two for a coffee and rest. What magnificent scenery, with its rolling green hills and overarching mountains.

After five hours of walking, it started to pour down rain. Soaked and tired, we reached our destination of St. Peter's Monastery in Vithkuq. After saying some prayers of thanksgiving, we visited a local fish farm and had a delicious lunch. By the end of our pilgrimage, our feet were aching, but our souls were soaring.

CHAPTER 8

ARCHBISHOP ANASTASIOS

*Throughout my ten years as a missionary, I have had many conver-
sations with Archbishop Anastasios, listened to his talks and sermons,
read his theological and scholarly articles, observed his witness within
the mission fields of Albania and East Africa, and noted his interactions
in a variety of other contexts, whether religious, political, or secular. He
is a brilliant theologian, an inspired hierarch, a practical missionary, a
Nobel Peace Prize candidate, and a humble Christian. From Orthodox
ecclesiastical settings, to ecumenical gatherings, to the political arena
at all levels and throughout the world, to totally secular meetings, I
observed his actions and listened closely to his words. In every situation,
I marveled at how the love of God shone forth from this holy apostle. His
patient, kind, attentive demeanor always offered the deepest respect and
dignity to the people with whom he spoke. His faith and experiences of
life taught him when to speak and when to stay silent, when to preach
with words, when to proclaim with his actions, or when to simply offer
a witness with his silent presence.*

*Following are a number of stories and sayings that I've heard first-
hand, or that I've read in his writings, that help reveal the spirit that lies
within this holy man.*

LIVING THE GOSPEL

"Is the Gospel really something that can be lived? This is the question of many skeptics in today's world," Archbishop Anastasios would say.

"Missionaries, however, offer an answer through the example of their lives. The ontological question is answered not by what we say and not even by what we do, but by what we are. Our life witness is what is most important! One of our greatest contributions is that we have tried to live with the people—in Africa or in Albania—and have offered our life to them. Our theological position has always been to live the mystery of the one, holy, catholic and apostolic Church. We have tried to live the mission of the Church with its proper universal and eschatological perspective—to live the life of the cross always with the hope of the resurrection."

IS GOD ENOUGH?

Archbishop Anastasios faced a serious dilemma as a young deacon back in the 1960s. As a lay theologian, he had preached about the need for the Orthodox Church to rediscover her apostolic calling of missions. In 1959 he started the bilingual (Greek and English) mission journal *Porefthentes— Go Forth,* and then in 1961, he founded the inter-Orthodox mission center Porefthentes, all as a means to reawaken the missionary conscience of the Church. Before his ordination to the priesthood on May 24, 1964, though, he faced the difficult question of whether he himself should actually go to Africa as a missionary or stay in his beloved homeland of Greece. "It was clear to me," he said, "that what you say, you must also do. How could I teach what I wasn't living?" He wrestled with this thought until he had a special revelation.

"I remember a young cleric who was on a prolonged retreat on the island of Patmos. Sitting in front of the open sea, he faced a challenging dilemma— to stay in his beautiful European country, within an environment he loved, and in which he was loved, or to obey the final command of the Lord, 'Go ye,' and to depart for Africa. No guarantee was offered for this latter course and its future. Gazing from his simple, ascetic cell, the horizon of the open sea called within him, seeking a satisfactory response for this major decision in relation to the will of God.

"The answer finally came in the form of a critical question: 'Is God enough for you? If so, then go. If not, then stay where you are.' A follow-up question, however, reinforced the first. 'But if God is not enough for you, in which God do you believe?' A peaceful decision followed, directing him on an innovative course into new missionary frontiers. My basic guarantee and comfort in my bleak hours was always the assurance of the resurrected Christ, with the promise that follows the command to 'Go and teach all nations'—'And lo, I am with you always, even to the close of the age.'"

The same night of his ordination, the newly ordained Fr. Anastasios flew to Africa and celebrated his first Divine Liturgy at the St. Nicholas Cathedral in Kampala, Uganda. His cross-cultural missionary work had begun.

WE BELIEVE IN MIRACLES

In 1959, the young lay theologian Anastasios gave a talk at the University of Athens in which he shared his vision for the creation of an Orthodox missionary center that would send out cross-cultural missionaries throughout the world. Many thought such a dream impossible, especially considering the reality of post-World War II Greece and the poverty of the country. Others dismissed such talk as romantic dreams of idealistic youth. Some laughed at his idealism, saying that such a vision would take a miracle. To which the young Anastasios responded, "Yes. You're right. But thank God that we Christians do believe in miracles!"

WHERE ARE OUR OWN MISSIONARIES?

Young Deacon Anastasios was the first Orthodox representative to take part in the WCC's Commission on Missions and Evangelism in Mexico City in 1963. Following that conference, he visited the Wycliffe Bible Translators' Training Camp in the jungles of Guatemala, staying among families who were preparing to serve in frontier missions among some of the most primitive Indian tribes of the world. His ecumenical openness to learning from others and observing the passion and love of Christ that others possessed remains a hallmark of his life. From that experience, he told me he still remembers a key phrase Wycliffe ingrained in their missionaries: "Accept life! No matter what unexpected challenges life brings, no matter how great the difficulties, accept life!"

The archbishop shared with me how a variety of figures across the Christian world touched him in his life. "I remember being affected by stories of Fr. Damian, the nineteenth-century Roman Catholic priest who dedicated his life to serving the lepers of the Hawaiian Islands. He offered his life to the point of becoming a leper himself and dying among his adopted people. And then I read of David Livingstone and his bold exploits throughout Africa. Albert Schweitzer was another figure. During the Christian camps we ran in Greece back in the 1950s, we would stay up late into the night, telling stories of such inspiring figures. But then, I began asking myself, what about missionaries from our Orthodox tradition? Who were our missionaries, and where were they? Why did we not have any contemporary missionaries to inspire us and bless us?"

These questions led Archbishop Anastasios to research and discover the incredible missionary exploits of the great Byzantine missionaries Ss. Cyril and Methodios, the evangelizers of the Slavs. He became fascinated with St. Innocent Veniaminov, the greatest of the Russian missionaries to Alaska, Siberia, and Asia. He learned of St. Nicholas Kasatkin and his incredible fifty-year ministry in Japan. The discovery of these missionaries affirmed his passion to help awaken the Orthodox Church to reclaim her missionary tradition.

He began to write provocative articles, emphasizing, "Indifference to missions is a denial of Orthodoxy. . . . A Church without mission is a contradiction in terms. . . . As unthinkable as it is to have a church without a liturgical life, it is even more unthinkable to have a church without a missionary life. . . . A static Church which lacks a vision and a constant endeavor to proclaim the Gospel to the world can hardly be recognized as the one, holy, catholic and apostolic Church to whom the Lord entrusted the continuation of His work. . . . How is it possible to celebrate Pascha and Pentecost without accepting the consequences of these feasts? Look at their theological perspective. These feasts proclaim that we must go!"

POREFTHENTES—GO FORTH

"When we began publishing the missionary periodical *Porefthentes— Go Forth* in 1959, people commented that it was something exotic. It is a fever that Yannoulatos has, and it will stop after a while. Others said this mission spirit came from some Protestant influences. This second accusation forced me to do serious studies, and to firmly show that missions was a central part of our Orthodox faith.

"We then created the mission center Porefthentes. Our vision for this mission center was not to create an entity outside of the Church structure, like a brotherhood or society. We wanted to educate, inspire, and motivate the Church from within, act as an impetus to reinvigorate the Church and help her rediscover her missionary calling. Porefthentes was to be the St. John the Forerunner. A mission center is not to be responsible for sending out missionaries, but the Church is. The mission center simply must act as an instrument of the Church."

MALARIA

On the very day the archbishop was ordained a priest in 1964, he traveled to Kampala, Uganda, and began what he thought would be his lifelong missionary work in Africa. He celebrated his first Divine Liturgy as a priest with a young African altar boy named Jonah. Years later, this young boy would become a co-worker and co-missionary of the archbishop's in Kenya, and then would become Metropolitan of Uganda.

During then Fr. Anastasios's first visit to Africa, something unexpected occurred. He came down with cerebral malaria. It first hit him while he was in Ethiopia at a missions conference. He didn't know what it was, and began to lose his balance, got the shakes, and developed a very high fever. He thought he was going to die. That night, he prayed, "O Lord, I have made many mistakes, but you know that I have tried to love You!" The next morning he was all right. He dealt with a second attack when he was in Geneva for another missions conference of the WCC. Thankfully, a doctor there diagnosed cerebral malaria, but not before Fr. Anastasios had a complete breakdown of health. The doctor gently told him that he shouldn't return to Africa because it could jeopardize his life.

This unexpected event radically changed his plans. "I thought I would spend the rest of my life in Africa. This news was like a second mortal wound for me." While one of his former professors and friends tried to direct him to further academic studies, telling him he could inspire others to become missionaries through his teaching and research, he wasn't sure. He questioned whether he could seriously challenge people to go to far-off places if he himself didn't actually go. "Always like the water, though, I tried to be free to flow wherever God directed me," he later confessed. "I tried to always say to the Lord, 'Here I am. I will do whatever You want and go wherever You want.'"

Thus, the path toward doctoral studies prevailed, and his passion for practical cross-cultural missions was put on hold for fifteen years.

During the next decade and a half, Fr. Anastasios traveled the world over as he studied the history of religions, became a professor of world religions, served as the general director of *Apostoliki Diakonia* in the Church of Greece, and accepted a position in the WCC's Commission of World Missions and Evangelism.

In 1972, Fr. Anastasios became both the Bishop of Androusa and a professor of world religions at the University of Athens. He told me, "I realized that I had two positions that could be very dangerous for my spiritual life. How could I avoid the great temptations of these positions?" So he prayed for God to protect him from the dangers these positions could bring. As he prayed, the Holy Spirit enlightened him to realize a truth that has remained with him for the rest of his life. "God reminded me to always remain a deacon (serving others) and a student (never stop learning). If I remembered these two things, and truly stayed a deacon and student, God would keep me safe."

Then in 1981, Patriarch Nicholas of Alexandria asked him to become the acting Archbishop of East Africa and help revive the flailing mission there. Archbishop Anastasios finally returned to Africa as a missionary. He became the acting Archbishop of Irinopoulis and East Africa (Kenya, Uganda, and Tanzania), opening up the first Orthodox seminary in sub-Saharan Africa, building dozens of churches, ordaining scores of new clergy, and revitalizing the mission there, while continuing in his ministry as professor of world religions at the University of Athens.

WHERE IS CHRIST PRESENT?

In 1990, Archbishop Anastasios's involvement in the ecumenical movement happened to take him to Leningrad in the Soviet Union, where he offered a lecture on "Dialogue and Mission" for a committee of the Council of Churches in Europe. It was Sunday, June 17, 1990, when he was invited to participate at the opening Divine Liturgy at the magnificent Cathedral of St. Isaac, a church that can hold 14,000 people. This is the third largest Christian church in the world, after St. Peter's in Rome and St. Paul's in London. During the seventy years of the Soviet Union, this church was used as a Museum of Science and Atheism. The archbishop narrated the following story.

"The luxury and magnificence was surprising. Twenty hierarchs and seventy priests attended, led by His Beatitude Patriarch Alexy II. Choirs comprised of more than one hundred members chanted brilliantly, and at various times throughout the Divine Liturgy, the thousands of people who filled this enormous and ornately beautiful church accompanied the chanting. It was spiritually uplifting. As the Divine Liturgy neared completion, I drew close to Patriarch Alexy and expressed my feelings of gratitude, giving glory to God. He embraced me in a brotherly manner, and summarized succinctly the events by saying, 'Christ is Risen!'

"At the official dinner that followed, given in honor of the patriarch, I was asked to make a toast. I started by saying, 'Following Holy Communion, near the end of this magnificent Liturgy which we experienced today in the beautiful Church of St. Isaac, I stood in a corner of the altar area wondering, "Where is Christ most comfortable? In the luxurious cathedrals of Europe or in the poor huts of Africa?"'

"The woman who was translating my toast stopped in mid-sentence, hesitating to translate something that appeared offensive to her. I asked her to continue, though, and a rather disagreeable silence followed. I continued, 'As I wondered about this question, I quickly found the answer—Christ is comfortable in both places. Christ is comfortable in a cathedral of Europe or a hut of Africa. What is most important is not the exterior luxury or poverty, but the Divine Liturgy, which transforms common bread and wine into the Body and the Blood of Christ. Holy Communion is what all believers share, irrespective of origin, tongue, or economic state. Christ is present both in the great cathedrals of Europe as well as in the simple village churches of Africa.'"

LEARNING FROM AFRICA

"From Africa," Archbishop Anastasios told me, "I learned an important lesson for Albania. Respect all that is good there, and don't try to impose our own culture. Offer what is best from our own culture, but respect and preserve what is good from theirs.

"This practical experience from Africa affirmed what my academic studies revealed. When the Church encounters a culture, it proceeds to initiate three processes: first, it accepts those elements that are in keeping with the message of the Gospel; second, it rejects other aspects that are irreconcilable with the

Gospel; and third, it transfuses new blood and a new spirit into the culture, fertilizing whatever is positive.

"Imprisonment in any of the cultural forms of this world is inexcusable; there is no justification for the closed circle of chauvinism. . . . Imposing a culture of uniformity and monotony always threatens to lead humanity to an appalling state of impoverishment."

WHY AM I HERE?

I remember a pastoral visit of Archbishop Anastasios to Western Kenya in 1988. Since I was living in this area with my Kenyan co-worker, Fr. Athanasios Karanja, I drove the archbishop around from church to church. After one week with him, I was exhausted from the constant travel, from early morning to late evening. He keeps such a non-stop pace.

During this trip, I almost committed one of the greatest sins of my life. As I drove, maybe a little too fast, along the mountain roads of western Kenya, a tire blew out, and the truck swerved out of control. I slammed on the brakes and stopped the truck inches from the side of a mountain. We got out of the truck and looked over the edge, the archbishop making his cross. I thanked God that I wasn't the one responsible for accidentally killing a saint of our times!

But that wasn't the most memorable experience of our trip. A few days later, we experienced something the archbishop would share in several of his international talks years later. "We were in a remote region in the highlands of western Kenya. It was night, and we arrived at a house that was in mourning. A little girl, stricken mortally by malaria, lay on a large bed, as if sleeping peacefully. 'She was such a good child,' whispered her afflicted father. 'She was always the first to greet you.' We read a short funeral prayer, and I said a few words of consolation.

"That night, as the rain fell on the banana leaves and tin roof of the schoolhouse where we stayed, I reflected on the events of the day. Away in the darkness, I heard a drum beating and knew it came from the house of mourning. In my weariness, I wondered, 'Why am I here?' Various thoughts about missions came into my mind—preaching, education, civilization, development, peace, love.

"Suddenly, a light flashed across my exhausted mind and revealed to me the essence of the matter. 'You bring the good news—the hope of resurrection! Every human being has a unique worth, and each will rise again. Herein lies human dignity, value, and hope. Christ is risen! You teach them to celebrate the resurrection in the mystery of the Church. You offer a foretaste of it.' And in a fleeting vision, I saw, once again, the little African girl run up and be the first to greet me, as she usually did. She helped me to understand more precisely the heart of our Orthodox witness."

The archbishop related this lesson to his ministry in Albania. "We live similar experiences in Albania. After the horrifying events under the shadow of death, which had crushed this land for 23 years, a new era has begun with the Paschal greeting, 'Christ is Risen,' and the responsive cry, 'Truly He is Risen.' This Pascha candle has become our symbol and guide in the struggle for religious freedom. It has helped us overcome violence and reminded us to respect all human rights, without distinction of peoples and communities. Here lies the essence of Orthodox witness—to infuse everybody and everything with the truth and hope of the resurrection and guide them into the new and abundant life in Christ.

"With Christ's Resurrection everything has become new again; everything is restored. From that point on, the question posed for every human being has been whether or not to participate in this restoration. In the code language of Christianity, this call to participate is known by the term 'repentance,' which calls on us to make the effort to change by becoming new, through the process initiated by the events of Pascha.

"What our brothers and sisters yearn for, in the isolated corners of Africa, Albania, or even in the outskirts of the large and wealthy cities of the West, are not vague words of consolation, a few material goods, some educational or medical programs, and other such crumbs of civilization. In their loneliness and depression, they consciously or unconsciously hunger for human dignity, hope, and transcendence of death. In the end, they desire the living Christ, the perfect God-Man who is 'the way, the truth, and the life.'"

I ASK FOR YOUR PARDON

Archbishop Anastasios recalled, "I remember being in Laikipia, Kenya, at an altitude of 2,000 meters near the equator, under the imposing summit of Mount Kenya. By the 1980s, we had created fifteen Orthodox communities in this area. Among the newly baptized were many men and women from the Turkana tribe, a tribe which until recently lived under primitive conditions.

"We celebrated the Divine Liturgy in a hut at Ol Moran in August of 1988, where the chanting intermingled with the strong mountain air and a gentle rain. Looking out at the sunburned figures of the newly baptized Africans that were coming ecstatically to Holy Communion, I felt the need to confess and said to them, 'My sisters and brothers, on behalf of the people and the Church to which I belong, a Church founded by the Apostle Paul, I want to ask for your pardon because we have delayed so long in coming—a delay of twenty centuries.'"

COMFORTABLE VERSUS AUTHENTIC CHRISTIANITY

During my first month in Albania in 1994, I remember stopping by Archbishop Anastasios's apartment to make a phone call, since my apartment still didn't have a phone. The archbishop's apartment and church headquarters were basically one. He lived on the fourth floor of a rundown apartment building where he had a private office, a bedroom, a room serving as a chapel, and a small kitchen. On the third floor was the four-room archdiocesan headquarters, with an office for the archbishop to receive people, a kitchen with a photocopy machine, and two other rooms for his translator, Vangjeli, the monk Fr. Justinos, and Fr. Spyridon, a 65-year-old former Greek judge who acts as the church's handyman. What an unimpressive and humble setting! I wondered how many bishops and professors in Greece would accept such conditions in their retirement years. Yet this is what makes Archbishop Anastasios unique.

When the archbishop saw me using the phone, he invited me into his office, and we talked for over an hour about a variety of topics. I can't describe what a blessing it is to be in the presence of this man. He exudes love and holiness. Sometimes I think, "Do I lift him up on a pedestal too much?" But each time I spend even a short time with him, I leave saying, "No, he really is that unique!"

I appreciate the way he combines a holy, prayerful, and peaceful presence with an open-minded, progressive, visionary, God-inspired attitude. He represents an authentic monastic spirit in his simplicity and prayerfulness, yet without a closed mind to the world around him. He refreshes me with his sincere critique about the narrow-mindedness of too many Orthodox.

His Beatitude Archbishop Anastasios in the Annunciation Cathedral, Tirana.

We began by talking about the difficulties Faith and I face with her family's unwillingness to accept her coming to Albania. I told him that many in America fear the "dangers" of Albania. He got a little annoyed with such portrayals of his beloved new home. "Is it more dangerous here than in Chicago, or New York, or one of the other major cities of America or Europe? One of the ways Satan tries to stop the work of God is through fear. What did Christ mean when He called His disciples to leave everything? By trusting in Him, we overcome all fear!"

I understood this comment to be not only for Faith and me, but also for those who love us. Are parents willing to offer their sons and daughters to faithfully serve God wherever He calls—whether as priests, missionaries, monks, nuns, or in some other special manner? How many parents will sacrifice much to give their children the best opportunities to succeed in the world educationally and professionally? So many of these same parents, however, will rebel at the thought of their children "denying themselves, taking up their cross, and following Christ." And this even from parents who faithfully go to church every Sunday and who call themselves pious Christians. Comfortable Christianity threatens authentic Christianity!

I confessed to the archbishop that I felt guilty about my adjustment time in Albania. All the missionaries seemed overwhelmed with work, yet during my first month I had been taking it easy, adapting to life and focusing on language learning. He encouraged me in this adjustment period, telling me to learn the language well. He even joked about how he was "jealous" that I had time to study. He longs to be fluent in the language, yet struggles to find time to study in his hectic schedule.

He told me to set my priority on the seminary and youth. "Help these students develop open minds, ready to grasp not only the Gospel, but also the reality around us. The youth make up the most vital part of the Church. Many of the people 30 to 60 years old are set in their ways and very slow to change their worldview. We must reach the young people! They have the open minds."

After saying this, however, he shared a story which reminded me never to lose hope in anyone. "We celebrated our first Divine Liturgy at St. Prokopi last August 15, for the feastday of the Virgin Mary. By the end of the service, I was hot and tired. A man entered the altar and demanded to see me. When I asked if we could meet another day, since I was extremely tired, the man became insistent. I sat down with him, and he began confessing that he was among the people who had turned St. Prokopi Church into a restaurant. He cried and asked for forgiveness for such blasphemy. I could see sincere repentance and joyfully accepted his confession. Afterwards, I thanked God. This is what I mean when I say, don't lose hope in anyone!"

Our conversation drifted to my African mission trip in 1993 and the situation there. We discussed the struggles the East African Church has faced since the archbishop's departure in January 1991. At that time, Ecumenical Patriarch Dimitrios asked Archbishop Anastasios to go to Albania as an exarch of the Patriarchate. Although the ecumenical patriarch wanted an immediate answer, the archbishop asked for an hour to pray about it. Although he had other commitments, the ecumenical patriarch understood that few people in the Orthodox world possessed the missiological experience and preparation that Archbishop Anastasios had. Albania presented an extremely difficult challenge, and the Church needed a unique leader.

After an intense hour of prayer, Archbishop Anastasios received the same answer he heard back in the 1960s. "Is God enough?" This same assurance comforted him once again, and he accepted the new challenge of Albania.

WAR WITH SATAN

I shared a very personal concern with the archbishop, related to slanderous accusations that a fellow missionary had leveled toward me after my year-long mission experience in Kenya in 1988. This missionary tried to defame my name and attack my integrity by telling some of her supporters in America, "Fr. Alexander Veronis's son wasn't a missionary. All he did in Africa during the summer was sleep around with women!"

The archbishop knew this woman well and warned me to learn an important lesson of life. "We are in a continual spiritual war with Satan. He is always trying to look for ways to tear down the Lord's messengers and to ridicule the Gospel. When you are involved in missions, be ready to face many types of persecution, false and absurd accusations, and attacks on your integrity and very personhood. Don't be discouraged. Strive to live in purity and truth, persevering even in the face of absolute lies!"

LIVING IN DIFFERENT WORLDS

One day, the archbishop travels to the most remote villages of Albania, dealing with such simple and poor people. The next day, he's flying first class, sitting next to a prime minister or president, being greeted at an airport by an ambassador or two, interacting with some of the wealthiest people in the world at the Davos Economic Summit in Switzerland or at a World Bank conference. The variety of people he deals with includes everyone from faithful believers to secular businessmen to communists. When I asked him how he deals with such different worlds, he humbly commented, "I have learned to adapt to wherever I am and with whomever I am. I never feel superior to anyone, and I never feel inferior. I am comfortable with all people, and try to love them all, regardless of who they are. I try to treat each person as a child of God. Remember, Christ is for all people and has a message of Good News for all."

THE OIL OF RELIGION

During the Kosovo War in 1999, the media and various political sides tried to portray the Balkan conflict as a religious war between the Serbian Orthodox and the Albanian Muslims. Tensions obviously ran very high as a half-million Kosovar Albanian refugees flooded into Albania while America bombed Serbia for three months.

Archbishop Anastasios acted as a key voice throughout the Balkans, trying to defuse the religious tensions and misunderstandings. "The oil of religion should never be used to ignite the fires of hatred," he repeated again and again, "but should be used to soothe and heal the wounds of others. . . . We wholeheartedly participate in the pain of those who are suffering because of injustice and violence due to the crisis in Kosovo. We are not in a position to make eloquent speeches or easy statements in this extremely difficult situation. But, interceding daily 'for those who hate us and those who love us,' we humbly pray to the God of truth and love to perform His miracle so that peace and justice prevail over our troubled area. We have already helped on a large scale and are continuously working to the best of our ability for the relief of the refugees of the conflict who take refuge in Albania."

ON PRAYER

I love praying with the archbishop. Whether observing his quiet and prayerful presence in the Divine Liturgy, praying with him in his personal chapel, or listening to his spontaneous prayers at various events, I always sense God's presence. I remember one specific incident while traveling with him to America. It took us fourteen hours to get from his doorstep in Tirana to our hotel in New York. We entered the hotel dead tired, yet before we went to our

Archbishop Anastasios celebrates the Divine Liturgy at the Dormition of the Virgin Mary Monastery in Svernec during the Rilindja boys' summer camp. Fr. Luke joins the archbishop, along with Deacon Emanuel, Deacon Jani, and Fr. Nikolla (later to become Bishop Nikolla of Apollonia).

respective rooms to sleep, the archbishop called me into his room to conclude the day (at 4:45 AM Tirana time) with an abbreviated Compline service. Earlier we had offered our morning prayers in the airport in Frankfurt. Of course, none of this surprised me. It simply reminded me that no matter where we are, or how tired we may be, we must be disciplined to offer our prayers.

Whenever I have prayed in a private setting with the archbishop, I have appreciated the way he ends his prayers. He will offer spontaneous words, starting with the prayer, "O God Almighty, O Lord, who is, who was, and who is to come, glory to you [Revelation 1:8]. Lord Jesus Christ, Son of God, have mercy on me a sinner. O Holy Spirit, grace us with the fruit of the Holy Spirit—love, joy, peace, patience, kindness, goodness, faithfulness, humility, and self-control." And then he proceeds with his own words, always remembering Faith and our kids, the other missionaries, the Church in Albania, and whoever else might be on his mind for the day.

When I asked him how we can stay spiritually healthy and alive, he responded, "Try to know God more, to love Him more, to serve Him more. Every day we need a time of silence, prayer, and Bible reading. Pray the set prayers of the Church, not only spontaneous prayers. Don't only read the Bible, but listen to what God is saying to you through the Scriptures. At noontime, and throughout the day, offer up even short prayers. And of course, end your day in prayer.

"Remember that freedom and love are the two most important elements of the Christian life. If God does not free us, then we will have no freedom. I sometimes pray, 'O Lord, free me from myself. Free me from fear! Let me be a free person in Christ.' God is always a God of love and freedom. Love and freedom must come first in our lives, and they lead us to God. You cannot love the other if you are not free from yourself. It is not easy. It is never finished. It may happen that you are only free a small part of the time. . . . Be like the water, free to flow wherever God directs you. I learned to say in my life, 'Lord, I will go wherever You want.'"

ON FUNDAMENTALISM

The archbishop often expressed to me his frustration with the fundamentalism or ultra-conservatism within the Church. We talked about how some Orthodox vehemently opposed praying with non-Orthodox Christians, gladly throwing around the term "heretics." The archbishop disagreed with placing every non-Orthodox Christian in the same context with the ancient heretics the Church Fathers battled. "One has to consider where someone has been raised, with what knowledge they have learned the faith, and what exposure they have had to the fullness of truth. One cannot simply ignore or reject their sincere love and commitment to Jesus Christ. . . . We have to be careful not to turn our church into a small 'pure' ghetto, which isolates itself from the rest of the world. Some monasteries may do this, but the bishop and the Church at large cannot embrace this mentality. The Church has to be open and welcoming to all!

"Certain people try to distort the authentic Orthodox perspective. They try to present themselves as the only bearers of Orthodoxy. I heard some people recently say, 'Archbishop Anastasios is doing good work in Albania, but true Orthodoxy is hesychastic monasticism.' Is this form of monasticism the only true form of Orthodoxy? Of course, monasticism has played and continues to play a central role in our Church, but we can't limit the expression of faith to only one form. Here is the danger of focusing only on a particular elder and his writings. We can't ignore the Spirit of the Gospels and of what Christ Himself established.

"Why are such people more Orthodox than we are? Why is a certain view of anti-ecumenism true Orthodoxy? They call me an ecumenist. I am, and have been for the last forty years of my life. I don't need to apologize for this. Some say it is heresy to pray the Lord's Prayer with other Christians. We can dialogue with them, but we can't say a common prayer together? What is this? The Church canon that stated we cannot say prayers with heretics referred to the Eucharist. Will we approach and reach our brothers and sisters by not praying with them? What is this type of Pharisaism?"

AN ANTAGONIST CONVERTED

An amazing thing happened once at a lunch with Metropolitan Theodosios of the OCA, the Foundos brothers, and Frs. Arthur and Nikon Liolin. At the end of a cordial lunch, Fr. Arthur commented, "Your Beatitude, I have told you privately, but now I want to say publicly, I'm very sorry for the way I acted towards you in the early years, and I am grateful that you are the Archbishop of Albania. I realize that no one else could have accomplished the work you have done in Albania over these past years."

What a miracle! Here is another example of the archbishop's charismatic witness—his patience, humility, and desire always to pray for the change and conversion of his antagonists. In the first years following the fall of communism, Fr. Arthur acted as an ardent Albanian nationalist when he rejected the archbishop's election to Albania. He joined other Albanians in fighting against Archbishop Anastasios because he is Greek. Of course, such critics ignored the fact that there was no available celibate Albanian cleric in the world who could become Archbishop of Albania. They ignored who Archbishop Anastasios was and what his credentials were. These fierce critics spoke harshly against the archbishop during his first years of leadership in Albania. Yet through much prayer, love, patience, and humility on the archbishop's side, as well as an openness from Fr. Arthur to see good where good was, a bridge of understanding and respect slowly developed. Then I saw a miracle happen that I didn't believe possible five years before.

Several months after this luncheon, the archbishop traveled to New York to receive the Patriarch Athenagoras Humanitarian Award from the Archons of St. Andrew. Before a crowded banquet of five hundred or so people, mostly Greek Americans, numerous speakers lauded the archbishop for his humanitarian accomplishments in East Africa and Albania. Although Fr. Arthur was not one of the programmed speakers, he asked the organizers if he could say a few words. He proceeded to describe his extreme hesitation toward the archbishop during his early years in Albania, which turned into a deep admiration. "There is no one else who could have done what you have done over these past ten years! Thank you, Your Beatitude, for all that you have done!"

OUR THEOLOGICAL CALL TO MISSION

At the Fifth International Conference of Orthodox Theological Schools in Belgrade, Serbia, in 2001, Archbishop Anastasios warned his fellow theologians and clergy about the danger of nationalism in our Church, which leads us to view one another with suspicion and doubt. "We are not different Orthodox churches, but are one Church in different countries. Our theology expresses this, but unfortunately our practice too often reveals the opposite."

He also challenged these theologians to make the apostolic spirit central to theological education. "We have a serious responsibility to continue in the work of the apostles, and we cannot hide the light of our faith under a bushel as we Orthodox have done too often." He stressed the difference between so-called internal mission, i.e. pastoral care of our own people within our own country, and the external mission of going outside our boundaries and taking the Gospel to others.

When one theologian tried to say that the authentic type of Orthodox missions was to simply stay where we are and shine a light so that others come to us, Archbishop Anastasios warned him that "we are in danger of creating spiritual ghettos only for ourselves and no one else. This has nothing to do with the 'apostolic, catholic' spirit of our forebears. If our theology is authentic and sincere, it must spur us on toward missions. Orthodox theology and missiology are not separate. Our theology motivates us for mission."

SAY A PRAYER, MAKE YOUR CROSS, AND GO

In 1994, I walked with the archbishop on the site of St. Vlash Monastery, the first church destroyed by the communists in 1967. The archbishop shared with me his vision of rebuilding a spiritual center for all of Albania. He wanted a seminary and monastery. When I asked him if he had the money to build such a dream, he shared with me his secret. "I believe that if God is calling us to do something, we shouldn't be frightened by any obstacles or negative possibilities. Simply say a prayer, make your cross, and go forward! Let us begin, and God will provide the rest."

Three years later, as we walked around the finished seminary and monastery, he said to me, "Look at this miracle of God. Who could have imagined such a place four years ago? Remember, say a prayer, make your cross, and go forward!"

WE NEED HOLY PRIESTS

"We don't need many priests, but we need holy priests," the archbishop told me. "I see a lack of discipline, laziness and apathy, greed, negligence with the sacraments and daily services, lack of cooperation with other priests, and a laziness to keep learning. . . . My greatest pain is not all the difficulties we've faced from the outside, but it is when I see priests who are not pleasing in the sight of God."

ENEMIES?

The archbishop came to the seminary for an informal meeting with the students. He sat in a circle with them, answering questions for two and a half hours. It was vintage Anastasios. He touched on many issues, but a central point he discussed for more than half an hour was the spirit we must have with people outside our Orthodox faith. "Focus on the good news, not on any bad news. Don't talk against others. Tell people of the special treasure we have."

He also warned that we must be careful about radical writings against Muslims, Catholics, or Protestants. "Even if some saint wrote something 200 years ago, we must take care not to interpret it out of its context. His saying may not be appropriate for Albania in 2004. If someone calls Muhammad the antichrist, or the Pope the antichrist, that is absolutely not appropriate for us today.

"Remember a Christian should never have enemies. Never call someone a 'bad communist,' a 'bad atheist,' or a 'bad so-and-so.' All people have the image of God in them, and they are all children of God! We pray 'for those who hate us and for those who love us.' Thus we cannot have enemies. How could we? If others want to see us as enemies, it is their choice, but we do not consider others as enemies. We refuse to punish those who punished us. Always remember that at the Last Judgment we are judged for loving Christ, or failing to love Him, in the least person. The message is clear. Our salvation depends upon respect for the other, respect for otherness. This is the deep meaning of the parable of the Good Samaritan; we see not that someone is my neighbor, but how someone becomes my neighbor. It is a process.

"How should we respond to hatred? Let us learn that often the best dialogue is silence; it is love without arguments. Only remember we cannot love without a great cost. It costs much to love Christ and to love the other.

"Everything in our spiritual lives comes down to our relationship with the Triune God. All is based on love and freedom. On the unconditional love of God, and the freedom we have to respond to that love with love. Love to all people, whether they are non-Orthodox Christians, or even non-Christians and non-believers. Respect for all. Love for all. Witness for the truth. This is what our faith is about. This is true Orthodoxy."

THE DANGER OF PROSPERITY

On a drive from the Athens airport to his home, the archbishop shared with me how much Greece has changed since his youth. He described the horrible years following World War II, and the poverty and suffering of the people. Yet over the past six decades, Athens has been transformed into a cosmopolitan European capital. As we drove through the city, the archbishop commented to me, "The people of Greece stayed close to God during their years of poverty. What will happen now during their years of prosperity? Will they forget God and make themselves and their egocentric pleasures their god?"

This obviously is a question for all of us in the West to reflect upon.

KEEP YOUR EYES ON ETERNITY

The archbishop shared that a crucial point in his life was his teenage years, when he sought answers for life's most fundamental questions. "Why are we here? What does God want from me during this brief time on earth? Where can I find authentic freedom and love? These are the questions that should direct our lives as we struggle to discover His will for us. When I was a teenager, many young people tried to find their answers in the communist movement of Greece in the 1940s. I could not imagine that freedom and love could result from the communist party or any other party. Very early in my life I had a longing for something authentic. . . . I can remember as if it were yesterday kneeling on the roof of our home and saying, 'Do You exist or not? Is it true that there is a God of love? Show me Your love. Give me a sign.'

"You can see why I have such a respect for teenagers. Our youth can be a time when we ask the most important questions in life. It can be a time when we make a total commitment to some ideal. That is why I will often tell the youth, 'Life is so short, keep your eyes on eternity.'"

MOTTO OF THE APOSTLES

Archbishop Anastasios refers to two passages from St. Paul's letters as the "motto of the apostles." This is the motto that all missionaries should live by:

For I think that God has displayed us, the apostles, last, as men condemned to death; for we have been made a spectacle to the world, both to angels and to men. We are fools for Christ's sake, but you are wise in Christ! We are weak, but you are strong! You are distinguished, but we are dishonored! To the present hour we both hunger and thirst, and we are poorly clothed, and beaten, and homeless. And we labor, working with our own hands. Being reviled, we bless; being persecuted, we endure; being defamed, we entreat. We have been made as the filth of the world, the offscouring of all things until now. I do not write these things to shame you, but as my beloved children I warn you. For though you might have ten thousand instructors in Christ, yet you do not have many fathers; for in Christ Jesus I have begotten you through the gospel. Therefore I urge you, imitate me. (1 Corinthians 4:9–16)

But in all things we commend ourselves as ministers of God; in much patience, in tribulations, in needs, in distresses, in stripes, in imprisonments, in tumults, in labors, in sleeplessness, in fastings; by purity, by knowledge, by longsuffering, by kindness, by the Holy Spirit, by sincere love, by the word of truth, by the power of God, by the armor of righteousness on the right hand and on the left, by honor and dishonor, by evil report and good report, as deceivers, and yet true; as unknown, and yet well known; as dying, and behold we live; as chastened, and yet not killed; as sorrowful, yet always rejoicing; as poor, yet making many rich; as having nothing, and yet possessing all things. (2 Corinthians 6:4–10)

"We should carry these passages as the motto of missionaries," he said. "We will face many struggles, many persecutions, many difficulties. It is not easy to follow Christ. Let us keep our focus on Holy Scripture, which reminds us to go forth, even when it costs much. Christ did not command His disciples to stay in one place. He did not create monasteries. Instead, He gathered men around Himself and called them His apostles, disciples whom He sent out into the world to radiate His love for the world.

"Life is not easy as a missionary. We shouldn't romanticize this life. Not everyone has the necessary patience. There are some missionaries who come full of their own ideas and too eager to impart solutions. This only creates confusion. I ask people who come from abroad not to come with answers to all our problems, but rather to come and see and listen and to discover first how to live when things are not working, when the water and electricity are not flowing. First, learn not why some people leave, but why so many people stay even though they could easily leave."

THE WORLD BANK

I traveled with Archbishop Anastasios to Canterbury for a conference for World Faith and Development Leaders, co-sponsored by the Archbishop of Canterbury and the president of the World Bank. It gathered world religious leaders—Orthodox, Catholic, and Protestant Christian, Muslim, Hindu,

Jewish, Buddhist, and others—together with secular development leaders, like the president of the World Bank, department heads of the United Nations, and Bono, the star of the rock band U2.

"Trips like this refresh me and remind us of who we are," the archbishop told me on our trip home. "When I sit with the president of the World Bank, who has thousands of people working under him, as well as the Archbishop of Canterbury, who is an important figure for England and worldwide Anglicans, it reminds me of how we should never live solely in our little worlds. There are many people with sincere desires to help the world, and who are doing good work. Too many Orthodox fall into the danger of staying isolated in their own little worlds. By interacting with others, we are forced to face the world, and all the people of the world, and see what they have to say, see what they are doing, and integrate that into our own worldview. This helps us stay humble, to remember how small we really are.

"I remember when I was a part of the Zoe Brotherhood [in the 1950s and 1960s]. We encouraged one another to write articles without putting our name on them, so that we would stay humble. And yet, if we really want to stay humble, all we need to do is go into one of the great libraries of Europe, like when I studied in Germany, and look at all the vast number of books. What have we done, what have we written, and should we not stay humble?"

A HERETICAL FORM OF ISLAM?

Archbishop Anastasios has received more than a dozen honorary degrees from universities around the world. In 2004, I traveled with him to receive an honorary doctorate from Boston University. On the day before Boston University's graduation, we unexpectedly attended the graduation ceremony at Holy Cross Greek Orthodox School of Theology, another school that had offered the archbishop an honorary doctorate a decade before.

Although Archbishop Anastasios was not scheduled to speak at Holy Cross, Archbishop Demetrios invited him to say a few words to the graduates. He challenged them by saying, "Although you are graduating today, remember to always remain students and deacons all your lives. Never stop learning, and never stop serving others. . . . Beware of turning contemporary Christianity into a heretical form of Islam. Islam looks at Jesus as a great prophet and teacher, but rejects His divinity. Islam accepts the fact that Jesus performed many miracles, but denies the central event of the cross. Too many modern Christians also deny the divine character of Christ and reject a life of the cross! We can never understand or taste the resurrection without the cross. The resurrection is not after the cross, but in the cross. . . . We must be ready to be crucified by the very same people whom we go to serve. We have to be ready for everything, especially our cross."

The archbishop has emphasized the centrality of the cross, especially in the life of missions, in many of his academic writings as well. "One of the greatest dangers for Christian mission is that we become forgetful in the practice of the cross and create a comfortable type of Christian who wants the cross as an ornament, but who often prefers to crucify others than to be crucified himself. . . . Missions will always be a service that entails acceptance of dangers, sufferings, and humiliations, the experience of human powerlessness and at the same time of the power of God. Only those who are prepared to accept, with courage and trust in Christ, sacrifice, tribulation, contradiction, and rejection for His sake can withstand. . . . How often we forget or consciously ignore St. Paul's words: 'We have the privilege of not only knowing Christ, but of suffering for Him as well' (Philippians 1:18). The privilege to suffer for Christ—this is the heart and essence of the Gospel.

"All those who ever made a significant contribution to mission and the pastoral ministry of the Church lived in ascetic vigilance, compunction, and penitence, in unceasing struggle against the dark abysses of the human ego—i.e. continuous, relentless, persistent struggle in the Holy Spirit. . . . Those who genuinely articulate the Gospel are not simply intellectuals versed in the books of Holy Scripture; they are people who comprehend and experience the mystery of the Gospel, constantly being transformed in the flame of the Holy Spirit's presence and radiating divine glory and love in their deeds and their existence."

A FOREST WITH MANY TREES

When Archbishop Anastasios began re-establishing the Church of Albania, other Orthodox churches tried to create their own jurisdictions there. A Romanian metropolitan tried to establish a diocese for the Vlach-speaking peoples. A Greek metropolitan claimed that parts of southern Albania fell under his jurisdiction. Certain Slavic peoples lived along the borders of

Montenegro and FYROM, and felt that they could go under the Serbian or Macedonian Church.

Archbishop Anastasios insisted that only one Orthodox Church existed in Albania, but it would be a Church for all peoples. The Greek-speaking peoples in the south would continue to use Greek. The Vlach-speaking peoples would use Vlach in their churches. The Macedonian or Serbian faithful would use Slavonic or their modern languages. The archbishop even allowed several churches to continue using the old Julian Calendar.

He noted that the Orthodox Church is one Church. "It is not correct to say that a Church is the 'Albanian' Orthodox Church, or the 'Russian' Orthodox Church, or the 'Greek' Orthodox Church. We are the Orthodox Church of Albania, or of some other country. We are one Church, with a variety of members. Do you think the forest is more beautiful if there is only one kind of tree? All the various trees must grow freely under the rays of the sun. The key to proper development is love and freedom. . . .

"We have to be forthright about the truth, even when it is critical to the Church. Too often people in our Church are ethnocentric. They think that God is Greek or Russian or Serbian or Albanian. I get criticized in Greece for making the Church of Albania too Albanian. Yet in Albania, the same type of nationalists criticize me because I am Greek. . . . Please stop this closed, ethnocentric Orthodoxy!"

CHANGING PERSPECTIVES

"It is nice to see how mentalities change within our Church," the archbishop shared with me after one ecumenical gathering. "I remember in the mid 1960s, when I became the first Orthodox representative to the WCC's Commission on World Mission and Evangelism. Metropolitan Nicodim of Leningrad told me, 'We Orthodox are not interested at all in this missions and evangelism agenda. We're only concerned about the Faith and Order group of the WCC. But we voted for you because we know you're interested in this topic, and we like you.' Twenty-five years later, Metropolitan Cyril of Smolensk [now Patriarch Cyril of Moscow] told me, 'The theme of missions and evangelism is of central importance. We are grateful for the efforts you've made in this area.'"

One can see this shift of emphasis in the third paragraph of the recent

Message of the Primates of the Orthodox Churches issued on October 12, 2008, in Constantinople. It states, "Inspired by the teaching and the work of the Apostle Paul, we underscore first and foremost the importance of the duty of mission for the life of the Church and in particular for the ministry of us all in accordance with the final commandment of the Lord: 'You will be my witnesses not only in Jerusalem, but throughout Judea and Samaria and to the uttermost parts of the earth' (Acts 1:8). The evangelization of God's people, but also of those who don't believe in Christ, constitutes the supreme duty of the Church. This duty must not be fulfilled in an aggressive manner, or by various forms of proselytism, but with love, humility, and respect for the identity of each individual and the cultural particularity of each people. All Orthodox Churches must contribute to this missionary effort, respecting the canonical order."

Archbishop Anastasios was appointed by the Synaxis of Primates to chair the drafting of this document.

AN INTERNATIONAL BEGGAR

The archbishop has brought in millions and millions of dollars to finance the massive reconstruction and resurrection of the Church of Albania. Along with being the spiritual head and leader of the Church, he is also the primary fundraiser. On this role as fundraiser, he would say, "I'm an international beggar, seeking alms from all people everywhere for the sake of my children in Albania. We may be a poor church, but we are rich in friends!"

WOMEN IN THE CHURCH

In the new constitution for the Church of Albania, which was approved in 2006, it is noted that a certain quota of women must be a part of all the administrative committees of the Church, except the Holy Synod. Archbishop Anastasios has always valued the role of women in the Church.

"Women have played an essential role in our church life," he often says. "There was a time when women stayed mainly at home, but today's reality is quite different. Women have many unique gifts to offer, and the Church must use their gifts to glorify God. During the early years, our Resurrection of Christ Theological Academy was for men, preparing them for the priesthood. After a few years, I decided to have women attend as well, because I wanted to have theologically trained women serving the Church and using their gifts. Today, many women have graduated from our academy and play an important role in the activities of the Church. We would have achieved much less without them."

CHAPTER 9

BEING THE CHURCH

THE REALITY OF OUR MISSIONARY TASK

When I reflect on the past decade of our missionary ministry, I realize how difficult it is to build up a church out of nothing. How many truly committed believers can we say we have helped nourish here? How many are struggling to stay the course, to walk the path and not get distracted? Over the past decade, the secular, materialistic spirit of Western Europe has entered full-force into Albania. Its spirit has enticed many who were involved in the Church in the early 1990s but have fallen away. We have seen some fall away only to return later. One girl shared with me, "As much as I try to run away from God, He won't let me. He keeps knocking on the door of my heart, and I realize I have to return home."

A danger for missionaries is to set too high a standard for these young believers. We want them to radically commit their lives to Christ, yet how long did it take us to make that decision in our own lives? When I was the age of many of these people, where was I? I have learned through these years not to be too harsh on those who fall away. Our responsibility as missionaries is to walk with these young believers, be there for them when they fall, and encourage them in their walk. And what we discover is that in the process, they will also help us in our own walk.

MISSIONARIES: ONE BODY YET MANY MEMBERS

"The number one reason missionaries leave the mission field is conflicts with other missionaries."

I remember reading that statement during my missiological studies. How can that be true? And yet, over the years, I have seen the wide variety of missionaries who have worked under Archbishop Anastasios for the Church of Albania. Monks from Mount Athos and nuns from Greece working side by side with American Orthodox converts and laypeople. Clergy and theologically trained servants working hand-in-hand with other missionaries who didn't have serious theological training, yet brought a sincere love for Christ and passion to serve Him. I have met some wonderful missionaries who had a style of ministry quite different from my own, while I have also seen some missionaries who did much more damage than good during their time in Albania.

Whenever some conflict arose among missionaries, Archbishop Anastasios inevitably would tell me he felt like a conductor of an orchestra. The conductor doesn't simply wave his arms, but guides and directs each person to perform their best while trying to keep each member of the orchestra happy and

The OCMC missionaries (Dr. Charles and Maria Linderman, Nathan and Lynette Hoppe, and Fr. Luke and Faith, along with their children) gather around Archbishop Anastasios in 2002, following their annual Pascha luncheon at the Archdiocesan Center.

content. It surely hasn't been easy for the archbishop to keep all personalities and characters content!

I look at our different missionaries and their differing styles as a blessing for the Church. St. Paul talks about the Church being one body with many members. This analogy proved to be so true from our own experience. We had monks and nuns, and we had married clergy. We had single lay men and women working side by side with married lay couples with many children. Our youngest missionaries were in their early twenties and the oldest in their eighties. Some missionaries had been lifelong members of the Orthodox Church; others were more recent converts. Our missionaries came from Greece, the United States, Great Britain, Wales, and Kenya. All together, we made up the body of Christ. Together, our witness seemed more authentic.

As the years passed, I learned to thank God for our diversity, although at particular times, I may have struggled with it. I did witness, though, how each missionary touched Albanians in different ways. Some Albanians felt more attracted to the monks or nuns, while others felt a stronger affinity for the lay missionaries. Some could relate to married couples from America, while others connected better with missionaries from Greece, or even from Wales or Kenya. All together we made up the body of Christ.

In our first years and up to the crisis of 1997, I remember our relationship with our long-term American missionaries. Fr. Martin and Renee Ritsi, with their children Stephanos and Nicole, welcomed us to Albania and helped us adjust to our new reality. They were the only American missionaries who had faced the rugged reality of Albania in its first post-communist years. They became family with us as they baptized our first son, Paul, and they helped us during the difficult moments of Faith losing her dad and of her first miscarriage.

Other longer-term missionaries included Penny Deligiannis, who capably ran the Diaconia Office, especially during the crises of 1997 and 1999, and our scholar, Dr. Peter Gilbert. Some of our shorter-term missionaries were Mike Stavropoulos, Jimmy Nakos, Christine Foundos, and Jim Bobis. We even had several co-missionaries from America who actually came from the Presbyterian Church USA—Sheila and Hal Mischke and Art and Eloise Ware. Their church sent them to work under the Orthodox Church in certain humanitarian ministries. And then we had our international team, not including the missionaries from Greece, complemented by Elekiah Kihali from

Kenya and Frank Garcia from Great Britain. When I think about it, many of these missionaries lived in our home at one time or another.

During those first years, the missionaries from Greece were mostly monks from Simonopetra on Mt. Athos, including Frs. Theologos, Tikhon, and Ephraim. Fr. Justinos served in Albania during all the years we were there. Fr. Theologos the architect and Fr. Spyridon the former judge each had unique personalities and gifts. The Monastery of St. John the Forerunner in Kareas sent nuns for many years, and we cherished the offerings of Sisters Galini, Dominici, Filothei, and the other nuns from their monastery. And the lay women from Greece who faithfully served included Sisters Agiro, Athanasia, and Eleni.

Before 1997, there were around twenty Orthodox long-term missionaries serving in Albania, while the Protestant/evangelical long-term missionaries numbered 700 and the Roman Catholics around 500. Many of these missionaries left Albania during the anarchy of 1997, not to return later. Others, however, continued to serve, and new ones replaced them.

In 1998, we welcomed Nathan and Lynette Hoppe. They represented the beginning of a new cadre of missionaries who arrived over the following six years. We became dearest friends with Nathan and Lynette, and our children became the best of friends. (You can read more of their amazing ministry and story in the book *Lynette's Hope*, published by Conciliar Press.)

Some of the newer missionaries served for a term of two years, while others stayed longer, and even planned to stay indefinitely. Hector Firoglanis came from our hometown of Lancaster following his years at Penn State, and would return to Albania as a long-term missionary with his wife Katerina after our departure from the mission field. Medwyn Roberts was one of the few Orthodox Christians from Wales. Shannon Robinson entered the mission field after many years of waiting to get married, and ended up meeting her husband, Panayiotis Sakelleriou, a Greek-American missionary from Athens, in the mission field. I was happy to play a little role in encouraging Panayiotis to open his eyes to our co-missionary Shannon! Their wedding in Albania was a tricultural ceremony and became another unforgettable memory.

Dr. Charles and Maria Linderman came with their five children and brought a whole new understanding of the international missionary family. And what a great witness for an American surgeon to leave his lucrative practice in the States to become a medical missionary! The architect Anthony

Callas and his lawyer wife Lara added another aspect to the understanding of lay missionaries. We had Pieter Dykorst and Jennifer Maples. Then George and Pauline Russell, with their children Christopher and Maddie, and mother Melanie Linderman came. George had quit his job as a vice president of the Rand Corporation in order to enter the mission field. The last missionary to come from the States during our time was Bishop Ilia Katre, who was a real answer to prayer.

With this last group of missionaries from the United States, I have to say we developed a unique bond of friendship. I remember how Nathan and Lynette Hoppe, both of whom grew up as "missionary kids" in Colombia and Uganda respectively, would comment about how special our team was. "We shouldn't take our fellowship for granted. We remember all the problems our parents had with their co-missionaries in the field, so we must cherish our relationship," they would say. This bond grew especially after our first OCMC missionaries' retreat in 2001. Following that inspirational event, we decided as a group to gather for a Bible study and Vespers service every Saturday evening. We would rotate to different missionaries' homes each week, pray the Vespers, and then study Holy Scripture together. Our busy schedules and different ministries often kept us from seeing one another throughout the week. But every Saturday, we came together to share in delightful fellowship. These missionary gatherings became very special memories.

Our unique fellowship continued in an expanded way every holiday. For Pascha, Thanksgiving, and Christmas, we would gather with our co-missionaries, together with a number of our Albanian co-workers and dear friends, and always invite a number of the beggars or poorer people we had helped throughout the year. For several years, we would empty out all the furniture in our small four-room house and set up tables to seat forty or so guests. When the numbers grew too large, we then took these feasts out to restaurants and celebrated in a truly Albanian way—with a delicious meal, lots of music and singing, traditional dancing, and fellowship over a four- or five-hour festivity.

Along with our long-term missionaries, we also had a number of memorable short-term visitors. Fr. Anthony Ugolnik, a professor from Franklin and Marshal College in our hometown of Lancaster, came the first year. Dan and Sue Tally offered their musical talents to bless people. Fr. Peter Gillquist visited Albania twice. Jim Forest stayed with us while he was writing a book on the resurrection of the Church in Albania. Fr. Vasilios Thermos, a priest and psychiatrist from Athens, came several times. Dr. Spiro Lazarou offered both his medical gifts and spiritual wisdom on numerous visits. Frs. John Breck, Harry Pappas, and Yves Dubois left lasting memories. And of course we had many others come through the various OCMC teams, Syndesmos groups, and youth groups from Greece.

Each of these people helped to make the body of Christ more authentic and real to our Albanian companions.

PREJUDICES AND OTHER RELIGIOUS COMMUNITIES

I spoke at the Roman Catholic seminary in Shkoder for one and a half hours. The twenty-five first- and second-year students included seven nuns and five monks. At one point, we discussed how we all have certain prejudices that can hinder us from understanding the essence of Holy Scripture. At this point, we diverted into a conversation about how our particular religious communities too often have prejudices and distorted preconceived notions of one another. I have seen this among our own Orthodox people and imagined it was the same for the Roman Catholic, Protestant, and Islamic communities. After a lively discussion, one younger student told me he had grown up in an all-Catholic village and very rarely met any Orthodox Christians. Such infrequent contact with Orthodox led him to develop strong negative feelings about them, especially whenever he saw the clergy with their long beards and robes.

After a stimulating conversation and a wonderful time of fellowship, I left the school, reflecting on the importance of such ecumenical interaction. In Albania, as well as in our pluralistic world in the United States, we cannot afford to stay closed in our little spiritual ghettos, judging others with our misperceptions and distortions of faith.

Several weeks after our visit in Shkoder, twenty students from the Protestant Bible Institute in Durres came to our seminary for the entire day. I offered a two-hour lecture on the Orthodox Church and answered their many questions. Following the class, we had lunch, and then all the students played hours of volleyball together. Some of the Protestant students shared with me how surprised they were by our warm hospitality. One shared some negative experiences he had had with the Orthodox priest in his village, but said he now had a new perspective on the Orthodox. We all have to work together at breaking down the walls we create between ourselves.

Our seminary dialogues also included a visit to the Islamic medresah in Tirana, where we listened to a Muslim theologian. We had a positive interaction that helped our students overcome their stereotypes of Muslims. We hope the director will reciprocate with a visit to our seminary as well.

There's nothing like face-to-face contact and the developing of relationships for breaking down walls of prejudice. We have to start seeing one another as brothers and sisters from whom we can learn and grow. We shouldn't let our differences or different beliefs create walls that nourish fear or uncertainty of the other. Our Orthodox faith teaches us to love others through encountering them, and to respect the freedom they have to believe whatever they choose. At the same time, our faith calls us to offer a bold yet humble witness of love.

As I reflect on this ecumenical interaction, I thank God that we have worked under Archbishop Anastasios for all these years and have witnessed his loving example—an example of never fearing the other, while always dialoguing and meeting with them. I grew up witnessing this same ecumenical spirit in my parents and their ministry as well.

ALBANIA'S HERO: MOTHER TERESA   OCTOBER 19, 2003

Today I traveled to Rome as a part of the official Albanian delegation invited to attend the beatification of Mother Teresa. Mother Teresa has played a significant role in my life. I have read at least fifteen books about her and continue to pick them up whenever I feel spiritually empty. Our work among the desperately poor here in Albania has also put us in close collaboration with her Missionaries of Charity.

We arrived the day before the beatification service, on a dreary, cold, rainy day. By the next morning, though, the sky opened up without a single cloud. An estimated 300,000 people packed St. Peter's Square. Since we were a part of the official Albanian delegation, and since Mother Teresa was Albanian, the Vatican placed us in the front row next to a hundred cardinals. Pope John Paul II was only fifteen meters away.

Three magnificent choirs—a Missionaries of Charity Choir, the Sistine Chapel boys' choir, and a third choir—sang hymns and songs while all the special delegates were arriving. The pope arrived in his wheelchair at 10:00 AM. The effects of his Parkinson's disease were clearly evident. He couldn't hold his head straight, he shook, and he slurred his words. He couldn't say the entire Mass, but prayed different parts. In response to his effort, people continually yelled, "Viva Papa!"

Most of the Mass was done in Latin, with certain readings and a sermon in English and other languages. In the English sermon, an Indian cardinal talked about how Mother Teresa didn't simply want to be the least, but to serve the least. "Greatness lies in the ability to give without counting the cost. To give until it hurts. Mother Teresa's motivation was to focus on God's longing for man. 'I thirst,' Jesus said from the cross. 'How can I quench Christ's thirst in my own life?' Mother constantly thought. 'What you do to the least of My brothers, you do to Me.' By serving the poor, she served Christ Himself. She saw Christ in the poorest of the poor. She highlighted the deepest form of service—caring for those in great need, but doing it all with love and joy. . . . She wanted to give herself completely to God and to others. She wanted to be a sign of God's love, compassion, and presence. We are created to love and to be loved. She brought souls to God and God to souls. For those whose vision of God had been diminished by their suffering, she tried to bring the presence and love of God to them."

At the end of the ceremony, the pope greeted everyone in different languages. In English, he welcomed all the pilgrims from the United States and India. He especially welcomed the one thousand Albanian pilgrims. It was nice to see how the Albanians took such pride in Mother Teresa. Metropolitan John, who was the Orthodox head of our Albanian delegation, said it well: "It is a blessing to have the world hear about holiness, sanctity, and goodness in connection with an Albanian. Usually the world only hears negative things coming from Albania. 'What good can come from Nazareth?' Well, we have someone coming from Albania that the whole world admires as a saint."

Following the beatification ceremony, we attended a lunch offered by the Albanian ambassador of Italy. I sat across the table from the former Albanian president, Rexhep Meidani. Two seats away sat the Albanian president Albert Moisiu, and on either side of me were Catholic bishops. I talked a little with former president Meidani, but the politicians didn't seem too interested in reflecting on the life of Mother Teresa. I found my conversations with the Roman Catholic archbishop, Rok Merdita, more fascinating because he shared with me some of his own interactions with Mother Teresa.

One positive impression I had from the entire service was that the Roman Catholic Church truly represents a worldwide community. How moving it was to see cardinals, bishops, priests, and 300,000 people from every continent and country of the world. Yet as I looked upon this army of cardinals, bishops, priests, and faithful, and especially as I looked at all the beauty, wealth, and majesty of these centuries-old buildings of the Vatican, I had an uncomfortable feeling—this church seemed to represent earthly power, might, and wealth, the greatest temptations that have forever plagued humankind. As I thought critically of the Roman Catholic Church, I also thought about the Byzantine Church and Empire, which must have displayed this same sense for more than a thousand years. And the Russian Church and Empire imitated this path of the first and second Rome.

This picture of a powerful and wealthy church contradicts the humble Incarnation of Almighty God. Imagine God being born in a small manger in a smelly, dark cave, living thirty quiet years as a simple carpenter in an insignificant village, willingly accepting to be rejected, ridiculed, humiliated, and ultimately beaten and crucified by the very people He created.

All the pomp and glory of this beatification service seemed to offer a stark contrast to the message and life of Mother Teresa herself, who epitomized the foolishness of the cross. She lived in utter simplicity and poverty while serving the poorest of the poor. She rejected the use of fans, washing machines, rugs, and other such "luxuries" for herself and her sisters. She chose a way of life that the world could not understand. Yet she became famous despite it all. And now, the rich and powerful, both of the Church and of the world, honor her in ways they themselves would like—with pomp and majesty.

For me, the humble path of love and service offers the true meaning of faith and life itself. "The Son of Man did not come to be served, but to serve" (Matthew 20:28). "A new commandment I give to you, that you love one another; as I have loved you, that you also love one another. By this all will know that you are My disciples, if you have love for one another" (John 13:34–35).

NEITHER ALBANIAN
NOR SERBIAN   FEBRUARY 14–15, 2004

I'm in the Belgrade Airport, returning from an unforgettable two-day trip to Banja Luka, Bosnia. It's hard to imagine that in a country of 3.9 million people, 250,000 died in the war from 1992 to 1995. Every person I met had family members who had died in that war. I try to think about the impact of the Vietnam War in American history, where we had 55,000 deaths in a country of 200 million people. The percentage of the Bosnian death total is hard to comprehend. I traveled to this Serbian city of Bosnia with two young Albanian students. Serbians and Albanians have extremely negative feelings and prejudices against one another.

The day before we arrived in Banja Luka, we had a twelve-hour layover in Belgrade. As I walked around this modern European city, I kept thinking about how we, the USA, could have bombed this city and country for three months without stop. What would it have been like to live with a family in this European city (and I emphasize European, because too often we're used to seeing war in Africa, in the Middle East, and in other places so different from our own) and hear bombing continuously for three months? It's quite scary to imagine.

The St. Sava Youth Association invited us to come to Bosnia. One of their leaders visited Albania this past summer during a Syndesmos Youth Conference and was so impressed with all he saw that he wanted us to visit his own city and talk about our work. The first evening we met with the leaders of this youth association, a group of ten men and women between the ages of 28 and 33. Some graduated from the Belgrade Theological Faculty, and others were simply devoted young Christians interested in getting other youth to discover the treasure within the Church.

The zeal and fervor of these young people greatly inspired me. I am reminded that in any country I have visited, I can always meet such people. Of course, this group has a unique challenge in reaching out to young people. They told me there are no youth groups in any of the local churches. All children in Bosnia and Serbia are taught religion in primary school, but that is the only religious education and ministry given to them. There is no catechism offered in the church, even to those who want to be baptized. No type of Sunday School. No youth groups. Nothing!

On Sunday morning, I celebrated the Divine Liturgy in the cathedral. Surely, it was the first time in the history of that city that Serbians heard Albanian spoken in the church. I offered greetings to the people from their "brothers and sisters" in Albania, and told them that today we were experiencing what St. Paul preached: "In Christ, there is neither Jew nor Greek, neither Serb nor Albanian. In Christ, we are one!"

In the evening, we gave a presentation in the city's main cultural center. The hall was packed. Two television stations interviewed us before the presentation. Almost all of these people viewed Albanians as Muslims and didn't know the Orthodox Church even existed there.

During our hour-long presentation, one fanatical Serb kept interrupting. He insulted me as an American imperialist and criticized everything we showed as un-Orthodox. At the end, he ranted like a drunken idiot. Thank God, though, everyone else in the hall started yelling at him to stop. Finally, a policeman escorted him out of the hall.

Afterwards, every speaker who had a question began by apologizing for that man's behavior. One elderly villager didn't understand our presentation at all, and commented, "You didn't mention anything about Serbs. How can you be talking about Orthodoxy and not mention Serbs?" Our host proceeded to tell him that Orthodoxy includes autocephalous churches in Greece or Russia or Albania where Orthodox Christians are not Serbian. This was literally shocking for the old man.

After this gathering, I understood what a sacred responsibility we have to share our experiences with others. So many people live in their tiny little worlds; we who have a different perspective must share this with others and challenge their parochialism. I include here the many people in America who have such a limited perspective on world reality. We don't know what war means, even though we're so ready to drop bombs. We don't know what poverty and suffering are on a national level. We don't realize how unique our situation is with our freedom, our wealth and comfort, our opportunities, and our life in America.

My entire experience in Bosnia offered a powerful learning experience. After our evening presentation, twenty of us went out to dinner at a beautiful restaurant in the city's castle. It was one of those truly unforgettable evenings of fellowship. We sat around the dinner table from 9:30 PM until 1:30 AM, talking, laughing, toasting, and singing. And the singing was so reminiscent of Albanians when they gather. Deacon Vladislav and his old seminary roommate, Darken, entertained us for at least two hours. I was mesmerized by traditional Serbian and Albanian songs, one after another. Such moments of fellowship and Christian love are some of my most treasured memories over the past ten years. To see Serbs and Albanians becoming friends, and by the end of two days, expressing such love and sincerity with one another was breathtaking!

This is the bond of Christian unity at its best. "There is no Jew or Greek," no Serb or Albanian! Here were men who fought in the Bosnian war, all of whom have extended family members and friends who were killed, who live in a society that emphasizes division, difference, and hatred towards the other, and yet these fifteen Serbs were sitting with an American and two Albanians in fellowship and love. Christ was truly in our midst!

MISSIONS AS RECONCILIATION

I was sent as a representative of the Orthodox Church of Albania to the Lausanne Forum on World Evangelization held in Thailand in the fall of 2004. I met amazing people on this trip.

Nico Smith was a white South African Dutch Reformed pastor and theologian who defended the system of apartheid for twenty years while he preached in an all-white church and taught at a prestigious university. One day in the 1960s, the famous theologian Karl Barth asked Nico a challenging question. "Are you free?" When Nico confidently responded that they have religious freedom in South Africa, Barth interrupted, "No. I mean are *you* free—free to live and preach the Gospel, even if your family and friends and society itself stand against you?" Like a self-assured young man, Nico thought that he was free. But as the years passed, this question kept haunting him. "Am I free to honestly live and preach the Gospel?"

By 1974, Nico finally realized he wasn't free. He started to see that the Bible didn't teach apartheid, and thus, he could no longer accept this unjust system. Uncertain about his future, yet sure about his newfound beliefs, he began to confront apartheid, preaching a message of reconciliation for whites and blacks. His parishioners, students, the university administrators, and even his family and friends began seeing his message as a threat to their way of life and a danger to the overall establishment. By 1981, he was forced to resign from the university and asked to leave his church.

Nico told me, "I realized that a true Christian cannot stay distant or indifferent to the sufferings of others. Authentic Christianity is not for those who want a comfortable, easy life. True faith costs much! If we follow Christ's call to bring good news to the poor, the afflicted, the oppressed, and the sufferer, then we must be willing to sacrifice and suffer with them!" This new understanding of faith led Nico and his wife to become the first white people to move into a black township, pastoring an all-black church.

When he did this, his extended family thought he had gone mad, and his former church condemned him as a traitor. The government attacked him as a communist, and the secret police tapped his phone, keeping constant surveillance on him, harassing and threatening him and his family.

"For the first time in my life," he said, "I tasted what it was like to be black. I realized then that we can never truly understand the oppressed until we actually live among them and try to become one with them. In the end, isn't this what Jesus Christ did, when He became incarnate as a human being?"

St. Paul tells us to "let this mind be in you which was also in Christ Jesus, who, being in the form of God, did not consider it robbery to be equal with God, but made Himself of no reputation, taking the form of a bondservant, *and* coming in the likeness of men. And being found in appearance as a man, He humbled Himself and became obedient to *the point of* death, even the death of the cross" (Phil. 2:5–8). Nico came to the point of sacrificing much in order to reconcile himself with Christ, and in order to try to reconcile enemies with one another.

My particular working group at this conference tackled the issue of how the Church needs to become more of an agent in reconciliation, especially in the many troubled parts of the globe. Although many people at the conference were more interested in how to preach and teach and convert and plant churches, our working group concluded that one of the most essential and crucial methods of preaching the Gospel was precisely through reconciliation.

St. Paul writes, "God . . . has reconciled us to Himself through Jesus Christ, and has given us the ministry of reconciliation. . . . Now then, we are ambassadors for Christ" (2 Cor. 5:18–20). If God desires the world to be reconciled to Himself and all people to be reconciled to one another, this means the Church needs to become an instrument of reconciliation. We need to heal the deep wounds of others.

"Blessed are the peacemakers," Jesus taught, not simply the peace-lovers. To love peace and to struggle for peace are quite different. I can love peace, yet too often I will stand at a distance from the problems and injustices of the world. To be a peacemaker and an agent of reconciliation means to consciously enter into the struggle and to become a part of an extremely difficult, slow, and painful process.

I discovered this as I worked within an amazing group of fifty people, only eighteen of whom were white Westerners. I heard stories of horror, tragedy, and unbelievable sorrow. There were Jews and Palestinians, Hutus and Tutsis from Rwanda, Sudanese, a Serbian, a Colombian, a North Korean, and one from Northern Ireland. Little superficiality here. No clichés or simple solutions as we talked about how to bring about reconciliation. Everyone agreed that true reconciliation is a long path of forgiveness and healing, and it only comes after much effort and struggle under the grace of God. The stories I heard were hard to imagine—full of terror, pain, and ongoing danger, yet they were also stories of hope.

Celestin Musekura is a Hutu from Rwanda. His wife is a Tutsi. Earlier this year marked the ten-year memorial of the genocide in Rwanda, when the Hutus killed 800,000 Tutsis within three months and left three million people as refugees. Although Rwanda was a country that had boasted of a great Christian revival, much of the killing was Christians killing Christians. "The blood of tribalism," they say now, "ran deeper than the waters of baptism."

In such unbelievable tragedy, many people cried out, "Where is God? Can we believe in a just God? How can we ever forgive? How can we ever be forgiven?" Celestin told his story about trying to preach the Christian message of repentance and forgiveness several years after the genocide. He brought the Hutu and Tutsi pastors together to discuss how the Church could be an agent of reconciliation for the country. Yet his own Hutu people accused him of siding with the Tutsis, while the Tutsis distrusted him since he was a Hutu. When he returned to Rwanda, he was arrested by the police and beaten for three hours by the Tutsis.

Later that year, seven members of his family were murdered, along with seventy members of his church. He agonized with God, "Where are You? Why did this happen when I'm trying to do Your work, trying to preach a gospel of reconciliation?"

Seven months later, however, he met family members of those who killed his family. It was extremely hard, yet he knew that he had to forgive them if he was going to continue preaching about reconciliation. And God gave him the strength and healing to do exactly that.

Such stories of hope made us all realize that the impossible is possible by God's grace. Christ's command to "love your enemy and pray for those who persecute you" is not a theoretical message. The people I met showed that even in the midst of the most unimaginable evil, hope remains.

After he shared this story, Celestin the Hutu and another member of our group who is a Tutsi, Emanuel, got up and embraced one another. With tears in their eyes, they asked one another for forgiveness on behalf of their own people.

Later in our meeting, we saw Jhan Moskowitz, a Jewish Christian whose father suffered in a concentration camp during World War II, and Bishara Awad, a Palestinian whose father was killed by the Jews during the war to establish the Israeli state, not only sit down at a table together as brothers, but even embrace one another, again asking for forgiveness for the sins of their people.

And then there was Grace Morillo, a young woman from Colombia, who was held captive for 68 days by the guerrillas of her country. Yet she showed no hatred or anger toward those who kidnapped her. In fact, she told moving stories about how the prisoners would pray together every day, and some-times their kidnappers would even join them, holding hands and praying the Lord's Prayer. She began to see these fearsome guerrillas as human beings. She started to think about how the injustices of her country often pushed the peas-ants to extreme actions.

After her release, she realized that as a Christian she could no longer stay indifferent to the injustices around her and remain at a comfortable distance from the sufferings of others. She needed to become an agent of reconciliation in her own country.

So many stories—stories about the genocide of the black Africans in Sudan today, of Northern Ireland, of terrorism, wars, and injustices throughout the world. During our conference, terrorists killed seventy people in northern

India, in the home city of one of our group members. He had to call home to make sure that no one from his family was killed or injured.

It is so easy to read about these dangers in the newspapers, yet to stay so distant from them in our own lives. The challenge for all Christians is to be aware of those who are suffering and to pray for those in need in our own country, as well as all parts of the world. Christians are called to leave our comfortable domains and enter into the suffering of others. And we can begin doing this by looking around our own areas and asking how we can be instruments of reconciliation.

What are we doing about the ongoing race relations in our own country? What about the need for reconciliation between the rich and the poor of our society? And what about our personal reconciliation in the broken relationships in our own lives and with those around us?

Many people are suffering and are in need. God has made very clear that we, you and I, are His hands, His feet, His love.

St. Francis of Assisi said it so beautifully in his famous prayer: "Lord, make ME an instrument of your peace. Where there is hatred, let ME bring love. Where there is sadness, let ME bring joy. Where there is darkness, let ME bring light. Where there is injury, let ME bring pardon. Where there is doubt, let ME bring faith."

One of the greatest ways to evangelize the world is for us to become instruments of God's reconciliation. This is our witness to the world. This is what missions and evangelism are all about. First, to reconcile ourselves to God. Then, to break away from our egocentric, comfortable lives and struggle to reconcile ourselves to our enemies, as well as to help enemies be reconciled with one another. O Lord, please make us instruments of your peace! Amen!

CHAPTER 10

SAYING FAREWELL

After more than a decade of service in Albania, we felt God leading us to return to the States. It definitely wasn't an easy decision, but we came to our conclusion after much prayer and discussion with our spiritual mentors and co-sojourners. Albania truly became our adopted homeland, and it was hard to imagine that we would leave people whom we love so deeply. What made this decision harder was the fact that we left a life we loved, a ministry in which we felt fulfilled, a mission that could still use our talents and gifts, spiritual children who were at critical stages in their spiritual growth, and dear friends who greatly enriched our lives.

We had come to Albania in 1994 with a commitment to stay for two to three years. In both of our minds, though, we felt that we would stay open to the Holy Spirit and realized that those two to three years could turn into something much longer. And they did. Yet even from our early years, we wrestled with the question of when to go home.

One thing that brought this question to the fore was the death of Faith's father in 1996. It was extremely hard for Faith to be so far from her mother and sister during this death. Her father was only 62, and although Faith had a ticket to return to America and see him during a critical point, he died several days before her arrival. This sense of loss always stayed close to us, and several surgeries and ailments for Faith's mother in the following years made the distance and loss even more acute.

Although we both loved our lives in Albania and even desired for our children to be MKs (Missionary Kids) for a longer time before returning to the States, we finally decided that after ten and a half years, it was time for us to be in the same country and more available to our aging parents. Possibly under other circumstances we would have stayed longer. We set July 5, 2004, as our departure date.

Faith and I put closure to our many ministries by April, having handed the leadership off to either Albanians or other missionaries who would continue the work. We used our final two months to travel around the country and really focus on saying goodbye to all our dear friends and spiritual brothers and sisters. We had seen, throughout the years, how some missionaries left the mission field in quite an abrupt manner. We never thought that was a good way to put closure to their work, nor did it offer an opportunity for them and the Albanians they loved to properly say goodbye.

We tried to encourage our Albanian spiritual children and spiritual brothers and sisters that we weren't abandoning them, but were passing on the torch of faith to them. The goal of missionaries is to work themselves out of their work and to raise up faithful indigenous believers who can carry on the ministry. We will greatly miss the fellowship and spiritual support of these people.

One group we tried to meet with during our final weeks were any people with whom we had had difficulty during our years of ministry. We tried to love everyone, but we surely made mistakes and had misunderstandings with certain people. One of the lasting memories we had during our final months was getting together with these people, asking once again for their forgiveness, and leaving in peace.

As a part of this chapter, I have included excerpts from a letter I wrote to our beloved archbishop, with whom I had thought we would continue serving for as long as he was the Archbishop of Albania. I have also included a letter to my children, whose entire lives had been spent in Albania. Although they may not remember their experiences, I wanted to include a letter which would help them realize what a special blessing they had as missionary kids.

A Farewell Letter to Archbishop Anastasios

Your Beatitude and my dearly beloved spiritual father,

As Faith and I prepare to leave Albania, we leave with many mixed emotions. [. . .]

You have truly been one of the greatest role models in my life—a spiritual and beloved father, a dear friend, and an exemplary archbishop and churchman.

I used to hope that we would never leave Albania until you died. Even though we won't realize this dream, we know that in spirit we will always be united with you. And we hope that your influence, prayers, and legacy will always be evident in our own lives and ministries.

Memories from Africa

You know well that you played a central role in the entire direction of my life. By allowing the first OCMC team to come to Kenya in 1987, when I was in my final year of university, you gave me a chance to experience firsthand the third world and a concrete mission setting. This experience challenged and enriched my entire worldview and understanding of life.

Such a life-changing experience filled me with the desire to return to Africa after graduating from the university six months later. Again, you gave an opportunity for a twenty-three-year-old kid to spend a year in Kenya and serve the Church in a simple way. Living in a village in Western Kenya, tasting the harsh life of the Africans, living with Fr. Athanasios Karanja, and having the occasional talks with you at the seminary in Nairobi all helped transform my vision of life. You and your example truly inspired and blessed me.

How I remember traveling with you in Kenya! I can't tell you how many times I have thanked God that we didn't crash when the tire of our truck burst. God was with us! One of my fondest memories of being with you, however, was when Fr. Paul's daughter died. As I have seen you in the midst of many tragedies and crises, you were at peace, and offered the "peace that passes all understanding" to all those around you. I know that you have reflected much on that incident, and I just wanted to tell you that it was a memorable one for me as well.

One of the lasting memories I have of you in Africa, however, is as an untiring apostle. Really, I remember your visits to Western Kenya, when I would drive you around the bush for a week. You would always want to go to the most remote village. By the end of the week, I was ready for you to leave because I was tired of keeping up with your pace! And yet, you never stopped. Even to this day, I am amazed at your pace of activity. It is obvious that God gives you the stamina and strength.

These memories, and many others, of Africa are indelibly stamped in my life, and I am truly grateful to you for making them possible.

Your Writings

Another way you have greatly influenced me in my life is through your writings. After leaving Africa, I began my studies at Holy Cross. My contact with you in Africa filled me with a desire to read your writings. I went through all the English missiological, theological, and ecumenical journals in the library, looking for your articles. As I gathered and read them, I realized that I had found a treasure. I read and reread many of your articles, and my practical mission experience was enhanced and deepened by them.

This is one reason I believe it is so important to make your writings more available to the general public. I not only want others to be inspired as I was, but I want those who are interested in missions to enter the field with a proper and serious understanding of what missions is all about. In English, we have so few missiological writings from an Orthodox perspective.

Memories from Albania

What a blessed decade these past ten years have been! [. . .] Each year has offered new and precious memories for Faith and me. We came to Albania in humility, knowing that we would first learn from others, like yourself. An unexpected blessing was to meet some of the living saints of Albania during our first years.

Our visits in the home of the Çiço sisters are among our most unforgettable memories. We would listen to stories of courage and faith as Demetra, Marika, and Berta told us how they kept their faith alive during the years of communism. And it was precious to see their deep love and respect for you. I remember when Fr. Anthony Ugolnik, a priest from America, came to Korça. He fell in love with the fervor of these women and said to little Berta, "I want to put you in my suitcase and take you back to America." She looked at him with all seriousness and said, "And leave my archbishop? Never!" You were a true answer to their years of prayer.

Over these past ten years, our greatest joys came from seeing how the Gospel of Jesus Christ has been planted and has grown in the hearts of numerous people. You told me during my first months here, "Focus on the youth and students!" We have tried to faithfully offer a Christian witness with our lives, in our relationships, as well as with our words. I'm sure we have failed at times, disappointing some, yet we hope that others could see our sincere love for Christ, for His Church, and for His people here.

I thank you so very much for all your support with our work among the youth. I know that at times we have created difficulties for you, especially when our methods of ministry contrasted with the ideas of some of the monastics. You often reminded me that you are a conductor who has to keep all the orchestra at peace. Please forgive me when I have caused ripples in the water. You know that I never did anything with ill intention—sometimes it was my carelessness, and at other times it was simply a difference in philosophy. I am grateful, however, that I have always felt your support and faith in me, and I believe that I have tried to the best of my ability to transmit your loving, tolerant, universal spirit to the youth.

Thank you also for making possible so many of our efforts among the youth. Without your openness of mind and ability to raise funds, we would never have been able to do many things, like run a seminary for both men and women. A year ago, I would have left the seminary with an unsettled heart. The arrival of Bishop Ilia has been an answer to prayer. His presence living at the seminary and his years of experience as a pastor in a community are invaluable.

Your vision and financial means have also allowed us to create dynamic summer camps and other youth programs. I have been a part of the best church camps in America, and what we have established here is just as good as what is available there. Our various visitors from Greece have said the same thing.

My university ministry will always be another unique memory for me. Over the years, hundreds of university students have gathered weekly to discuss the faith and discover God. Thank you for allowing me the freedom to run this ministry. I was reminded of its importance last summer, when I found out that six of those students who regularly came to our meetings are now judges around Albania. [. . .]

How will I ever forget the hundreds of baptisms I have performed here—mass baptisms in villages and baptisms of many people from Muslim families. The most incredible thing, however, was to see how some of these youth who accepted Christ later led their parents, and in some cases even their grandparents, to the baptismal font.

The various crises in Albania will always hold a special place for me. I remember November 1994, when we all thought you would be kicked out of the country. At one of the last meetings before the referendum, I remember how you radiated a sense of peace. [. . .] The crisis of 1997 was another wonderful example of how your inspired, dynamic leadership guided the Church to offer a powerful witness of love in the midst of chaos. Your faith and trust in God comforted and strengthened us few foreigners who didn't evacuate the country, as we lived together in uncertainty at the archdiocesan headquarters.

The Kosovo war offered another example of your holistic understanding of mission. Your witness and vision for outreach to all, regardless of faith, guided and inspired me in an unforgettable way.

I have also learned much from the way you have dealt with those who attacked you unjustly. Whether they were Albanian nationalists, Greek nationalists, or any other type of fundamentalist, you always dealt with them in the same way. I remember you telling me, "Let us just do our work, and our work will be our answer to their accusations!"

I liked your words when you said, "We Christians should never have enemies. Others may hate us, but we never hate anyone!" I wish more Christian leaders had lived by such a vision throughout history.

I also have learned much from the way you have handled those who have hurt you and betrayed you. Every time we go to America, you are ready to meet one of these people and give him another chance. Seeing you help an antagonist get a job, even after all the pain he caused the Church, was another unforgettable lesson. I pray that I can imitate this spirit of love in my own life.

I have been privileged, like few others, to travel with you around the world. I thank you so much for this opportunity to be close to you. I have learned invaluable lessons watching how you interact with people at all levels. I always admired the way you were at ease with the simple people in the most remote villages of Kenya or Albania, treating each one with respect and dignity. Yet I have also seen how comfortable you are among the rich and powerful, never judging others, but trying to offer a witness of God's love to all.

Thank you so much for allowing me to travel with you. I loved being in your presence, praying with you each morning and night, listening to your occasional explanation of an Epistle reading, hearing your impressions of life in other parts of the world, and always marveling at the way you were constantly open to learning new things about new people and places. These experiences are truly among my fondest. [. . .]

I want to conclude by expressing from the depths of our hearts our gratitude for your continual and overflowing love for us. Faith and I will never forget how you blessed us personally during our various struggles or crises, either with your wise advice and comforting words, or by your concrete actions of love. How can we ever forget your visit to the Tirana hospital at 11:00 at night to see how Faith was during her appendicitis? And your visits to our home at every feastday of St. Luke, or your occasional call to see how we were doing, are memories we will never forget.

We will sorely miss your love and spiritual shepherding from up close, but of course, we know that we will be united in spirit through our prayers and through the Eucharist. You will always be remembered in my proskomidi and in our family prayers.

Please remember us in your prayers, especially as we try to adjust to a new life in the United States. It is not easy raising children with a Christian mindset in the midst of an affluent, materialistic, egocentric society. We want our children to dedicate their lives to Christ and serve Him with a spirit of love and sacrifice. Please pray for us as we try to stay faithful to our calling of cultivating a missionary spirit among our churches, and of serving the Lord in a fruitful and blessed manner.

Our wish for you, along with a wish for many more blessed years, is the prayer of St. Paul, which you yourself often offer to others:

May God grant you in accord with the riches of His glory to be strengthened with power through His Spirit in the inner self, and that Christ may dwell in your hearts through faith; that rooted and grounded in love, you may have strength to comprehend with all the holy ones what is the breadth and length and height and depth, and to know the love of Christ that surpasses knowledge, so that you may be filled with all the fullness of God. Now to Him who is able to accomplish far more than all we ask or imagine, by the power at work within us, to him be glory in the Church and in Christ Jesus to all generations, forever and ever. Amen. (Ephesians 3:16–21)

We love you dearly.
With the warmest love and deepest respect,
   Your spiritual son,
   +Luke

A Letter to Our Children

Dear Pavli, Theodora, Panayiota,
and our baby-in-the-womb, Nicholas,

   We are leaving our home in Albania, the only home that each of you has known. Two of you were born in our hometown of Lancaster, Pennsylvania, and one in Boston, but each of you came to Albania when you were only two or three months old. Paul and Theodora, you both have learned Albanian quite well, and feel comfortable speaking to and understanding all our Albanian friends. You have not only adjusted to life here, but in reality, this is the only life you've really known. You've gotten used to living without electricity for hours a day. [. . .] By living here, you've come to appreciate some of the most basic things of life.

   You love your missionary friends, like Tristan and Katherine and the Lindermans and Russells, but it is great to see how much you love your Albanian friends as well. Every morning at seven, little Ana, our neighbor, comes knocking on our door, and you play with her for hours. You have developed a nice bond with the neighborhood children, especially through the little preschool that Mommy has run in our home. Some of the church kids, like Petro and Spiro, hold a special place in your hearts. Of course, some of your closest friends have been your two babysitters—Alexandra and Marina. Alexandra played such a central part in your lives during the first few years, and then her sister Marina became your big sister afterwards. Every day you loved seeing Petraq, and especially wanted him to sing you lullabies when you took your naps. Then you interacted with all our co-workers who would come by the house to work with Mommy in the children's office or camp, or with me in the university ministry or seminary. You have so many surrogate big brothers and sisters. Although you have not spent much time with your cousins and extended family in America, God has blessed you with a huge extended family here in Albania that dearly loves you!

One of your highlights each year has been our six weeks in the summer at camp. You loved being out in nature, running around with Tristan catching bugs and exploring the grounds, taking part in the Olympics by carrying the torch, making arts and crafts with Alexandra and Marina, helping set up the campfires, or simply sitting in the little baby pool and splashing all the campers who came by. Paul, you grew up with a hundred girls kissing and hugging and holding and squeezing you from the time you were nine months old. Maybe you overdosed on all that affection, and that's why you now don't like it when people show too much affection to you! And Theodora and Panayiota, you experienced all that affection at six months old.

Of course, along with all our great memories of camp, we also remember how you, Theodora, once got 110 mosquito bites all over your body, or how we were always a little nervous that one of you might get too close to the scorpions we would inevitably find each summer.

Paul, we loved how each year at camp you wanted us to buy you the blue plastic sandals that all the village kids had. You thought these sandals made you run fast, because you saw how fast the village kids ran wearing them. What we appreciated is that you didn't realize these sandals cost a dollar. Even when you wore those sandals during our visits to America, you never thought of style and fashion. You have not yet been tempted by the materialism that will face us in America.

Theodora, you developed a nice friendship with your village friend Elona. During your first years at camp, you couldn't communicate well with one another, yet you still loved playing together. As you got older, though, it was nice to see how you could communicate with her. And of course, Panayiota, you were only at camp for one year, but even that first year you brought your sunshine to all the campers.

It was at camp, Paul, that you began serving as an altar boy at the age of two. It was at camp that you children had a hundred girls chanting your names and singing to you in the cafeteria or during the talent shows. It was at camp that you each received so much love and affection.

Not only at camp, but in Tirana, you got so used to being around all types of people. Along with villagers, our lives were filled with many other types of people. Almost daily we had various beggars come by our home asking for help. When you would go to the door and see these people, you would excitedly inform us of their arrival and then carry a bag of food to them. The beauty is that you came to know these "beggars" by name and considered them your friends.

The beauty of life here is that our lives have deep meaning. Everything is about relationships, and you children have played a central role in these relationships. Our lives have not centered solely on you and your activities. More importantly, our lives have centered on serving our Lord Jesus Christ, and you have participated in that service. Of course, you played and have had lots of fun with your friends, but your lives have revolved much around the Church. Every morning and evening we can hear the church bells ring from our house. You loved walking to church, giving money and talking to the beggars in front of the church, getting the archbishop's blessing along with all the other children at the beginning of the Divine Liturgy, touching the robes of the priests as they pass by in their processions, and sitting on the steps right in front of the iconostasis throughout the service. You attended services on most feast days, and that seemed normal.

You also have gone on visits to the poor and needy, you came to the university for our early morning liturgies, and you went out to the seminary when we had special events. Paul, you tagged along with Mommy into the refugee camps during the Kosovo war, while you, Theodora, were in her womb. For one Christmas celebration, how can we ever forget that you, Theodora, even went with your mommy into the prison to bring joy to the prisoners there. [. . .]

Up to this point in your lives, you are not only PKs (priest's kids), but you truly are MKs (missionary kids). You are bicultural children who comfortably identify with the Albanian culture, as well as our American culture. In fact, you also identify with our Greek-American culture. One of our prayers is that you will always maintain this bicultural identity and cherish the diversity life offers.

Yet we realize that all these wonderful experiences you have had have come at a stage in your lives when you will not actually remember many things. This saddens us. In some ways, we wish that we could have stayed here for another ten years so that these experiences would be

engrained in your minds and hearts. That's why we are writing this let-
ter. We want you to remember something about this time in your devel-
opment, and realize what a blessed childhood you have had!

Our greatest prayer for you will always be that each one of you will
discover in the depths of your hearts the priceless treasure of our faith,
and that you, on your own, will one day commit your lives in a radical
way to serving our Lord Jesus Christ in whatever way He may call you.
As you grow up in the United States, many temptations will assail you.
You will no longer have this beautiful and dynamic missionary faith
community to nourish and bless you. We pray, though, that we will dis-
cover and help create other such communities of faith wherever we may
live in America. As ironic as this may seem, we are afraid that it may be
harder to find or create this same spirit or atmosphere in the States as we
had here in Albania.

Whatever awaits us in our return to America, we pray that we will
always cherish this memory of Albania, and carry the good lessons we
have learned here with us wherever we will be.

We love you, Pavli, Theodora, Panayiota, and our baby-in-the-
womb Nicholas!

With the deepest love and affection,
Babi (Albanian for Daddy) *and Mommy*

OUR LAST SUNDAY: MISSIONARIES TO AMERICA   JULY 3, 2004

Archbishop Anastasios needed to travel to Greece for some health
issues on the Tuesday before we departed Albania, and although the doctors advised him to stay in Greece for some rehab, he insisted on returning
to Tirana so that he would be in church for our last Sunday. I gave a sermon
recalling all our wonderful memories, thanking everyone for all the blessings
they have given us, and emphasizing that we did not view these ten years as a
sacrifice but truly as the greatest blessing. At the very end, I got so choked up
I couldn't say my last two sentences. After a few tears, I struggled and blurted
them out.

At the conclusion of the Divine Liturgy, the archbishop offered very
warm and loving words. The main point he noted was that the church

On their last Sunday before departing Albania in 2004, the Archbishop says farewell to the Veronis family in front of the Annunciation Cathedral in Tirana.

community was not saying goodbye to us. "Fr. Luke was ordained here. Fr. Luke and Prifteresha Fotini have faithfully served here for more than ten years. They are ours and a part of our church. Therefore, we do not say good-bye, but we are giving them a sendoff. We are sending them as our missionaries to America!"

RE-ENTRY INTO AMERICA   JULY 15, 2004

We've been home for a week and a half, and have been in constant transition. Few people, other than my parents, have really asked us in any serious manner about Albania or how we feel about our return. Faith and I read a great book on missionary re-entry, and we sort of expected this type of welcome; yet it makes us sad. Our best conversation has been with Dr. Tom Miller, who came over and talked for two hours. He shared with us his own experiences when he returned from the mission field after five years in Tanzania. He could relate to our feelings.

Our main reason for coming home was to be closer to family and be available to care for our aging parents. Our timing couldn't have been better. Last week my mom had chest pains, went to the hospital, and discovered that one of her three main arteries was ninety percent blocked. This could have led to a massive heart attack. The doctors put in three shunts, and she is recovering fine. I had the opportunity to spend the night with her in the hospital.

Being back in the States has reaffirmed that I feel more comfortable in Albania and don't fit in so well here anymore. I'm not interested in many things that occupy the attention of others—the sports, television, entertainment, and superficialities of life. I'm interesting in talking about the Gospel and how to share the faith, but I see that so many people don't seem to have time to talk about such things. A few will say, "It's hard to be back, huh?" but most think it is normal that we are back, and we must be happy. Besides my parents, George Maragakes showed a keen interest, as well as Hector and Katerina Firoglanis, who are considering going to Albania as missionaries themselves.

This experience teaches me an important lesson. We need to reach out to others who return from the mission field, listen to their stories, show an interest in their struggles of readjustment, ask how they feel to be back, and not be too busy to spend time with them.

Welcome home!

ABOUT THE AUTHOR

Fr. Luke A. Veronis has been involved in the Orthodox Church's missionary movement since 1987, including serving as an OCMC missionary for twelve years in Albania and different parts of Africa. He presently pastors Ss. Constantine and Helen Greek Orthodox Church in Webster, Massachusetts, where he has led church groups on short-term mission teams, working with Project Mexico to build homes for the poor in Tijuana, Mexico. Fr. Luke teaches as an adjunct instructor at Holy Cross Greek Orthodox School of Theology and Hellenic College. He serves on the Board of Directors for the Orthodox Christian Mission Center (OCMC) in St. Augustine, Florida, and the Overseas Ministries Study Center (OMSC) in New Haven, Connecticut. His other published works include *Missionaries, Monks, and Martyrs: Making Disciples of All Nations* (Light and Life Publishing, 1994) and *Lynette's Hope: The Witness of Lynette Katherine Hoppe's Life and Death* (Conciliar Press / Ancient Faith Publishing, 2008). He has published articles for the *Cambridge Dictionary of Christianity* (Cambridge University Press, 2009), *The Encyclopedia of Christianity,* Vol. 3 (Eerdmans, 2003), *Evangelical Dictionary of World Missions* (Baker Books, 2000), as well as numerous articles for professional missiological journals and lay magazines.

OTHER BOOKS OF INTEREST

Lynette's Hope
The Witness of Lynette Katherine Hoppe's Life and Death
Compiled and edited by Father Luke Veronis,
with a foreword by Archbishop Anastasios of Albania

"Now we have to live whatever we have ever preached to others," Lynette Hoppe wrote in her journal. "I have been classified as having Stage 4 cancer (of four stages), and my prospects are rather grim. Nonetheless, I remain cheerful and hopeful and want to spend what years God grants me in joy and thanksgiving, serving as and wherever I can." With these sober yet hopeful words, Orthodox missionary to Albania Lynette Hoppe began the last journey of her fruitful life. In frank and poignant prose, Lynette's journals, newsletters, and website chronicled her struggles in the "valley of the shadow" as she faced impending death. Close family friend and fellow missionary Fr. Luke Veronis briefly tells the story of Lynette's life, then lets her writing speak for itself, showing how Lynette's radical faith and love for Christ transformed the tragedy of a young mother's untimely death into a powerful witness to the love and saving power of her Lord. Those who witnessed Lynette's passing agree that hers was truly a "beautiful death."

Paperback, 276 pages, plus a 16-page photo section (ISBN 978-1-888212-99-0)

Drita
An Albanian Girl Discovers Her Ancestors' Faith
By Presbytera Renée Ritsi, illustrated by Cameron Thorp

As this beautifully illustrated story opens, we meet Drita, a young Albanian girl, whose family has lived for years under repressive communist rule. After decades of religious oppression, Drita is finally able to discover the faith of her ancestors. As she experiences God's love for her through the example of her grandparents and the teachings of missionaries, she turns her heart toward Christ. At the story's joyful conclusion, Drita is baptized and lives in an Albania where all are now free to openly worship, praise, and glorify God in His Church.

Paperback, 32 pages, 8-1/2" X 11" size (ISBN: 978-1-888212-94-5)

Dimitri's Cross
The Life and Letters of St. Dimitri Klepinin,
Martyred during the Holocaust
by Hélène Arjakovsky-Klepinine

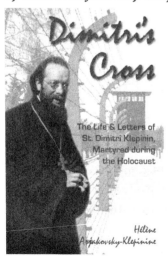

In February of 1943, Fr. Dimitri Klepinin, an Orthodox priest serving the Russian émigré community in occupied Paris, was arrested by the Nazis for issuing false baptismal certificates to Jews. One year later, he died in the concentration camp at Dora, near Buchenwald—a camp known as "the Man-Eater." Fr. Dimitri, an associate of Mother Maria Skobtsova, was glorified by the Orthodox Church on January 16, 2004. In this volume, his daughter, born only five years before his arrest, lovingly tells the story of her father's life: his early search for faith and meaning in a life upended by revolution and exile; his decision to enter the priesthood; his devotion to his wife and children; his sacrificial service to his parish at the rue de Lourmel; and his heroic decision to do all within his power to save the Jews who came to him desperate for protection from the growing Nazi menace.

Paperback, 200 pages, including an 8-page photo section (ISBN: 978-1-888212-33-4)

Royal Monastic
Princess Ileana of Romania (The Story of Mother Alexandra)
by Bev. Cooke

The life of a princess isn't all glamour, handsome princes, and beautiful clothes. It's also devotion to duty, sacrifice for your people, and a lot of just plain hard work. And if your country happens to suffer two world wars and a communist takeover in your lifetime, it means danger and suffering, exile and heartache as well.

Princess Ileana of Romania endured all this and more. But her deeply rooted Orthodox faith saw her through years of change, and eventually led her to the peaceful repose of monasticism. But that life included sacrifice and hard work too, because as Mother Alexandra she was called to build the first English-language Orthodox women's monastery in the United States—the Monastery of the Transfiguration in Ellwood City, Pennsylvania.

Princess Ileana's story is a thrilling tale of love and loss, danger and rescue, sacrifice and reward. Her inspiring life stands as a beacon of faith and holiness for young women of all times and nations to follow.

Paperback, 200 pages (ISBN: 978-1-888212-32-7)

Please call Ancient Faith Publishing at 800-967-7377 for complete ordering information, or order online at store.ancientfaith.com.

CPSIA information can be obtained
at www.ICGtesting.com
Printed in the USA
FSOW04n1327091117
40769FS